PRIMITIVE
INTERNALIZED OBJECT
RELATIONS

PRIMITIVE INTERNALIZED OBJECT RELATIONS

A CLINICAL STUDY OF SCHIZOPHRENIC, BORDERLINE, and NARCISSISTIC PATIENTS

VAMIK D. VOLKAN, M.D.

INTERNATIONAL UNIVERSITIES PRESS, INC.

New York

Library of Congress Cataloging in Publication Data

Volkan, Vamik.
    Primitive internalized object relations.

    Bibliography: p.
    1. Psychoanalysis—Cases, clinical reports, statistics. 2. Schizophrenia —Cases, clinical reports, statistics. 3. Pseudoneurotic schizophrenia—Cases, clinical reports, statistics. 4. Narcissism—Cases, clinical reports, statistics. I. Title
RC504.V64   616.8'982'09   75-18608
ISBN 0-8236-4995-4

Manufactured in the United States of America

For Elizabeth Palonen Volkan

CONTENTS

[vii]

ACKNOWLEDGMENTS

Since this book grew out of my clinical experience I want to acknowledge here my gratitude to those who taught me what I know about clinical matters—my teachers, my colleagues, and, by no means last, my patients. I owe a debt to many people, only a few of whom can be named in a statement necessarily so brief.

When I was a medical student at the University of Ankara in Turkey, Dr. Rasim Adasal was Chairman of its Department of Psychiatry. Rasim Hoca, as we affectionately called him, spoke Turkish with an accent since he was a Turk from the island of Crete. A Turkish Cypriot, I had also come to the Turkish medical community from an island, and as I listened carefully to his lectures on Freud and psychoanalysis I felt a special bond with him, hearing in memory the voice of my teacher father with its insular accent and recalling the presence in my father's black chest of valuable books one volume, probably the first Turkish translation of Freud. I suppose it had made an impression on me then because it was about sex; it could very well have been the *Three Essays on the Theory of Sexuality*. There was no actual practice of psycho-analysis or psychoanalytic psychotherapy in Turkey in the mid-fifties, and there is little to this day, but Rasim Hoca's lectures excited our curiosity about something that remained rather mysterious even as it beckoned. I began to dream of becoming a psychoanalyst; my dream took shape when I came to the United States after completing medical school in Turkey.

I take full responsibility for what appears on the pages to follow, but I must acknowlege a debt for con-sultative or supervisory help, in at least four of the cases I describe, from Drs. D. Wilfred Abse, Edith Weigert, William L. Granatir, and Rex E. Buxton. The first of these four teachers, now a colleague at the University of Virginia, was enormously influential in my early psychi-atric work, and in my decision to become a teacher myself. The others supervised my clinical work at the Washington Psychoanalytic Institute. I want to remem-ber here my own analyst also; he was good to me in so many ways, and my realistic admiration of him helped me form a firm psychoanalytic "work ego" of my own.

After my days as a psychoanalytic candidate were over, I benefited from the encouragement of colleagues on the national scene. I owe special thanks to two of these, Drs. William G. Niederland of New York City and L. Bryce Boyer of Berkeley. They were both extremely generous in corresponding with me and giving useful criticism of earlier papers which were the precursors of this book. My special thanks go to Dr. L. Gordon

Kirschner, Jr., of Washington D.C., and Dr. Seymour Rabinowitz of Charlottesville, who read drafts of the manuscript and offered suggestions. For years I commuted between Charlottesville and Washington with Dr. Kirschner when we were both candidates at the Washington Psychoanalytic Institute, and some of the ideas I put forth here arose from the discussions we had while traveling together.

The professional environment in the University of Virginia's Department of Psychiatry is one in which the investigative spirit is nourished, and for this I must thank Dr. David R. Hawkins, its Chairman. I appreciate the kindness of Dr. Arvell S. Luttrell of Knoxville, Tennessee, for sharing his notes on the case of the "mechanical boy" seen at the University; and of Dr. William M. Cseh of the University of Virginia for permitting the inclusion of a vignette from his treatment of the "turtle man."

Mrs. Irene Azarian, of International Universities Press, gave me truly supportive and kind encouragement from our first discussion on the writing of this book, and contributed significantly to its completion. My secretary, Miss Sara McClure, demonstrated great skill and patience in preparing the manuscript itself, and I am most grateful for her always willing help.

I want to express a basic indebtedness to Mrs. Virginia Kennan, editorial assistant of the University of Virginia's Department of Psychiatry, with whom I entered into a close working alliance several years ago. She made it possible for me to write this book, since not only was she able with amazing speed to "decode" my rough handwritten drafts, polish my English, and edit the manuscript as it approached completion, but in her I found the necessary intelligent reflections and responses to my writing as I worked on it.

FOREWORD

This book will be of interest to the practicing psychoanalyst, the psychoanalytically oriented psychotherapist, and the behavioral scientist who wants to learn about new developments in psychoanalytic theory. Dr. Volkan has here made an important contribution to the application of psychoanalytic object-relations theory to the treatment of severely regressed patients. This theory may be defined in three progressively more restricted ways. Most broadly, it is concerned with understanding the nature of present interpersonal relations in terms of past ones — with the study of intrapsychic structures deriving from, fixating, modifying, and reactivating earlier internalized relations with others. What is usually included within this broad definition is the general theory of those mental structures that preserve interpersonal experiences, and the mutual influences of these intrapsychic structures and the over-all vicissitudes of expression of instinctual needs in the psychosocial environment. Psychoanalytic object relations theory, at this level, represents a general focus or approach occupying an intermediate field between psychoanalytic metapsychology proper, on the one hand, and clinical analyses of normal and pathological functioning, on the other.

A more restricted definition would describe object relations theory as a specialized approach within psychoanalytic metapsychology, one that stresses the building up of dyadic intrapsychic representations — "self-" and "object" images — reflecting the original infant-mother relation and its later development into dyadic, triadic, and multiple internal and external interpersonal relations in general. This focus stresses the simultaneous building up of the "self" and of "internal objects" (or object representations), with particular emphasis on the essentially dyadic — or bipolar — nature of all internalizations, which are established in the context of a particular affective disposition or interaction.

Whereas the first, broad, definition applies to practically all psychoanalytic approaches, the second reflects the views of such theoreticians as Erikson, Jacobson, and Mahler within the ego-psychological approach; Fairbairn, Winnicott, Bowlby, and Melanie Klein within the so-called British schools of psychoanalysis; and, to some extent, Harry Stack Sullivan and the more relevant work of Talcott Parsons.

A third, still more restricted definition of psychoanalytic object relations theory would limit the term to the specific approach of Melanie Klein and Fairbairn, including those close to Fairbairn, such as Winnicott, Wisdom, Guntrip, and Sutherland.

Dr. Volkan's application of psychoanalytic object

relations theory falls mostly within the level of the second, intermediate definition proposed, and, as Dr. Volkan points out in his introduction, is quite close to my own approach. Although Dr. Volkan relies considerably on my theoretical formulations, his approach is a flexible one and encompasses contributions from authors other than those included in my theoretical frame. He is, hence, his own man. This original book illustrates his attempt to develop new theoretical formulations in the light of the psychoanalytic treatment of severely disturbed or regressed patients. Dr. Volkan's formulations are open-ended; he uses object-relations theory, but does not make it a theoretical straitjacket.

Dr. Volkan's book is predominantly clinical, and psychoanalysts and psychoanalytically oriented psychotherapists will find in it perspicacious and thought-provoking clinical observations, as well as bridging of these observations with theoretical formulations, which, in turn, crystallize into particular technical approaches to these patients. Dr. Volkan's observations regarding emotional flooding, his discussion of transitional object relations, and his general focus on affect theory from a clinical viewpoint are among the original theoretical contributions he makes within an essentially clinical context.

Dr. Volkan correctly stresses the importance of differentiating psychoanalysis proper from psychoanalytic psychotherapy. Many analysts might, however, define psychoanalysis proper more restrictively than he does. This issue is particularly relevant in the treatment of patients with serious character pathology, borderline conditions, and psychoses, where parameters of technique and modifications of technique often raise the question of whether the treatment is still psychoanalysis. In agreement with Gill, I think that psychoanalysis proper is characterized by a neutral setting permitting the full development of the transference neurosis and the resolution of the transference neurosis by interpretation alone, and I would particularly stress the need for the psychoanalyst to maintain a technically neutral position. In contrast, psychoanalytic psychotherapy, while also requiring a technically neutral setting that permits full development of the transference, does not involve systematic transference interpretation (in the sense of the systematic interpretation of an orderly sequence of transference paradigms that jointly constitute the transference neurosis). The interpretation of the transference in psychotherapy would depend upon the moment-to-moment dynamic constellation or the combined impact of the predominant transference paradigm, the urgency of immediate life problems, and the specific goals in each case. Although transference interpretation is a crucial tool of psychoanalytic psychotherapy as well as of psychoanalysis proper, and although psychoanalytic psychotherapy and psychoanalysis both require a neutral psychotherapeutic setting, it is questionable whether one can call a treatment "psychoanalysis" when systematic analysis of the transference cannot be carried out, and where a great number of parameters of technique have shifted the stance of the analyst into a non-neutral behavioral position that cannot be fully resolved by interpretation alone.

Some of the treatments reported in this book are

psychoanalytic psychotherapy rather than psychoanalysis proper. Dr. Volkan's cases nevertheless illustrate how the application of psychoanalytic object relations theory to the theory and practice of psychoanalytic technique may broaden the indications for psychoanalysis proper, while also broadening the application of modified psychoanalytic psychotherapy.

All in all, *Primitive Internalized Object Relations* constitutes a significant enrichment of the general field of treatment of borderline conditions and psychoses.

Otto F. Kernberg, M.D.
Director, General Clinical Service,
New York State Psychiatric Institute,
and Professor of Clinical Psychiatry,
College of Physicians and Surgeons,
Columbia University.

INTRODUCTION

Great interest has been shown in recent years in the theory of internalized object relations and in its use to facilitate the understanding of clinical observations. This volume explores the clinical correlates of the pathology of internalized object relations, with considerable reliance on the theoretical concepts of Otto F. Kernberg. Kernberg proposes a bridge between the traditional psychoanalytic instinctual drives theory and the psychoanalytic object relations theory. The first views object investment as secondary to the expression of libidinal and aggressive instinctual needs; the second stresses the primacy of the infant's attachment to the object. Kernberg sees the earliest expression of instinctual drives in behavior that involves interaction between the infant and others in an "average expectable environment." He holds that subsequently the instinctual drives are expressed in internalized object relations which in turn are crucial organizers of all other psychic structures.

Internal object relations bring into play representations of self and object undifferentiated from one another at the outset. The undifferentiated self-object representations of the "all good" type are established as a result of perceptions and memory traces of experiences in which the mother's behavior was need-satisfying. Corresponding "all bad" undifferentiated self-object representations are at the same time built up out of any painful psychophysiological states. Libidinally tinged "all good" constellations and aggressively tinged "all bad" ones are polarized by the mechanism of primitive splitting. Within each constellation a differentiation between representations of self and representations of object becomes possible later, and when the developmental course is normal "all good" and "all bad" internalized object representations coalesce — between the end of the first year of life and the last half of the second year. Self-representations also come together at this time, and as soon as this process takes place the individual leaves the arena of primitive internalized object relations because he now has a stable self-concept as well as an internalized representational object world that is integrated.

A number of attendant "conditions" need consideration when we study fixation in or regression to the arena of primitive internalized object relations. For example, cathectic processes involving self- and object representations are reflected in introjective-projective relatedness. Denial is brought in to support primitive splitting; competence in reality testing is crude or altogether absent; emotional flooding may take place, since libidinal and aggressive drive derivatives do not interpenetrate; and the individual controls his psychological distance from the external object, which is tinged with his own projections and externalizations.

Clinical illustrations of psychopathology of primitive internalized object relations are drawn from my 16 years of experience with schizophrenic patients and those with borderline or narcissistic personality organization. Soon after I finished my psychiatric training at the University of North Carolina I was assigned for two years to a state institution for the mentally ill, which was at that time segregated and used for black patients only. I felt that most of my patients there had been admitted only after their behavior had become bizarre to the point where it could no longer be tolerated in the neighborhoods in which they lived. Since I lived on the grounds of the hospital, which was rather remote and greatly understaffed, I was immersed in clinical observations of psychotic behavior. Subsequent academic appointments at the University of Virginia and psychoanalytic training prompted me to systematic, in-depth observation of patients classified as schizophrenic, borderline, or narcissistic.

I do not try here to review the differences between psychoanalytic therapy and psychoanalysis proper or to point out their similarities. I use the term "therapy" for the former and "psychoanalysis" for the latter in instances where one or the other approach has been chosen. I focus on specific aspects of treatment to show the patient's attempt to create for himself an integrated internalized world. Obviously, such patients as I write about present many manifestations that deserve consideration, but I choose to make a systematic exploration of their primitive internalized object relations with little reference to other phenomena. This is not strictly designed as a textbook on the subject but I have tried to serve the needs of the student by tying each chapter with one that follows by pertinent introductory and summary statements.

The review begins with the clinical observation of an internalized, unintegrated, and "living" archaic structure — the "little man." The identification of an unassimilated internalized presence, and curiosity about it, serve to introduce the second chapter, which reviews the developmental stages of internalized object relations and the "conditions" already seen to accompany the pathology of primitive internalized object relations. Subsequent chapters examine these conditions one by one or in combination. It is my purpose to go far beyond the clinical reflection of primitive internalized object relations to show how such object relations are reactivated in the transference situation, and to give examples of the analyst's involvement in the patient's introjective-projective cycle, in the split transference, and so on. Technical suggestions are provided. Special attention is paid to the mending of the primitive splitting so essential in the treatment of such patients. Chapters III through VIII discuss the clinical correlates of primitive internalized object relations in the case of schizophrenic or borderline patients. Chapters IX and X deal with the narcissistic personality from the standpoint of primitive internalized object relations. The last chapter deals with transsexualism and neurosis and poses the question as to whether a "weakness" in mending a primitive splitting can contribute to the perniciousness of a neurotic situation.

The kind of patients I discuss may develop the classical transference neurosis once their primitive splitting is mended. I refrain from describing in any detail the usual issues involved in transference neurosis in order to focus on the transference psychosis (which reflects the failure to differentiate between self- and object representations and between one object-image and another), the primitively split transference (which reflects the interplay between the "all-good" and the "all-bad" analyst and the "all-good" and the "all-bad" patient), and the narcissistic transference (which reflects the idealization of the analyst as an extension of the patient's grandiose self—or, contrariwise, his devaluation as an empty husk). Although elements of the transference neurosis may coexist or alternate with other types of transference from the start, they may receive only secondary attention until other transference paradigms are resolved.

CHAPTER I

IN SEARCH OF A "LIVING" ARCHAIC STRUCTURE

Psychotic patients may communicate aspects of their internal reality, often with exceptional clarity. Such communication permits us to share their observation and to learn about their inner dramas and processes of change. This chapter opens with a vignette of a neurotic patient who referred symbolically to his inner attempts toward further structuralization by means of a childhood habit of building empires in a toy world by conquering and consolidating scattered islands. Some psychotic individuals unable to integrate early ego segments, which have formed self- and object representations and affective ties between them, not only refer symbolically to the drama of attempted integration of these ego segments, but at times become these different segments, and behave accordingly. Thus they present a clinical picture that changes in accordance with which segment is dominant at the time. Such a segment, a very archaic ego structure, can be seen in the "little man" phenomenon as the patient becomes the manikin. The "little man" is an archaic ego segment established under certain traumatic experiences in childhood, and retains a sort of autonomous existence. Thus it allows the investigator to study a "living" inner archaic structure.

A game of empire building

Toward the end of his first year in psychoanalysis, Gable, a man in his early twenties, recalled in vivid detail his childhood games and preoccupations. As a child he had played on the floor of a large bathroom with his toy soldiers and warships; the scatter rugs were islands to be fought for by his miniature navy. The object of the game was to acquire one island after another and then to integrate all of them into an empire, the units of which were connected with one another by using the ships as bridges. Each island had a name, and the consolidated empire did also. Gable had been deeply absorbed in this game.

Gable's efforts to unite a string of islands into an empire came to mind when, some years after work with this patient had terminated, I visited Hawaii and learned of the way King Kamahameha I had finally put all of these islands under one rule. Gable's focus on island conquest compelled him to continue the game even when the rugs were not available to him. He would draw the islands on paper, name them, then remove their boundaries and bind them serially into nations and then into an empire. His battles were always won by the "bad guys," and during his analysis he expressed curiosity about this ascendancy of the "bad guys."

[2]

He had begun his analysis with me when he was a student in English literature. He had developed "heart trouble" while playing basketball, on the eve of a visit from his parents, who had been living overseas. He had been married for a year, and the pending visit was to give his parents their first glimpse of the home he had made with his wife. He had always been pampered by his mother. His father was a military officer often assigned to foreign duty. As the oedipal father he remained for Gable a brutal, cruel, and cold man, and in the phallic phase — and later as an adolescent and a young man — Gable felt such anxiety in his presence that he felt impelled to avoid him and would not stay alone in a room with him. It was only toward the end of his analysis, after the father transference toward the analyst had been worked through, that he discovered that his actual father was a gentle man with whom he could have a warm friendship.

It is not surprising that this patient's analysis began with a fantasy, in which he was on a mountain top (which I came to believe represented his mother's breast), engaged in defending his country from a foreign invader. During the psychoanalytic hour after this disclosure, Gable "fell victim to the foreign invader," the analyst being of foreign birth. He and his analyst were to re-enact the inconclusive childhood war games. He desired as much as he feared invasion by the "bad guy" — analyst/father. When he regressed and recalled his preoccupation with war games he referred symbolically to the inner aspect of a continuing but incomplete psychic process, his attempt at further structuralization. Although other meanings may have been condensed in

[3]

Gable's childhood games, it was obvious that he was fixated in his attempt to integrate his inner structures, and that the "bad guys" represented his superego. The maps he saw on the bathroom floor or in his drawings were symbolic images of the process of his psychic structuralization.

Once his analysis had eroded his defenses and led him to reactivate in the transference and in his recall of memories the unfinished business of his childhood, Gable changed his college major from English to one in city planning. Once more he was at the drawing board, making maps, outlining boundaries only to erase them, and putting units together to create integrated structures. In spite of my interpreting his new enthusiasm as a representation of his childhood games, he continued studies in city planning. I believe that his map-making represented a sublimation. After concluding his analysis he obtained employment as a city planner, and, as I learned from others, greatly enjoyed his work.

If we look closely at Gable's islands we can see that each was a definite structure in its own right. Each had a name, definite boundaries, and its own military force. With this analogy in mind one might consider the antecedents of the island's structuralization. Whence did they come, and what kind of fluid boundaries might they have had before taking definite shape?

Gable was a neurotic who had the ability to use symbolism in a mature way. He could observe and symbolize an inner process unconsciously, and echo this process in action, but from day to day he had continuity of a stable ego identity. Had he been psychotic he would not have referred symbolically to his unfinished attempt to integrate his already largely differentiated psychic structures, but would himself have *been* his fragmented islands—some of which were quite amorphous; and he would have behaved in a fragmented fashion. A truly psychotic person would change according to whichever of his islands were currently dominant. For comparison I will now turn to a psychotic individual, the details of whose situation were reported by Abse (1955). The "islands" of this patient were not in the service of analogy; they represented actual psychic fragmentation.

Primitive ego nuclei

Abse's patient was a young woman, diagnosed as paranoid schizophrenic, who was oriented to "islands" like my patient Gable. However, phenomena referred to symbolically by Gable became an actuality to her in her psychosis; she became her islands and behaved accordingly. She conceptualized many "souls" (islands, some of them hostile to her, others warring against them on her behalf. She complained that her soul had trouble holding her body together, and reported that she had left parts of herself scattered from New York to California. Abse discusses the patient's symptoms in terms of Glover's (1932, 1950) conceptual model of the historical modifications of ego structure.

Glover might describe such "souls" as "ego nuclei," his conceptualization being that the primitive ego is polynuclear. An ego nucleus is a psychic system that has libidinal relation to an object (or part object); it can

[5]

discharge tension (aggression) toward this object and reduce anxiety. For example, an "oral" nucleus gratifies the instinctual drive on a mother's nipple (a part object); it can discharge aggression against the nipple as in biting, and can thus reduce tension. First nuclei also represent various erotogenic zones—cutaneous, respiratory, alimentary—in active function, as well as muscular reactive systems that discharge aggression. In the beginning, then, there is a cluster formation of ego nuclei that develop into cohesive organization as the anal-sadistic level of libido organization is reached. Glover suggests that the "decomposition products" of schizophrenia reveal the operation of primitive ego nuclei appearing in early life in the typical course of development. Abse states that Glover's conceptual model corresponds with the verbal reports of certain patients with schizophrenic psychosis, and with what they imply. "Disconnectedly, such patients work over ideational derivatives from the operation of disintegrated primitive ego nuclei established at oral, anal, auto-erotic and homosexual phases, as well as reporting on the total experience of the disintegrating process" (p. 232). Abse provides a theoretical formulation as to how such schizophrenic patients are able to observe and report their inner dramas, of which the battle of souls described by his patient is an example. After reminding us that psychoanalytic theory has identified the superego with an inwardly directed scrutinizing function, he suggests that in his patient who left "souls" scattered here and there:

. . . ego-feeling has become largely invested in the super-ego as part of the total defensive operation.

The patient strives to identify herself with the super-ego fraction of her total personality, and to a very large extent, one might say to a pathological extent, she succeeds. It is this achievement which enables us to share her scrutiny of what goes on within, for in her own way she formulates and communicates this scrutiny [p. 232].

One might re-emphasize that such schizophrenic formulation and communication of the inner struggle are not entirely symbolic. What is described, like the many souls of Abse's patient, not only stands for other representations, but is something that the patient has *become,* as this patient *became* her souls. Communication is possible only through primitive symbolization — in "pre-symbolization."

In one sense the analyst is fortunate when a severely regressed patient communicates, even when the communication is so primitive that the patient becomes what he inwardly perceives his psychic state to be. This process provides disclosure of the nature of such manifestations as "fragmented islands." By using such terminology as "primitive ego nuclei" we can put these structures in perspective and assess the advance of the therapeutic process by listening to the patient's remarks about changes in them — as the islands became nations and then empires, for example.

Glover's conceptualizations were based largely on an early concept of Freudian ego psychology as it was before being influenced by Hartmann (1939, 1950) and others. They were concerned with the cortical layer of the id and the development of the ego from this layer, rather than with the more commonly accepted contemporary notion of an undifferentiated id-ego matrix from which the ego and the id became differentiated. The latter formulation states that, regardless of whether its energic aspect is wholly or only partly traceable to the instinctual drives, once formed, the ego disposes of independent psychic energy (Hartmann, 1950). It should be remembered, however, that Glover (1966) later reiterated his formulations about ego nuclei and disputed Hartmann's position.

Before proceeding with further theoretical formulations and studying the process whereby the "islands" are integrated, one must ask whether it is indeed possible to study one island, an early unintegrated ego segment. The pathological ego formation known as the "little man" phenomenon (Kramer, 1955; Niederland, 1956; Volkan, 1965) provides a clinical example.

The "little man" phenomenon

In 1955 Kramer reported aspects of the analysis of a very ill middle-aged man in order to show the early experience one undergoes in moving toward the discovery of one's ego — or, rather, those segments of the ego that "embody the sense of one's identity" (p. 47). He used the term "identity" to denote "the awareness of one's self as an entity separate and distinct from one's environment, specifically, earliest environment" (*ibid.*).

At a point well along in his treatment Kramer's patient began to refer to a part of himself as "the little man," and, alternately though less frequently, as "the little king" or "the little lord." At first glance reference to "the little man" seemed to be his way of describing a

[8]

primitive, archaic, and harsh superego, but being an isolated part of the ego—"an area of condensed narcissistic reaction to the early perception of the patient's own weakness and helplessness" (p. 59)—was fundamental to this phenomenon. At first this ego segment did not contain the kind of identifications that enter into superego formation; these were added subsequently. In this way, features of the primitive superego were condensed in the "little man." Throughout the life of the patient Kramer described, his "little man" underwent no basic modification, since this ego segment was separate from the rest of his ego, apparently coming into the clinical picture as the patient became aware of the resistance to treatment this segment manifested.

Kramer tells of the traumatic events in his patient's childhood. The patient had had a severe organic illness (double pneumonia) during his first year, and the arrival of a sibling when he was 20 months old evoked rage against the mother and her newborn child. It forced an interruption of the unity that had existed between the patient and his mother, and did not permit its dissolution to come about gradually. The patient had "interpreted" his displacement by a sibling as evidence of the mother's hostility toward him. From this point on, development was precocious; a premature ego "extremely narrow in scope and limited in its capacity for further growth" was formed. Observations showed that the "little man" had come into being "as part of the discovery of the patient's separateness from his mother, at a stage when the mother was not yet felt as an external object, but was perceived as one with the child." It separated from the rest of the ego as he completed his third year and passed through different stages of libido development, each of which inflicted its peculiar trauma, aspects of which accrued recognizably to the "little man." The "little man's" main function, however, was to make available to the rest of the ego a mother equivalent from which separation would never be required. A price was being paid for the restoration and preservation of the omnipotence lost in infancy. The price paid for this success was clearly a heavy one,

> . . . as so often it is, when, to borrow a description from Freud, a prehistoric ego structure remains preserved as a fossil in the body of the ego, alien to its more advanced and differentiated elements [p. 69]. . . . The isolated existence of this ego segment interfered with the development of a properly integrated ego, and impaired its function of synthesis. In this fashion there came to exist a house divided within the ego itself, and the total effect was that of a weak, helpless, impoverished and limited ego, even though actually a part of it, the "little man," gave every evidence of possessing great power. Here it was not only the superego that opposed the ego as harsh taskmaster, but an isolated part of the ego itself that was not the result of an identification with the parents, but a segment split off in consequence of the necessity to sustain life with a support suddenly lost [p. 71].

Two contributions by Niederland (1956, 1965) and one by me (1965) followed Kramer's paper and further established the existence of "the little man" phenomenon. In one of Niederland's cases (1956) it emerged for the first time in a dream in which the patient saw an ugly and deformed little man in a dirty cellar. In his associations the patient referred to the dwarf Alberich who presided over the golden hoard in the saga of the Nibelungs, and to other dwarfs in mythology and literature such as Rumpelstilskin in Grimms' fairy tales, and Victor Hugo's hunchback of Notre Dame. At last the patient indicated in his associations recognition of the fact that "the little man" was himself, and he gradually identified more and more with "the dwarf" whenever he mentioned any kind of shady deal in which he had been engaged. Like Kramer's patient, this man learned to distinguish between the "dwarf" segment of his ego and the ego proper as time went on.

The appearance of "the little man" phenomenon in this case came about, as in the case of Kramer's patient, as the end result of a succession of narcissistic injuries on every level of early development. These included gross nutritional disturbances from birth, separation from the mother during her prolonged hospitalization, and the birth of a sibling, all of which undermined the feeling of infantile omnipotence. The "little man" accordingly had the illusion of omnipotence and formed no true object relations "in the sense of an investment of genital, or aim-inhibited libidinal energy in the object" (Kramer, 1955). Niederland's patient had been severely rachitic in infancy, but later gave no physical evidence of this except perhaps in a head proportionately large for his body, which had led his classmates at school to call him "big head," "little monster," or "shortie." Accordingly, this patient's "dwarf" was depicted by him as a creature less than a foot tall, ugly and hunchbacked, with a large square head resting on a body without bone or muscle.

The "little man" as these writers have described it is first an autonomous "fossil" separated from the rest of the ego. Its primary function is to deal with separation anxiety, but it is used subsequently as a defense against castration anxiety at the time when, following the anal phase, phallic components are added. Niederland's (1956) patient had serious disturbance in the integration and development of the body ego. "The at least partial blocking of the skeletomuscular system of discharge at a period when such avenues for discharge were most urgently needed, had far-reaching effects. The child entered the phallic phase with a few minor bodily defects, but with a severely disturbed body image" (p. 387). The "dwarf" was now utilized as an "internalized fetish" (p. 385). Thus it seemed, to use Freud's (1927) formulation on fetishism, like a token triumph over the threat of castration and a safeguard against it.

The "little man" in mythology and literature

"Little men" with magical powers are common in folklore and mythology. Murray (1960) wonders that our ancestors were so afraid of the power of fairies, since everything about them is miniature, and it would hardly be an alarming experience for a mortal to meet a fairy, a creature he could crush between his finger and thumb. To solve this puzzle, she traces fairies and elves—the "little people" of folklore—to the Horned God, the most ancient of all known gods, an omnipotent deity.

[12]

In his associations to his dreams about "the dwarf" Niederland's patient mentioned Rumpelstilskin among other magical little people. Heuscher (1963), who made a psychological study of fairy tales, associates this ugly and powerful manikin with the "new ego," holding that the new meaning he offers does not need to conflict with a more one-sided psychoanalytic interpretation which would see in the story a personal drama of the growing girl.

Abse (1966) notes that the early stages of body image change as one grows up—and as one ages—may involve symbolic reference to mythological figures through projection and condensation. He cites the Egyptian belief that every man has a *Ka,* an exact counterpart of himself in features, gait, and dress. Egyptian monuments represent the confrontation between king and deity, and in these each king has a little king standing behind him. So exact is the likeness of the manikin to the man—that is, of soul to the body—that fat, thin, long, or short bodies are accompanied respectively by fat, thin, long, or short souls. The *Ka* foreshadows the homunculus of later folklore, the dwarf with magic powers; but the exact doubling revealed in the *Ka* demonstrates a central psychic validity without ambiguity or adornment. A core of real truth lies behind the projective condensation of superstitious belief, just as is the case in the more idiosyncratic delusions symptomatic of mental disease. The *Ka* is a representation of a representation, for it represents the psychic representation of the body, the so-called body image, an essential part of the mental ego. Thus it is

[13]

logical that Niederland's patient had a "little man" who was deformed since it was modeled on the body image of a rachitic child.

Alice

The case of Alice is introduced at this point to illustrate in some detail the phenomenon "little man." Alice was the only child of a couple with such age disparity that her maternal grandfather, the "omnipotent" leader of his family, had been the same age as her father: indeed, she called him "Papa." He and the child's mother worked side by side in the country store he owned, and he was an integral part of his only grandchild's life. His death when she was 15 precipitated her psychiatric illness. Two years after her grandfather's death, Alice was rejected by a young man with whom she was having a platonic love affair. She lost 25 pounds in a month, with accompanying amenorrhea, was diagnosed as suffering from anorexia nervosa, and hospitalized. She derived little benefit from her treatment in the hospital, which included supportive therapy and 68 modified insulin treatments within four months' time. She continued hallucinating—seeing her dead grandfather—and remained suicidal. Her weight, assessed daily, ranged between 87 and 107 pounds, but her nurses soon realized that she was stabilizing herself at 99 pounds, refusing food when she weighed more, and stuffing herself if she fell below that weight. The meaning of this maneuver escaped her physicians and became clear only after she came into treatment with me after leaving the hospital, still very ill.

[14]

It was disclosed then that after the grandfather, a huge man, entered the hospital for care during what was to prove his final illness, the family "protected" the child from the shock of seeing him there, so she was totally unprepared for the sight of his shrunken body, which someone said weighed only 99 pounds, as it lay in the casket. She fainted, and, as she disclosed later in early therapy sessions, "became tiny" before losing consciousness. Although she had referred to a diminutive being at the outset of her difficulty, the meaning of the "little man" phenomenon emerged gradually during the first year of her treatment.

Congenital or early acquired malformations

Alice's mother had given birth to her only after she had been in labor for 48 hours, and throughout her pregnancy she had been constantly nauseated. Alice heard all about these maternal trials as she grew up. Her own eating difficulties had begun during the week in which her mother tried unsuccessfully to nurse her, but had been obliged to give up and resort to the bottle. During the first six months of her life the baby was dehydrated, constipated, and colicky. To make matters worse, she had been born with an umbilical hernia which was treated during her first nine months by strapping the anterior abdominal wall with adhesive tape. The mother had been obsessively concerned with this hernia, and often told her daughter about her anxiety long after the defect had healed. Thus the child not only had a body that was defective at birth, but her mother kept alive her defective body representation as Alice internalized her

[15]

mother's crystallized perception of her child's early body image.

The body defect was important in this case, as it was in that of Niederland's rachitic patient, and Kramer's patient who had double pneumonia. Niederland's (1965) work on narcissistic ego impairment in patients with early physical deformities shows the development of body ego affected virtually from the beginning in patients whose physical defect either existed at birth or appeared in the first year of life. Although many kinds of psychic traumas suffered in childhood may find solution through mastery in the course of subsequent development, Niederland suggests that an early body defect tends to leave an area of unresolved conflict because of its concrete nature, its permanence, and its cathectic significance. His study thus supplements the extensive work of Greenacre (1952, 1953, 1958) on this subject. She refers to primitive "body disintegration anxiety" in the serious disturbances of the early body image, and proposes that defective development of the body image contributes significantly to fetishism. Interestingly, both Kramer and Niederland see the "little man" as an "internal fetish" or "fossil."

I want to emphasize here the mother's role in the crystallization of the child's image of his own body. The mother's perception of a child's physical deformity may persist long after the deformity has been corrected; it may thus be given back to the child within the interaction of the mother-child unit. One of my patients, Ricky, to whom I will have occasion to refer in Chapter IV in some detail, was born with a deformity of one of his hands and its fingers. The part the mother played in his development of ways to deal with this deformity is apparent in the fact that on each of his birthdays, beginning with the fourth, she presented him with a golden ring like a wedding band, always too large for him to wear on his rather shrunken fingers. The mother of a child with a body defect can further traumatize her child if the mother-child unit functions poorly and she overestimates the child's body or attempts various physiotherapeutic or orthopedic maneuvers (A. Freud, 1952).

One of Alice's symptoms was her excessive preoccupation with pregnancy and her idea that if she became pregnant her abdomen would burst; these were directly related to her representation of her herniated abdomen and her mother's account of being torn apart in the effort to bring Alice into the world. After bearing Alice, the mother had developed many somatic complaints and had become a "polysurgical addict" (Menninger, 1934). She underwent six operations, five on her breast and one involving the uterus, the last being performed when Alice was at puberty. Both mother and child regarded these as having been necessitated by Alice's birth.

When she was a little girl, Alice often played that she was pregnant, stuffing a pillow under her dress in a representation of pregnancy and fantasizing having dozens and dozens of children. The counterphobic nature of this gesture is obvious. By the time she reached her late teens she felt that a penis would tear her apart during intercourse, and she was horrified at the idea of becoming pregnant by genital means. As is usual in anorexia nervosa (Meyer and Weinroth, 1957), she disclosed a highly oral concept of sexuality. Fantasies of becoming

[17]

pregnant by oral means appeared during her treatment. As shown in the literature (Waller, Kaufman, and Deutsch, 1940; Jessner and Abse, 1960; Volkan, 1974a), one way of looking at anorexia nervosa is to regard it as an acting out of the wish to be pregnant. On the one hand the patient wants to demonstrate pregnancy through amenorrhea (or, in the male, impotence), constipation, and overeating; on the other, whenever anxiety or guilt arises in relation to such gratification, the patient rejects the idea of pregnancy by means of starvation.

Aspects of the way Alice handled the consequences of her congenital hernia resemble those of a patient described by Niederland (1965). This patient, who lacked normal musculature in his anterior abdominal wall, acted out fantasies of magic oral incorporation in order to make the congenital body image intact, licking and even eating pages from sports magazines with photographs of muscular men. This was seen as a magical attempt at narcissistic replenishment. He also formed the habit of bathing for hours before retiring, repeating the performance when he awakened in the morning; by this enactment of his rebirth fantasy he hoped his deficiency would disappear.

Congenital or early body defects may, as in Alice's case, contribute to the development of the "little man" phenomenon. The autonomously existing split-off ego segment, containing "infantile features of invulnerability, grandiosity, timelessness, magic power, and other narcissistic attributes" (Niederland, 1965), becomes the reservoir, an "inner fetish" to deal with separation anxiety in its broadest sense—that is, with body disintegra-

[18]

tion anxiety (Greenacre, 1953) at one end of the spectrum and castration anxiety at the other.

Alice's "stick man"

I have given a full account of Alice elsewhere (Volkan, 1965). On one level her remark about having turned into a "stick man" (tiny person) before she fainted at the sight of her grandfather's wasted body seems to be an attempt to identify with it. In 1897 Freud (1887-1902) wrote to Fliess about the hysterical patient who imitates rigor mortis and sustains the imitation with tonic spasms. Alice, for whom her grandfather was not "resting in peace," found it necessary to keep in touch with him by internalizing him as well as hallucinating his presence. It soon became evident that the old man, as head of his traditionally oriented family, had been the reservoir of Alice's infantile omnipotence. He was for Alice the one who could "fix" anything, and it was impossible for her to surrender to death this helpful and protective giant.

When Alice attempted the process of mourning in the security provided for her by treatment, it was frozen at the initial phase of denial. I became aware of her intense separation anxiety as it appeared in the transference, as well as in her childhood memories of her mother's many hospitalizations. It was when she felt helpless and weak that references to the "little man" were made during her treatment, as a defense against her helplessness.

When she had been told as a child that Jesus "died and came to life again," she felt that she need lose no one in her family to death, and that she need never be

[19]

separate from her mother altogether. When she was about six, a visiting preacher had explained to her that a dead human being was like a "little seed"; seeds planted in the ground would come to life as beautiful flowers. Alice began to make interchangeable her references to the "stick man" and the "little seed." She recalled the death of childhood pets who had been buried in the back yard. She had grown roses on their little graves to keep them from "dying." Recalling this, she said her "stick man" was fashioned out of rose canes.

A little later in her therapy, associations were made to the "little seed." When she was in first grade, she had been shown a diagram of a fetus within the womb. Since this disclosure was made at about the same time she was told about death and the "little seed," Alice tried to picture herself as a little seed in her mother's womb. Further associations indicated that the main function of this tiny Alice was to deny separation — at one level, from the grandfather who was the reservoir of her projected omnipotence, and on another level, from the early mother. Alice was, in a way, stating that the freedom at issue in separating from her mother was available if she regressed to a phase in which intrapsychic separation was not required, a phase symbolized by union as a "little seed" with her mother. This patient, like the one observed by Kramer, was symbolically illustrating that the "little man" phenomenon could occur as a feature of the discovery of separateness from the mother "at a stage when the mother was not yet felt as an external object, but was perceived as one with the child" (Kramer, 1955, p. 63). Further evidence of this meaning appeared subsequently as she described the characteristics of the stick man.

One of her dreams seems to represent the split in the ego; she dreamed of two girls, one of whom represented her "little seed" aspect while the other was a mature woman who flirted with married men. The first of these girls was sick in bed. Her hair spread around her "as if she were coming up out of the sand" — like a plant growing from a seed. Associations to this indicated that her "little seed" segment could contribute also to handling conflicts from the oedipal level, and that by regressing to union with the mother she would be saved from the oedipal guilt of separating married men from their mates. As she worked on this dream, during the second half of her first year in treatment, Alice confided with some anxiety that her transformation into a "stick man" at her grandfather's funeral was not an isolated incident, but that since that time she had been in the habit of turning into a "little seed" or a "stick man" for a few minutes now and again, or for as long as several hours at a time.

Mirror, mirror on the wall

The characteristics of the "little man," "little seed," or "stick man" emerged from her account. When she looked into a mirror she saw herself as no more than an inch or two in height. The tiny creature she beheld was a precise miniature of herself, somewhat like the Egyptian *Ka*. When in reality she was sitting on a chair, looking in the mirror, she could see the chair reflected truly but her own person as diminuitive; its miniaturization made everything else enormous by comparison. When Alice was

[21]

being a "little seed" anything that approached her would itself shrink before touching her. If it failed to do so she became panic-stricken with fear of being ground beneath something of horrendous size, perhaps beneath a huge foot.

When she was tiny her perception of distance altered so that she felt it would take a long time to move only a short way. Nevertheless, she did move if it was necessary to do so to seek shelter. Usually she took shelter in her bedroom, where she locked herself in and became the "little seed" in the womb, omnipotent and capable of fulfilling her wishes magically. She need fear nothing, since as the "little seed" in its home she could restore her dead grandfather to life and defy separation.

Ferenczi (1913, p. 186) once described omnipotence as: "The feeling that one has all that one wants, and that one has nothing left to wish for. The foetus ... could maintain this of itself, for it always has what is necessary for the satisfaction of its instincts, and so has nothing to wish for: it is without wants." Ferenczi added, "The childhood megalomania of their own omnipotence is thus at least no empty delusion." The child demands nothing impossible; he is demanding only "the return of a state that once existed." Although he has spoken thus of a first "unconditional omnipotence" which persists as long as there is no conception of objects, "the omnipotence of human beings gets to depend on more and more 'conditions' with the increase in the complexity of the wishes ... as the wishes take more and more special forms with development, they demand increasingly specialized signals" (pp. 190, 191).

[22]

As Freud (1930) indicated, traces of the belief in an unlimited omnipotence (the oceanic feeling) of the objectless period persist in many people. In some, regression to it could be a defense against narcissistic injury; in others — those who have the "little man" phenomenon — the isolated segment of the ego has as its primary aim the restoration of the lost early infantile omnipotence and its continuation and preservation.

The figure in the attic

As Alice became able to distinguish between her "living" archaic structure and the rest of her ego, I could interpret to her the function of her "little man," especially the ways in which it protected her from facing separations. She came to understand that her grandfather was her "little man," a protector from narcissistic injuries, and that when she had seen his dead body in the casket she had re-internalized the "little man" and become the "stick man" herself. She understood the difficulty of grieving in order to let the old man go. Now she was ready to grieve fully, and she revisited the memories of their life together. She went on her own initiative to the attic of their house and spent hours poring over his scrapbook and photographs. Her therapy had brought on this physical search during which she found the original of the "stick man" in an old school workbook from the first grade. It was an illustration of a stick man holding a sign on which appeared the legend, "Hello! Look at me! I can help you. Watch my mark (*). I will tell you where to start."

This picture had been given to the students by their

teacher. It appeared to be an omnipotent helper, since it always pointed to the right answers and helped with school work throughout the year. Drawings in the workbook suggested that the students had drawn many stickmen figures every day. Alice's crystallized and split-off ego segment, which included the omnipotent self-representation that had been projected for so long on the grandfather, apparently drew its name from this symbolic figure the memory of which had been repressed. Another symbol—"the little seed"—had attached itself to the same concept at about the same time.

The death of the "little seed"

Once the magic of the "little seed" or the "stick man" had eroded in treatment by means of reconstructions, interpretations, and working through my loss of omnipotence in the transference, Alice seemed to be actively testing separation from the mother. Certain physical separations represented her anxious efforts to accomplish intrapsychic separation. During the time Alice was hospitalized her mother had formed a therapeutic relationship with a sensitive and warm psychiatric nursing instructor who met with her regularly during most of the time I worked with Alice. This meaningful relationship was responsible, I believe, for the mother's willingness to let her child, now nearly 18, have time to struggle toward more integrated individuation without external interference.

Just before her eighteenth birthday Alice went to her church for the first time in some years, and heard a sermon describing how all of the dead awaited resurrection at the end of the world, with all sinners being penalized by a seven-year delay in their becoming acceptable to God. This doctrine was at odds with the teaching she had heard as a child from the preacher who compared death with planting a seed, and who promised that the gates of Heaven open to all at death. This church visit provided the day residue for the following dream:

> I had just died and was lying on a bed. I saw two preachers. One of them was standing at one end of the bed, the other was at the foot. The first was waking my soul up, repeating the idea that after death one became a small seed first and then a blossom. The other was pushing me back into death. Both were taking turns, one after the other.

Her associations indicated the inner struggle between surrendering her belief in omnipotence or clinging to it.

When she became 18 Alice received a thousand dollars from an insurance policy. For a few days she gave way to "excessive feelings, now laughing and now feeling anger." She experienced the kind of strong emotion that had in the past made her turn into a "little seed." She declared that the "stick man" was dead. "I feel something missing in me now," she said. "I feel a little sad about it, but I want to jump for joy, too. I am 18 years old. I am a grown-up. I can feel angry and have sexual feelings."

The death of a President

One swallow does not a summer make, and a few months after "the death" of the "little man" a tragic event in the external world reawakened the "stick man" and

[25]

necessitated another round of examining this phenomenon. When she heard of President Kennedy's assassination Alice found herself thinking that he was like the "stick man" (or the "little seed") — an omnipotent figure. She imagined his power as being strong enough to hold the whole world together in harmony as her grandfather had held the family together. Now he was dead. Although her response to his death did not turn her into a "stick man," she had a dream which recalled her earlier dreams about her grandfather's funeral, except that Kennedy lay in the casket in place of the old man. She examined again, through this dream, the loss of her projected omnipotence, which had been represented in the "stick man" phenomenon. At her grandfather's funeral she had quickly internalized her projected omnipotence, and she showed a tendency here toward slowly taking in the omnipotent President. In therapy, she reported a localized pain in her head, and became sleepy. Then she remembered a fight among some children she knew, recalling that one of them had a toy machine gun. It became clear that the pain in her head was associated with the President's head wound, and she spoke of "going to sleep" as he had done. I interpreted her attempt to identify with the dead President who, as her dream had suggested, was associated with her grandfather and her own projected omnipotence.

Working through her reactions to these events enabled Alice to cry hard — something she had been unable to do for some years — both for President Kennedy and for her grandfather. "I am very sad about the President's death," she explained, "but I am very proud that I can allow myself to experience this sorrow." After this her associations to her dreams dealt for the most part with oedipal conflicts as they were reflected in her transference neurosis. In her dreams she competed with her girl friends.

Two months after the assassination she visited Washington with a friend, and felt pleasure that she could take such a trip without her parents. This trip provoked another dream about the "stick man":

> I was in the White House and saw President Kennedy lying there in a casket. I wasn't scared. In a way I felt sad, but I was very proud that I was allowed to see the body.

She associated Kennedy with the "stick man" without help from the therapist. "The stick man has been dead for about three months now," she said, and went on to talk about problems connected with her sexual feelings.

Whatever happened to Alice?

I have deliberately referred only to the pregenital aspects of Alice's "stick man" as she focused on them during the first year of her treatment. After she had acquired the ability to make a definite distinction between the pathological ego formation and the rest of her ego, she was able to achieve — ultimately — an ego that was more integrated. It became possible to focus on conflictual issues on a higher level. Alice's penis envy then became evident; on the higher level it was her penis that the "stick man" represented.

After two years in therapy Alice was a rather well

integrated young woman who fell in love and married. Although I felt she would benefit from further treatment, she moved away and I never heard again from her directly. Two years after she terminated therapy, however, I heard from her gynecologist that she, her marriage, and her newborn baby were prospering.

CHAPTER II

INTERNALIZED OBJECT RELATIONS

To grasp the character of a patient's "released" ego segments in day-to-day clinical practice will be impossible without taking into account self- and object representations they constructed, and the affective interplay among them. This chapter reviews the developmental stages of the internalization of object relations. The internalization of object relations plays the most important role in ego-superego development. It can be said that when a stable self-concept and stable object representations are formed, internalized object relations have matured and reached a higher level.

Object representations are not at the outset differentiated from self-representations. Even when differentiation between self-representations and object representations is reached, internalized object relations are considered primitive *when: cathectic processes that involve object and self-representations are reflected in introjective-projective relatedness; primitive splitting supported by denial rather than repression is the dominant mechan-*

ism of defense; and the presence of primitive splitting indicates failure to achieve a tolerance of ambivalence. Reality testing is not adequate. Patients who reactivate primitive internalized object relations during their treatment may develop transference psychosis and are prone to emotional flooding.

Another grandfather dies

The first chapter deals with a "living" archaic structure encountered in the course of therapy. Much can be learned from such phenomena; they provide a clinical understanding of the formulation of the islands described in the first chapter, for example. The isolated island Alice called the "little man" included an omnipotent self-representation constructed at a time when no definite differentiation between the child and the mother had been established; its primary purpose was to deny such differentiation. The "little man" included no "true" object relations at its initiation other than those objects Niederland (1965) referred to as narcissistic pseudo objects. In Kohut's (1971) terminology they might be self-objects. Kohut maintains that the existence of object relations does not exclude narcissism, but that, indeed, some of the most intense narcissistic experiences relate to objects. However, the objects referred to by Kohut as self-objects are themselves experienced as part of the self (See Chapter IX for further elaboration of Kohut's formulations).

In day-to-day clinical practice the character of "islands" is impossible to grasp without consideration of the patient's internalization of early object relations. In order to explore psychic structuralization and development profitably we must examine what the experience with objects has been. In pointing to the external origin of the superego that ultimately becomes an internal structure, Freud (1923) also made reference to the character of the ego, saying:

> At the very beginning, in the individual's primitive oral phase, object-cathexis and identification are no doubt indistinguishable from each other. . . . It may be that by . . . introjection . . . the ego makes it easier for the object to be given up or renders that process possible. It may be that this identification is the sole condition under which the id can give up its objects. At any rate the process, especially in the early phases of development, is a very frequent one, and it makes it possible to suppose that the character of the ego is a precipitate of abandoned object-cathexes and it contains the history of those object choices [p. 29].

It is experience with objects that makes it possible to lay down memory traces that can be utilized for thinking and facilitating the efficient functioning of the psyche at both memory and motor levels. Interaction with the environment promotes the ability to test reality.

It is, of course, an absurdity to think of psychic constructs literally as though they could be touched and measured in the physical sense, although certain patients—Gable and Alice of Chapter I, for example—describe theirs as if they had concrete reality. However, the psychoanalyst may be as well justified in using "map-making" techniques to communicate a concept as is the business executive who teaches his staff by means of a flow chart, or the demographer whose ascending bulge on a graph represents the presence and aging through time of population cohorts. That is not to say that the psychoanalyst has access to all the pieces of the puzzle, the segments of which take on size and shape as he works with his patient's disclosures; he continues to work with ever-changing dynamic forces and affective processes. When the patient discloses himself by what Bychowski (1956) calls "the release of internal images," the information about his inner archaic structures appears in complex ways, of which the defensive maneuvers against threatened anxiety in transference provide an example. When we put boundaries around ego segments, give them names, and indicate that they contain such constituents as the "released image of the nursing mother" or the "released image of projected infantile omnipotence" we resort to symbolism and metaphor to introduce necessary simplification to a situation that is itself far from simple, and to relate it usefully to our theoretical knowledge.

A clinical vignette will illustrate. The history of this patient resembles Alice's in many ways, and invites comparison. George, an extremely narcissistic man in his early twenties, referred to himself as "the last Renaissance Man." Like Alice, he had "torn" his mother during an unduly protracted delivery, and had been told so often about this that he had internalized a representation of his fantasy of this stressful event. His castration anxiety was condensed with his concern about the disintegration of

[32]

his body, counterphobic expressions of this concern appearing in a series of accidents of which he was the victim.

As a child he had witnessed brutal physical combat between parents who divorced subsequently. A flashy, "omnipotent" grandfather provided an external arena for the child's infantile omnipotence, so essential for him to maintain if he were to handle the stresses of his life and their internalized representations. He entertained the little boy by talking to him on the telephone, pretending to be some nationally celebrated movie star; the child knew and at the same time did not know that the caller was one of his heroes. Once when the two were attending a circus the child saw "in the flesh" one of the heroes with whom he had supposedly had a telephone conversation. The man's name came over the loudspeaker, and he appeared on horseback, evoking an "aha" experience that symbolized the crystallization of the boy's narcissistic character structure. He had access to omnipotent heroes — in fact, he himself belonged to that rare breed of men!

In the face of severe family problems the child and his grandfather paired, and acted like supermen. The boy was, in fact, handsome, highly intelligent, creative, and successful in dangerous sports; his narcissistic views of himself did not represent an altogether false reflection of his daily life.

When George was 21 his grandfather was murdered by an unknown assailant. The boy went into a psychotic break and became involved in the drug scene. Although later he was able to reorganize his narcissistic way of life to a great extent, he could not cope with his daily responsibilities. When he came to analysis his grandfather had been dead for several years. Alice had been able to reclaim from her dead grandfather the "encapsulated" omnipotent ego segment by means of the "tiny Alice" phenomenon. It became almost real enough to point to in space. The released image of the grandfather cherished by the "last Renaissance Man" was, by comparison, more complex and fluid, but it was nevertheless highly typical of this type of phenomenon. After eight months of analysis George became disoriented and helpless after a summer interruption of a few weeks' duration. In the working through of his helplessness the omnipotent grandfather image (which included his own projected infantile omnipotence, his "good mother" image as well as his ego ideal) appeared. In the transference I was the early "bad" mother who could not soothe his tensions. He canceled one hour and flew to another city on an "unbelievable" business deal involving the purchase and resale of African beads, a venture he expected to triple his investment of some $900 but which involved financial risk. This curious speculation made no sense on the surface, but during the next hour with me my patient spontaneously began talking about the *depression* years. His helplessness seemed to have left him, and his reminiscences of his grandfather's life in the difficult thirties surfaced without conscious awareness of any connection between the bead venture and an unusual exploit of his grandfather's that had become legendary in the family. The grandfather had been briefly jailed for some unexplained infraction of the law. While in jail he gambled with the sheriff and won his gun; he then purchased some

[34]

furs from a fellow prisoner, selling them later at such a profit that his transaction started him on the road to acquiring a fortune.

I then understood that my patient was by his behavior "releasing," through a dominant identification which directed his present behavior, a segment of his ego that included the image of the grandfather extricating himself from "depression" single-handed. The force of this memory could be seen in the patient's "remembering in action," his reaction to helplessness, and his use of the analyst as the unsoothing mother. Certainly the ego segment involved had gained the upper hand, even without the concreteness characteristic of the "little man" (George's case and his analysis are examined in detail in Chapter IX).

Self- and object representations

Although one of the main functions of the ego is to relate to objects (either to seek or to avoid them [Balint 1955]), object relations are crucial for the development of the ego and the superego; the nature of these structures is determined to a maximum extent by the internalization of object relations. Hartmann (1950) distinguishes the ego (as a psychic system in contradistinction to other substructures of personality) from the self (as one's own person in distinction to the object). At the outset, object representations are not differentiated from self-representations. The term "representation" is used to refer to "an enduring schema" (Moore and Fine, 1968) constructed by the ego from a multitude of impressions, realistic or distorted images of the self and the object.

[35]

Thus, for example, self representation: "includes enduring representations of all the experienced body states, and all the experienced *drives* and *affects* which the individual has consciously perceived in himself at different times in reaction to himself and to the outer world. Together with object representations, it provides the material for all the ego's adaptive and defensive functions" (p. 88). Object representations basically consist of a complex of affective and ideational components. The earlier ones have more dominance of affectual aspects because early object images, as well as the enduring schema in which they appear, are established within the foundation of a primarily affective relation between the infant and the mother (Novey, 1961). According to Jacobson (1964):

> The meaning of the concepts of the self and self representations, as distinct from the ego, becomes clear when we remember that the establishment of the system ego sets in with the discovery of the object world and the growing distinction between it and one's own physical and mental self. From the ever-increasing memory traces of pleasurable and unpleasurable instinctual, emotional, ideational, and functional experiences and of perceptions with which they become associated, images of the love objects as well as those of the bodily and psychic self emerge. Vague and variable at first, they gradually expand and develop into consistent and more or less realistic endopsychic representations of the object world and of the self [p. 19].

Kernberg (1966) suggests that the ego comes into

[36]

existence—in the sense in which Freud (1923) described it, not in the sense of primary autonomous apparatus (Hartmann, 1939)—when the internalization of objects (introjection) is used for defensive purposes, specifically, in an early defensive organization against overwhelming anxiety.

Since the ego's integrative function and the self- and-object representational differentiation are reciprocally developing and mutually enhancing processes, it would be appropriate to define each of Gable's islands as dissociated ego segments containing a certain primitive self-image constructed by the ego, each connected with a complementary object image and whatever affective disposition was uppermost at the time that particular internalization occurred. Moreover, in psychosis there is no differentiation made between self- and object images, and the islands are fragmented. The islands of patients with borderline personality organization are apt to be clustered, the "all good" clustering together, and the "all bad" splitting off into groups of their own. In this connection I use the term "splitting" as Kernberg (1966, 1967, 1970b, 1972b) uses it, applying it in a definitely more restrictive way than do the Kleinians.

Kernberg made the formulation that patients with borderline personality organization have a pathological fixation of an early ego constellation, and that the object and self-images they build up under the influence of the libidinal drive are not integrated with those built up under that of the aggressive drive. This division in the ego was at first a simple defect in the integration of "introjections" and identifications of opposite quality; it was subsequently to be used for defensive purposes. In order to distinguish this type of splitting from other applications of the term in psychoanalytic literature (Lichtenberg and Slap, 1973) I shall refer to it as *primitive* splitting, recognizing it in Kernberg's (1967, 1970b) schema of a *lower* and *intermediate* level of organization in contrast to a *higher* level.

The notion of fragmented islands clustering into constellations that are primitively split one from another recalls Jacobson's (1964) description of that time in childhood when:

> Libido and aggression are continuously turned from the love object to the self and vice versa, or also from one object to the other, while self and object images as well as images of different objects undergo temporary fusions, and separate and join again. Simultaneously, there is a tendency to cathect one such composite image unit with libido only, while all the aggression is directed to another one, until ambivalence can be tolerated. These cathectic processes are reflected in introjective and projective mechanisms based on the child's unconscious fantasies of incorporation and ejection of the love object [p. 44].

This is an account of the primitive internalized object relations that become evident in the clinical setting in adult patients when such relations are reactivated. While object representations are not differentiated from self-representations or from one another in psychosis, the patient with borderline personality organization can differentiate between representations of self and object except in *intimate* relationships, in which differentiation is blurred, or disappears. In the narcissistic personality the tension between the actual self, the ideal self, and the ideal object is eliminated by the fusion of all of these images into an inflated self-concept (see Chapters IX and X). In sexual perversions, object representations are retained, protected, and invested with libidinal and aggressive or neutralized energy, in spite of fused body image or fused genital representations (Bak, 1971). Primitive internalized object relations in transsexualism, which is one form of sexual perversion, are discussed in Chapter XI.

The following summary of a young borderline patient's cathectic shifts and changes as they were reflected during treatment in her introjective and projective mechanisms illustrates how the reactivation of primitive internalized object relations may appear in a clinical setting. I shall present the case of Jane in detail in Chapter VI. I wish here to show only the surface manifestations of the clinical material involved in the third year of her treatment. Moreover, this surface material will be examined only from the point of view of introjective-projective movement of her libidinally and aggressively invested self- and object images or representations. I shall not comment upon the condensed higher-level symbolism attached to this material, nor shall I remark about its genetic underpinnings. It will be noted that one clear manifestation of primitive splitting is a split transference. The patient perceives the analyst, who stands for the patient's libidinally and aggressively invested self- and object images or representations, as "all good" or "all bad" alternately. When the analyst is "all good," the "all bad" unit is attached to another external object or kept within the patient; as "all good" the analyst is seen by his patient as engaged mainly in protecting him from the "bad" units.

My patient opened one hour by reporting that "bad air" was trapped in her body, and that she wanted her analyst to stab her with an icepick to let the raging "evil" out. By the end of the hour she heard my voice as an inner hallucination as she took me in as a "good," soothing object image that would combat the "evil" within. During her hour on the following day the patient reported feeling dead inside. Her self- and object images had become undifferentiated; they appeared to be serving her in an autistic defensive maneuver. She then talked about wanting to be a surgeon, her associations pointing to a desire to excise the raging images within. As the hour went on, "all bad" images were projected onto me; then the patient wanted to murder me because my annihilation had become necessary for her protection. But this goal produced anxiety because my death would represent her own death, at least in part, inasmuch as I represented part of her own self-image. The patient finally relaxed when she remembered having written a request for "good music" to the local radio station. This represented the possibility of auditory introjection of "good" object images to protect her from her analyst seen as externalized "badness."

Jane filled the next hour with detailed and colorful descriptions of the furnishings in her room at home. (She had had at the beginning of her analysis a series of dreams about a room without structure but recognizable to her as a room nevertheless. In what she termed her "plug-in" phase, electric outlets appeared in it to furnish energy. Later, the room, although empty, had a discernible ceiling, walls, and floor. Furniture appeared as therapy progressed.) I felt that her changing the furniture in the room represented the shifts of her self- and object images from the inner to the outer world and back, and from one side of the primitive splitting to the other; these shifts occurred in her effort to control any eruption of primitive affective states.

The next day I was "all bad" and she seemed panic-stricken. As the hour went on she spoke of wanting to be fat, associations indicating her notion that fatness would protect her against instrusion by the "bad" analyst. On the next day, however, she reported that her muscles were filled with evil. Once more she begged to be "taken out of her body."

Systematization of stages whereby object relations are internalized

Kernberg (1972a) divides the process of the internalization of object relations into four stages, and then examines the psychopathology characteristic of fixation at any one of them. His thinking is consistent with that of Greenson (1954) and Jacobson (1964), who differentiate among those introjections and identifications that pertain to different times of life. They are thus able to indicate the relative maturity of patterns of internalized object relations throughout the developmental sequence.

[41]

Kernberg tries to bridge traditional psychoanalytic instinct theory and psychoanalytic object relations theory. The first places object investment secondary to the expression of libidinal or aggressive instinctual needs; the second — particularly among such spokesmen as Fairbairn (1954) and Bowlby (1969) — stresses the primacy of the infant's attachment to the object (mother). Kernberg (1972a) suggests that it is possible to bridge these two points of view if one takes into consideration an additional dimension of early development.

> ... the differentiation of "rewarding" (libidinally gratifying) and "punishing" (painful, frustrating, frightening experiences triggering aggression) experiences in the early mother-child interaction into early intrapsychic structures culminating in a set of structures representing "internal object relations...." instincts are expressed *first* as inborn behavior patterns that release in an "average expectable environment" [Hartmann, 1939] mothering functions and interpersonal interactions; and *later* are expressed as internalized object relations that, in turn, are a crucial organizer of all other psychic structures [p. 233].

He states that the first stage of the internalization of object relations is characterized by memory traces of the pleasurable, gratifying experiences provided the infant in interaction with his mother during a time when the primary undifferentiated self-object constellation has not yet been established. When the infant's relationship with the mother is unsatisfactory, autistic psychosis or a malignant type of "affectionless character" may result;

the personality structure may very well become anti-social. The mother must provide adequate stimulation and gratification of psychophysiologic needs if the child is to pass successfully into the second stage, which begins somewhere between the fourth and twelfth week of life.

In the second stage, primary undifferentiated self-object representations of an "all good" type are established as a result of the multiple perceptions activated by the need-satisfying behavior of the mother. Any painful psychophysiologic experiences build up correspondingly "all bad" undifferentiated self-object representations at the same time. The fixation of internalized object relations at this level is likely to impair the subsequent ability to test reality, and to preclude awareness of ego boundaries. Here the term "ego-boundary" is used by Kernberg to refer to the function of the personality that differentiates the origin of intrapsychic experience according to whether it arises from inner fantasy or memory, or from a perception of external reality.

While Stage I refers to the developing ability to differentiate between the stimuli that are significant and those that are not, and between the "all good" and the "all bad," Kernberg's Stage II implies further differentiation of "good" from "bad," and the further task of differentiating self from nonself, and the human from the nonhuman.

Fixation at or regression to this stage results in symbiotic childhood psychosis and "acute types of adult schizophrenia." At this stage there is excessive primitive splitting and defensive disorganization of cognitive process. Primitive projective mechanisms lead to paranoid distortion of important others. Since fixation at Stage II leads to symbiotic childhood psychosis, it must correspond to symbiosis as Mahler (1968) describes it. Giovacchini (1972a) questions whether one should consider the "symbiotic phase" one of object relatedness or one of "pre-object relatedness." He argues, "since the child is 'engaged' in a relationship (even though he is fused with someone else), this has been considered a primitive form of an object or part object relationship. One can argue that the process of fusion requires some concept (even though vague) or something outside the self in order to be able to fuse with it" (p. 153).

Modell (1963, 1968) suggests the term "transitional object relationship" instead of "symbiotic object relationship" for this phase, since the use of "symbiosis," taken from biology, is misleading, implying as it does an emotional bonding of the object to the subject. He points out that "the emotional attitude of the object to the subject may be quite irrelevant" (p. 41). In describing his "transitional object relationship" Modell depends on Winnicott's (1953) description of the transitional object which is not a hallucination but something that exists physically in the environment. In it, the child creates a substitute for his mother, and invests it with the qualities of life. It is not only the child's first possession, it is the first not-me (but not totally not-me) possession. According to Modell (1968):

> Winnicott's observation of the transitional inanimate object of the child—an object that is a substitute for the maternal environment but is itself created, invested with life, a life that is given form

[44]

by the child's own inner world—is analogous to certain types of adult love relationships ... [p. 33]. The relation of the subject to the object is primarily exploitive, the subject feels no concern for the needs of the object and cannot acknowledge that the object possesses his own separateness and individuality. The transitional object relationship is dyadic—it admits no others [p. 40].

Kernberg also acknowledges that "The playful control of nonhuman objects may have important functions in the self-nonself differentiation" (p. 240). In Chapter VIII, I shall examine aspects of the utilization of nonhuman objects in some detail.

Kernberg's Stage III, from six to eighteen months of age, is announced by differentiation between self-representation and object representation. This occurs first within the "all good" undifferentiated core, later within the "all bad" one. The differentiation within the "all bad" core is complicated "by the development of early types of projection; that is, intrapsychic mechanisms that attempt to externalize the 'bad' self-object constellation and probably determine the intensity of 'stranger anxiety' between six and ten months of age" (p. 235).

In this stage, in which "good" self- and object representations and "bad" ones are separated by primitive splitting from one another, there exists as yet no integrated concept of the self. However, ego boundaries do stabilize, because self-images are separate from object images now, and therefore self becomes differentiated from nonself. Integrated conceptualization of other human beings is not yet possible at this stage, since

[45]

"good" and "bad" constellations referring to the same object remain separated. Accordingly, Kernberg suggests the presence of "part-object relationships" so designated by Klein (1946). Failure to pass through this third stage successfully may cause borderline personality organization. Superego integration is not achieved until Stage IV is reached. Moreover, a fantastic "ideal self" representation without any correspondence to reality produces difficulties.

In the final stage an integrated self-concept is achieved and the separation of "good" from "bad" self-representations is mended. This process commences somewhere between the end of the first year of life and the last half of the second, and progresses throughout childhood. An integration of object representations accompanies the integration of self-representations as "object-images coalesce into more realistic representations of significant others seen as integrated individuals. An integrated self-concept 'surrounded,' as it were, by an integrated conception of others, with ongoing modification of self-concept and concept of others in the process of interpersonal relationships, constitutes 'ego identity' in the broadest sense" (Kernberg, 1972a, p. 236).

Psychopathology that arises from Stage IV of the development of internalized object relations will involve neuroses and the "higher level" (Kernberg, 1970b) of organization of character pathology, i.e., hysterical, obsessive-compulsive and depressive-masochistic character. At this level the previous fantastic ideal self and sadistically distorted images of parental figures coalesce to establish new structure, the superego with a concomitant

[46]

tamed ego ideal. At Stage IV infantile genital and oedipal conflicts rather than pregenital ones dominate the clinical picture.

Reality testing

As the ego boundaries become stabilized, reality testing — the differentiation of what is internal from what is external (Freud, 1940; Nunberg, 1955) — can be maintained. This capacity becomes available at Stage III; patients with borderline personality organization thus have considerable competence in reality testing. However, it is only in the last stage that the function is refined. J. G. Jacobson (1973) indicates a broader scope for reality testing than that contained in the formal definition I have given here. He itemizes four aspects of reality testing: "(1) the perception of the differentiation of self from object and the broader distinction of internal from external; (2) the perception of differentiated objects; (3) the perception of differentiated states of the self; and (4) the perception of affective experiences in the inner world, especially those derivatives which approach the drives themselves" (p. 399). These functions, he says, have two developmental lines; the first is "the primary autonomous line, the development of the perceptual apparatus that furnishes raw perceptual data." The second comes from "the emotional meaningfulness, the felt belief in the perceptions" within the matrix of separation-individuation experiences. There may be difficulty in reality testing in any one of the four aspects. The synthesis of all four gives way to a fifth factor, "the capacity to differentiate the present from the past" (*ibid.*). I

[47]

believe that until Kernberg's Stage IV is reached, the four component functions involved in reality testing cannot be synthesized and thus there is a tendency of the past to intrude into the present. For example, when the perception of differentiated objects is not strongly established one may often see a relatively indifferent object provide a stimulus that sets off strong affective response in the ego. Novey (1961) refers to "the principle of suitability of representations" to explain this phenomenon. He suggests that the impact of the relatively indifferent object rests on its affectional coincidence with an internalized object on the basis of this principle.

The following case demonstrates many aspects of the stages of internalized object relations short of Stage IV. It illustrates how an intolerance of ambivalence and the related mechanism of primitive splitting lie at the heart of the clinical picture.

A cat person

I call Samantha a "cat person," using the phrase employed by Sanford (1966) in her engaging description of her patient Elsie, who was so enmeshed with her pet cats and so involved in living through them that she always appeared in her analyst's notes as "the cat girl." Elsie not only displayed feline qualities herself but assigned important psychic roles to her pets, and even on occasion cast her analyst in a feline role.

Samantha was a 31-year-old married woman whose case I have described elsewhere in detail (1964). Here I highlight only those aspects that illustrate how one can

[48]

understand the clinical manifestations of primitive internalized object relations. She was the firstborn in a musical and "temperamental" family in which the father was only marginally involved, being passive and rather colorless. The mother was contemplating a professional career as a concert pianist when she became pregnant with her first child; she was unprepared for motherhood emotionally, and reared her daughter according to a book that advised leaving babies alone and refraining from unnecessary handling or affectionate play. To her the child was a lovely doll who would, in the course of time, gratify her mother by becoming a famous musician. As the child lay in her crib or played in her playpen, without tactile stimulation or body contact, the mother played the piano endlessly, perhaps feeling that through her music she was communicating with her baby. Practical competence in dealing with the child was so lacking that the baby had long crying spells at the age of a few months; the physician who had to be called said the infant was "hungry," and advised bottle-feeding.

The mother continued her "musical communication," and tried to teach her child to play the piano at an early age. The little girl's limited musical accomplishment disappointed her mother's hopes, and when another girl was born, 13 years after the first, the mother transferred her musical interests and ambitions to the latter child. By this time, however, the patient was caught in hostile dependency on her mother. When she married at the age of 17, she had difficulty dealing with the ordinary responsibilities of wife, housekeeper, and mother, and from time to time retreated under stress to her mother's home, near which she and her husband had made theirs.

Seven years before she came to see me, Samantha had moved with her husband and only child, a young daughter, to Europe, where Samatha's husband's business took him. The necessity of living at great distance from her mother represented an intrapsychic separation to Samantha. The European move, however, placed her in what she called "the most musical countries of the world." Her neighbors were musically inclined and often played the piano. It is possible that the musical environment provided in a distant land acted as one of the precipitating factors in the development—on a clinical level—of Samantha's psychosis.

The family took their cats—Maxie, a male, and Marie Jane, a female—to Europe with them. As she described them to me seven years later when she was a hospitalized psychiatric patient, I was struck by her identification with them, her behavior as a "cat person." When she felt gentle she worked her hands like the paws of a kitten kneading its mother's belly while nursing; and she expressed her aggression in clawing gestures. Once she made a significant slip of the tongue, saying that she "tasted" her cats when she meant to say she "chased" them. Sanford's (1966) patient Elsie, whose mother was psychotic, had consoled herself with the neighbor's cat, but I was unable to learn whether Samantha had so compensated herself in childhood for her mother's shortcomings.

She anthropomorphically endowed Marie Jane with

gentle and playful qualities, Maxie, with strength and power. Marie Jane met her end by falling from a window and going into convulsions. It was unclear whether or not Samantha had pushed her, although in therapy she blamed the maid for the accident. When it happened, Samantha did not weep, but assumed Marie Jane's purported stillness and composure. She had become greatly concerned about and fearful of the "wildness" she saw in Maxie after his mate died. She pondered whether he should not be destroyed, and felt that she would be liberated from her own aggression if the animal who reflected it in her perception were done away with. Her husband was persuaded to have the cat done away with and afterward she felt "killed inside," and regressed to a point she designated as "the complete backwards." In this state she assumed the fetal position and refused communication, adopting autistic regression as a defense.

Clinical manifestations of the "cat person's" internalized object relations

When I began seeing Samantha she complained of having too many "selves" or "frames of mind," much like Abse's (1955) patient, described in the first chapter. These diverse "selves" that made up her personality came and went, none remaining for any length of time. They were under two "main controls"—her left side and her right—and she referred to these "sides" as components of her "double personality." She continued to complain also of being often in the "complete backwards" state mentioned above.

It became clear in therapy that when Samantha was

mastered by her "left side" she spoke softly, with seductive and gentle behavior. When the "right side" dominated, she spoke roughly, exhibited temper to the point of throwing things at her therapist and on the floor of his office, and became generally aggressive. Occasionally she brought an accordion to the office and played it. Her music ranged from gentle to aggressive according to which of her two "main controls" dominated at the moment.

When her verbal communication in therapy became more meaningful she reported a division between her two "main controls" and named it the "bar." In order to communicate her perception of the "bar" as a gap she explained, "there is no place to land on it." I believe that the "bar," perceived as a chasm or hiatus, represented the primitive splitting that separated her two "main controls," and that one of the two "sides" represented her aggressively determined self-object conglomeration and the other represented its libidinally determined counterpart.

Neither "side" was static; she could go forward and backward on each. The "bar" had to be taken into account in all forward movement, since the patient had not achieved Stage IV, and could support only primitive internalized object relations because of the persistence of primitive splitting. In forward movement on either side, however, she could manage greater differentiation within her self-object constellation; backward movement was in the direction of a general blurring of these differences, and such regression wound up at the "complete backwards," the extremity of the "bar." Here she was "in balance" in the sense that her "sides" were then "equal" and the "good" and "bad" self-object representations were lost. When observed at the "complete backwards" or, as she put it, "before the dual thing starts," the patient was speechless. Her eyelids were heavy, and she lay motionless in the fetal position oblivious of others in the environment. She exemplified the first stage of the internalization of object relations. One might expect that a 31-year-old woman attempting to recapture a state of such extreme regression would retain an observing ego, however shaky. In the state itself she was incapable of verbal reporting, but she was later able to verbalize something of what had happened to her. As long as she was at "complete backwards" her thoughts came only "in music"; she had no words.

The transitional tune

Some years after I had the therapeutic relationship with Samantha, McDonald (1970) wrote her paper on "transitional tunes." This was based on Winnicott's (1953) transitional object, the first "not-me" possession, selected as somehow unique from among the child's belongings. It appeals to sight, smell, touch and taste. Noting that Winnicott in his original identification of this phenomenon did not altogether overlook auditory aspects, McDonald points to the transitional tune, which has to be:

> . . . a familiar tune, frequently filling the atmosphere between parent and child. It has to provide a shared and comforting experience. In that the infant hears it himself, he probably initially ex-

periences the sensation as though it were a part of himself, just as mother herself does not at first exist as a person distinct and separate from himself. At first he does not, and indeed, is not capable of, asking about the tune's origins or who "possesses" it. When he finds a way to reproduce the tune ... he can feel himself to be in charge and the originator of the experience [p. 513].

Music provided the bridge for Samantha to cross over, to acquaint herself with the external world, the mother. We see elements of this "first object" in "the complete backwards," which was not totally autistic in the technical sense since it included the precursor of an object representation that was to be separated from the self representation. Moreover, the patient must possess a split-off, shaky observing ego at this level to be able to describe it later. Before she arrived at the end point of "the complete backwards" Samantha would play certain nursery tunes or folksongs on her accordion, confirming the hypothesis that her relatedness to object began with the music that had "filled the atmosphere between parent and child" many years earlier.

Further evidence of primitive splitting in the cat person

For Samantha her cats had become, respectively, her libidinally and aggressively invested self-object represent- ations. They were involved in introjective-projective re- latedness; she could "taste" them as well as externalize them. As long as they were alive she could maintain the illusion of a balanced distancing of her libidinally in- vested self-object representations from those invested with aggression, and thus handle her intolerance of ambivalence and the tension that stemmed from her bisexuality, which kept her from fully developing female sexual identity. She perceived her "right side" as male; under its domination she was mannish. Her "left side" was female. Elements of bisexuality were later condensed also in the cats of the opposite sex. She felt at the mercy of "bad" self-object representations — aggressive affect (the male cat) — once her "good" unit (the supposedly passive, female cat) died. Aware that her aggression was dangerous, she had the "wild" cat done away with also, and defensively regressed to an almost objectless and undifferentiated state by destroying the cats' separate representations once and for all. By using transitional tunes she could achieve this almost objectless state, but she could nevertheless move out of it toward more highly developed stages of internalized object relatedness by means of her "musical thinking." As in Modell's (1970) reference to the uses of the transitional object, the transitional tune was Samantha's "watershed" (see the expansion of this idea in Chapter VIII).

Samantha's reactivation of primitive object relations was exhibited in other ways also in her day-to-day life. She spoke of having a "double personality" represented in her "sides," but she actually had many personalities since her many "selves" or "frames of mind" were included on either side of her "bar," each having varying degrees of differentiation between self- and object images and separate affective dispositions — her "ups" and "downs," in her terms. That her "multiple personalities" "knew" each other was evidence that it was a failure to integrate

[55]

(primitive splitting) rather than repression that was at issue. This type of "multiple personality" can be differentiated from the hysterical multiple personality that appears on a higher level by the fact that in the latter repression permits one or more of the personalities to remain unaware of the existence of the others.

At times Samantha included her bodily self-representation in her primitive splitting. Different sides of her face seemed to her to be pulling in or out, and she tried to protect her face or her head from splitting apart by using her hands to pull at her hair or to quiet the muscles of her face. Her only escape from the tensions so evidenced was to regress defensively to "the complete backwards." Elements of primitive splitting appeared in her daily productions. In one dream that had been recurrent since she was a child she saw twins, whom she associated with her "sides." When, during her 10-month hospitalization, she completed a rug in occupational therapy, a faulty line that divided the rug into two parts could clearly be seen. She kept in her room a magazine on the cover of which a brain was depicted as being divided in two; she explained her interest in it by saying that her own brain was so divided, and that at any given time she was sustained by only one half. Since she could not tolerate ambivalence, she adhered to the perception that her "left" and "right" sides were not coexistent but had separate being.

Primitive internalized object relations

My basic focus in this book is the study of clinical aspects of primitive internalized object relations, with

[56]

particular reference to Stages II and III. This leads me to an examination of patients who have not developed tolerance of ambivalence; for them it remains impossible to relate to the same object with love and hate simultaneously. This "crucial juncture" (Klein, 1946) has not been reached. Klein, who made no discrimination between external objects and endopsychic object representations, but to whom we owe much for her study of internalized objects, writes, "The synthesis between the loved and hated aspects of the complete object gives rise to the feelings of mourning and guilt which imply vital advances in the infant's emotional and intellectual life. This is also a *crucial juncture* [italics added] for the choice of neurosis or psychosis" (p. 100). At Stage II of internalized object relations self- and object representations are not differentiated. Even when object representations are differentiated from self-representations as well as from each other (Stage III), the internalized object relations are considered *primitive* when they are associated with the following conditions: reflection in introjective-projective mechanisms of the cathectic processes of object and self-representations, and separation of "all good" from "all bad" object representations by means of primitive splitting; separation of self-representations in the same pattern. When primitive internalized object relations are reactivated, primitive splitting, rather than repression, is the main defense mechanism. Moreover, other primitive defense mechanisms such as denial and global control of external objects come to the aid of primitive splitting.

There are other related "conditions." The patient,

having reached Stage III, may develop reality testing ability that is not refined and is ineffective in *intimate* relations. Patients in this stage and in lower stages are apt to exhibit manifestations of transference psychosis. Because they cannot interpenetrate derivatives of libidinal and aggressive drives, they are prone to emotional flooding during treatment. In the following chapters I shall examine different "conditions" which, when found in a clinical setting, reflect the existence of reactivated *primitive* internalized object relations.

CHAPTER III

INTERNALIZATIONS AND THE "ANALYTIC INTROJECT"

This chapter describes aspects of fusion of self- and object representations, as well as introjective-projective mechanisms that involve differentiated self- and object representations. The terms internalization, incorporation, introjection, and identifications are defined. Introject is referred to as special, already differentiated, object representation that strives for absorption into the self-representation in order to achieve identification. It is functional and may play a role in the formation or alteration of the psychic structure. Although patients speak of their introjects as if they are concrete foreign bodies, it would be a mistake for the analyst or psychotherapist to view them in this light, since such a view may lead to "mechanical" treatment maneuvers likely to become seductive intrusions.

Ego or superego building in patients who predominantly reactivate in treatment their primitive internalized object relations resumes on levels close and similar

*to those of their early child-parent relations. While the
introjection-projection cycles perpetuate the pathological
early object relationship, the gradual differentiation of
the analytic introject from the archaic introjects opens
the way for therapeutic results. It is in identification with
the analytic introject that the analyst's special functions
become the characterological modality of his patient and
thus build on and alter the patient's existing psychic
structure.*

Merging [fusion] and introjective-projective relatedness

In the preceding chapter I itemized the "conditions"
that justify calling internalized object relations primitive.
In this one I begin an examination of aspects of these
conditions, the fusion as well as the introjective-projective
relatedness processes that involve self- and object representations. When there is an absence of differentiation
between self- and object representations the situation reflects a fusion between them. When some differentiation
does occur, cathectic processes that involve these seg-
mented representations are reflected in introjective-projective relatedness. It may be very difficult to determine
the point in normal development at which the child's
introjective-projective relatedness terminates, but it
seems certain that this is the dominant form of relatedness throughout the first year of life.

The newborn's "ego" is submerged in the id-ego
matrix and, thus undifferentiated, has no object world.
The infant is protected from the mass of stimuli by the
stimulus barrier (Freud, 1920) provided by the not yet

developed state of the nervous system as well as the primitive state of the mental apparatus, which nevertheless has the capacity to differentiate between pleasurable and unpleasurable states. It is with the development of the perceptual functions and closely connected motor actions (Freud, 1925) that the pleasurable and unpleasurable sensations slowly become connected through memory traces with gratifying or frustrating (part) objects.

Fenichel (1945) summarizes the primitive reaction to the "first objects":

> . . . the infant wants to put them into its mouth. It was hunger, repeatedly disturbing the peacefulness of sleep, which compelled the recognition of the outside world. The experience of satiation, which first banished this tension, then became the model for the mastery of external stimuli in general. The first reality is what one can swallow. Recognizing reality originally means to judge whether something helps to gain satisfaction or whether it raises tensions, whether one should swallow it or spit it out. Taking-into-the-mouth or spitting-out is the basis for all perception, and in conditions of regression one can observe that in the unconscious all sense organs are conceived as mouth-like [p. 37].

This taking-into-the-mouth or spitting-out competence underlies the mechanisms of introjection-projection which exist first in the service of drives and later facilitate the infant's relatedness to his earliest external objects prior to and along with the ego's use of these mechanisms for defensive-adaptive functions. If we were more seman-

[61]

tically precise we would not speak of introjective-projective relatedness as existing before the establishment of awareness of external objects, however dim; it might, indeed, be more accurate to describe the relation between undifferentiated self- and object representations before awareness of any differentiation as merging or fusion. The child's ego perceives and experiences his impressions of external objects by fusion, and then in richer fashion by entering into introjective-projective relatedness with them. However altered they may be by investment of drives and fantasy, it is out of such multitudinous recognitions and experiences that the ego constructs object representations, which constitute an "enduring schema" (Moore and Fine, 1968) of objects other than the self.

The state of being like the object and undifferentiated is usually referred to as primary identification; this state pre-exists the discovery and cathecting of objects in the external world. Because of the ambiguity of the term, Jacobson (1964) avoids this definition, preferring to speak of "primitive affective identifications" instead. She notes: "The fact that the mother is able to directly induce affects in the baby by way of her own affective expression—a fact on which Sullivan's anxiety theory is based—is well known, but difficult to explain" (p. 42). She suggests that prior to these events there occurs a mutual "tuning in" of the discharge patterns of both mother and child that stimulates and prepares the awakening emotional life and ego functions of the infant. She continues: "We may surmise that the child's imitation of parental emotional expression arises on this basis and that early reciprocal affectomotor identifications between mother and child precede and usher in the child's imitations of the parents' functional activities" (pp. 42-43).

Winnicott (1953) describes the mother's tuning in with the child in terms of her "at the beginning, almost 100 per cent adaptation" to the child's immediate needs. This helps the infant to have the "illusion" that the mother's breast is not only part of the infant itself but is, as it were, under his magical control: "the breast is created by the infant over and over again out of the infant's ... need.... The mother places the actual breast just there when the infant is ready to create, and at the right moment."

As time goes on, the near perfection of the mother's adaptation to her infant's needs diminishes increasingly. The infant experiences frustration, which, in turn, plays an important role in the earliest attempts at reality testing. Winnicott says: "*If all goes well* the infant can actually come to gain from the experience of frustration, since incomplete adaptation to need makes objects real, that is to say hated as well as loved" (pp. 94-95).

Once the boundaries between the inner and outer worlds are established, introjective-projective relatedness serves the purpose of maintaining a close tie with objects. Introjection may lead to identification, which serves to make the self-representation like the object representation, but independent of it. Although one of the earliest tasks of the new ego is to differentiate between self- and object representations, early identifications in which part of the self-representation becomes like the already differentiated object representation provide the materials for

[63]

the ego's adaptive and defensive functions thereby allowing the ego to grow. Anna Freud (1936) noted this when she said: "Introjection from the outside world into the ego could not be said to have the effect of enriching the latter unless there were already clear differentiation between that which belonged to the one and that which belonged to the other. But the situation is by no means simple" (p. 51).

Incorporation and internalization patterns of introjection and identification

I must speak further about identification although I have no intention of reviewing all of the ramifications of this concept. Critical reviews of this subject include a collaborative work by Miller, Pollock, Bernstein, and Robbins (1968), and the series of papers by Meissner (1970, 1971). Knight (1940) claimed that the term "identification" has probably been used in more different senses than any other psychoanalytic label, and Koff (1961) cautioned that any individual member of the family "identification" should be introduced by the first as well as the last name. Some types of identification can be seen as defensive mechanisms of the ego, and others are hysterical (symptomatic) manifestations that appear when the symptom represents fulfillment of the wish to resemble someone else in some way — and the punishment for the wish at the same time. I shall limit myself here to those identifications that can be seen from a developmental perspective — especially with reference to earlier developmental stages.

Although Freud in 1896 and 1897 spoke of identification (hysterical) in his letters to Fliess, it was not until the *Three Essays on the Theory of Sexuality* (1905) that he made a theoretical formulation about identification, referring to the experience of sucking as an essential gratification tied to the oral zone and linked with the function of nutrition. The sexual aim of the oral phase, the oral taking in of the external object, became a prototype of identification. (Here he began to see identification from the standpoint of development also.) After Ferenczi (1909) used the term "introject," Freud (1917) applied the concept it named to the analysis of mourning and melancholia, which signaled the beginnings of the study of internalized object relations. A libidinal relationship should not be given up when its object is lost, since the ego identifies with the lost object. Moreover, the loss of a love object provides an opportunity for any ambivalence that had characterized the relationship to surface and make itself felt with some force. In 1923, while describing the external origin of the superego, which ultimately becomes an internal structure by means of taking in, Freud referred to the ego as a precipitate of abandoned object cathexis. Hendrick (1951) described the fundamental differences between identifications responsible for the formation of the ego and those accounting for the superego. Identifications that lead to superego formation involve the more mature object relatedness of a child going through the resolution of the Oedipus complex, but ego-forming identifications result from the more primitive relations with the object that occur in early infancy and childhood. "In contrast to superego formation, the early ego identifications are derived

[65]

largely from the mother's way of doing things, rather than from the prohibitions against what the child wants to do. Ego-identifications therefore contribute largely to growing capacity to deal effectively with the external world" (p. 56). Moreover, Hendrick reminds us that earliest ego-identifications involve only partial functions of the infant's ego, since at this level the infant is obliged to deal with only partial object perceptions and partial functions, being as yet unable to integrate them and to cathect the total object.

> . . . ego-identification may either produce the capacity actually to exert power originally attributed to another, e.g., to handle a spoon in the way the mother handles it, so the baby will not be frustrated when she delays feeding it, or, when the baby's physiological capacity to reproduce the actual function is inadequate, identification may result in the use of substitute partial functions; this is illustrated by Freud's (1920) example of the baby who throws a ball and pulls it back in order to achieve in fantasy the power of bringing mother back when she has left the room [*ibid.*].

Furthermore, the infant, through fantasies, attributes omnipotence to the object. Identification with such an object produces an ego in quest of omnipotence and may in adult years produce behavior which is not adaptive.

Koff (1961) approaches "true" identifications metapsychologically. From the economic point of view, identification is an attempt to conserve libido by shifting it from an external to an internal object. From a structural point of view, true identification results in changes in the

[66]

self to resemble an object. Seen dynamically, it conserves libido by offering one portion of the self as a substitute for an external object. The latter is renounced, and the ego unconsciously experiences identification as a movement of the object from the external to the internal world. It may be more precise to say that in some instances the external object is renounced as a result of identification; identification in this case replaces the object relationship. In other identifications, like those in the service of super-ego formation, identification with the external object permits the continuation of the relationship with the same object in a form now "delibidinized and deaggres-sified" (Greenson, 1954).

A major contribution was made by Hartmann (1939) when he enlarged Freud's ideas about taking part of the external world into the internal world. Hartmann main-tains: "In phylogenesis, evolution leads to an increased independence of the organism from its environment, so that reactions which originally occurred in relation to the external world are increasingly displaced into the interior of the organism. The development of thinking, of the superego, of the mastery of internal danger before it becomes external, and so forth, are examples of this process of internalization" (p. 40). Later, Hartmann and Loewenstein (1962) spoke of internalization as existing when regulations brought into play in interaction with the outside world are replaced by inner regulations. This suggests that internalization is functional-regulatory; these aspects are further elaborated in the scholarly work of Schafer (1968), who states: "Internalization refers to all those processes by which the subject transforms real or imagined regulatory interactions with his environment, and real or imagined characteristics of his environment, into inner regulations and characteristics" (p. 9). Schafer sees identification as a subclass of internalization. Later (1973) he argued that internalization is a "pseudospatial" metaphor "that is so grossly incomplete and unworkable that we would do best to avoid it in psychoanalytic conceptualization . . . it refers to a fantasy not to a process" (p. 434). I continue to refer to his 1968 contribution since the concept of internalization as a process contrasted with a process of externalization provides useful insight into clinical manifestations and a tool for the planning of technical maneuvers.

The terms "introjection," "incorporation," and "identification" were not clearly defined after Freud, and indeed seem to have been used interchangeably. Schafer, like others (Greenson, 1954), sheds light on the differences among them; he sees identification and introjection as two distinct types of internalization. The latter refers to the process whereby object representations become introjects, and in this representation the object carries on an internal relationship; whereas identification refers to modifying the subjective self or behavior, or both, in order to increase one's resemblance to an object taken as a model. The term "incorporation," on the other hand, is not used as a synonym of internalization. Schafer uses it to refer to a specific wishful *primary process ideation* of taking in the object through the mouth or other body orifice. Such ideas then express either the wish to continue one's relationship with the other person within oneself (to introject him) or the wish to assimilate (to identify with) some aspects of his being. Such ideas are usually accompanied by ideas of being incorporated by others, like those appearing in Lewin's (1950) well-known triad of eating, being eaten, and falling asleep—or with the expelling of incorporated objects in feces, vomit, etc. (Abraham, 1924).

I agree with Schafer's (1968) view that primary-process ideation concerned with incorporation appears not only in such conditions as mourning and melancholia but, "There is reason to think that the primitive infantile identifications, those in which self and object representations merge directly, are wished for and experienced as incorporation of the object by the self or of the self by the object. But this is not necessarily or altogether so for the later identifications—those, for instance, that go to make up the superego" (p. 22). I shall deal with this type of primitive identification in Chapter IV, indicating how it manifests itself in actual clinical experience.

Linking objects and introjects in relation to self- and object representations

It is necessary that I define the term "introject" as I use it, before continuing. There is little agreement among contemporary psychoanalytic writers as to what this entity is. Some, notably Jacobson (1964, 1971) and Kernberg (1967), conspicuously refrain from using the term where others would find it appropriate. Giovacchini (1972a) seems to regard it as the same thing as the object representation and uses the terms interchangeably, in spite of providing a rather specific definition of the introject as "experiences and objects that have become part of the ego but have a structure of their own that distinguishes them from the rest of the ego" (p. 157).

I propose to examine the introject concept first from a clinical-descriptive point of view and then from the theoretical standpoint. My work (Volkan 1970, 1971, 1972, 1974b) with adults responding pathologically to the death of a loved/hated intimate indicates that people in bereavement keep within themselves a representation of the one they have lost. Some even refer to having buried the deceased within their breast. Such a representation has, in the eyes of the patient who is established in pathological mourning, an independent existence that may persist over years and provide an opportunity for continuation of the past relationship. Although this relationship is of necessity conducted internally, it involves — as the patient perceives it — interaction that, to all intents and purposes, is between two persons (or their representative parts such as face, head, etc.) on an ambivalent plane.

One of my patients whose half-brother drowned kept a representation of the dead boy's face and voice within his bosom and carried on inner conversations with it as he drove to work. Other patients being treated for pathological responses to loss by death have exhorted the representation of the dead, resident as a foreign body within them, to "Get out! Get out!" (Volkan 1971, 1972; Volkan, Cillufo, and Sarvay, 1974).

It is usual to call the inner representations in all such circumstances "introjects." The psychoanalyst understands this phenomenon in metapsychological terms but patients in established pathological mourning describe these as concrete entities, foreign bodies. The patient feels the introject with his own mind and body as part of the other person, i.e., a voice, a face, etc. Children and psychotics describe such "inner presences" (Schafer, 1968).

I agree with Schafer's (1968) report that: "Objects appear to become introjects (to be introjected) in crises — for example, when they are urgently needed and are unavailable, or when they get caught up in storms of ambivalence. Both the coming into being of an introject and its continued existence represent attempts to modify distressing situations with the external object" (p. 73). Such inner presences are referred to in psychoanalytic literature in the accounts of episodes in which the analyst becomes an introject that competes with pre-existing introjects or is gradually assimilated into the maturing ego-superego organization. This psychoanalytic process will be examined in Chapter IV.

Although I have said that the established pathological mourner feels his introject to be a foreign body that is nothing more than the representation of the dead person, the situation is considerably more complex, as I shall indicate. A consideration of "linking objects" (Volkan, 1972) that are actual *external* inanimate objects put to magical use by the pathological mourner, will contribute to the understanding of the type of introject at issue, and its relation to object and self-representations.

The adult established pathological mourner is "frozen" at that stage of uncomplicated grief that Bowlby and Parkes (1970) and Parkes (1970) refer to as "the yearning to recover the lost object." This phenomenon can be seen years after the loss has occurred. It is patho-logical in that it is accompanied by a dread that such a recovery will in fact take place (Volkan, 1974b). The polar opposites of the yearning to recover and the dread of doing so reflect the ambivalent conflict that character-ized the mourner's relationship with the deceased. I observed also that in established pathological grief the adult patient's process of searching for (as well as dread-ing) the return of the dead "is unconsciously intensified, and ... is habitual and specific enough to be called a mechanism of defense—and defense mainly against the tension of ambivalence and the eruption of derivatives of those aggressive and libidinal drives originally directed toward the deceased" (Volkan, 1972, p. 216).

The patient's search and concomitant dread coalesce in his choice of the specific inanimate object he will use as a linking object, and the way in which he will use it. Although the established pathological mourner may pick a "last-minute object"—something at hand when the death news came and which therefore marks the last moment in which the deceased was considered to be living, it is more usual for him to select something that had belonged to the dead one, perhaps something he wore. The object may have been a joint possession, in fact or fantasy. It may be a symbolic representation of the departed, as simply a photograph.

One patient had as a linking object a red robe of her own that her mother wore constantly during her last months. This patient, a single woman, was in her thirties at the time of her mother's death, and although she realized intellectually that her mother was no longer

[72]

living, her behavior denied the fact. She yearned for her mother's return but dreaded it also.

She was the youngest of six. The mother had been severely burned when her last child was six months old. Bedridden for a year, the mother had been unable to carry out her mothering functions. The early mother-daughter relationship which contained elements of un-resolved separation-individuation manifested itself in later years as sadomasochistic. Although her siblings left home, the patient stayed with the mother, who was widowed, and, during the last ten years of her life, an amputee because of diabetes. The patient had surrender-ed all independent social life, a college scholarship, and opportunities for marriage to care for her parent. Al-though she sometimes wished for her mother's death, she kept in touch with her day and night at regular intervals "to see if she was all right," phoning her from work several times daily and sleeping at the foot of her bed and checking regularly during the night.

After the mother died she appeared often in her daughter's dreams and fantasies, clad in the red robe in which she had died. The patient had purchased it for herself on one of her infrequent holidays but gave it to her mother at her request. It became a linking object, an ambivalence-strained link that had to be externalized but also put aside. The daughter became actually afraid of it and took pains to avoid contact with it.

I have dealt elsewhere (Volkan, 1972, 1974b) with the distinction between the linking object and fetishes, and between linking and transitional objects. (For further examination of these topics see Chapter VIII.) The linking object is specifically associated with a loss; its primary purpose is to deal with separation anxiety. Although it might be said to represent the reappearance in adult life of an early transitional object, it is "distanced" in a unique manner, i.e., locked in a chest or hung out of sight in a closet, never required by the transitional object in childhood or the fetish in adulthood. The mourner insists on being aware at all times of its whereabouts, although he may be as much interested in avoiding it as in giving his attention to it. It induces eerie feelings, and is seldom put to use in the usual way of wearing or using a keepsake to which only manageable sentiment is attached.

My study of the linking object has persuaded me that it provides an external locus in which part of the patient's projected self-representation may meet externally with part of the projected object representation of the deceased. This meeting provides a link in which the ambivalent object relationship is not renounced but "frozen." Although great care may be taken to keep it out of sight, it is important to know where it is at any given moment; the ambivalence of wanting to annihilate the deceased and simultaneously longing for him is condensed in it, and it provides an external reference for the painful and unresolved work of mourning. It makes it possible for internalized object relations with the dead to be maintained externally.

One of the most interesting ramifications of the linking object concept is the merging of parts of projected self- and object representations within it. The kind of introject earlier described as pertaining to established pathological mourning serves much the same purpose; from the point of view of the patient the foreign body in his bosom is a locus (this time internal) in which self- and object representations can meet. With the exception of transient experiences of merging with the dead one, the established pathological mourner's main inner link with him is through the introject, and the outer link with him is through the linking object.

It is true, of course, that the established pathological mourner had had an object representation of the now dead intimate during the time he was alive, but this was invested with vastly more psychic energy after the death and loss occurred. Uncomplicated mourning might involve not only the gradual decathecting of the object representation of the deceased but undisruptive identification with parts of it. Greenson (1954) holds that one can observe in patients suffering from depression the introjection of the ambivalently regarded object without transformation that would indicate identification. This is the state of affairs that I call established pathological mourning, in the belief that the typical patient suffering from pathological mourning does not accomplish total identification. Pollock (1961) has also demonstrated this circumstance. I believe that in depression there is a total identification and the self-representation changes by identification with those parts of the object representation (of the deceased) that include disruptive elements; thus the self-reproach of the mourner is clinically evidenced. The adult caught up in established pathological mourning is in a continuing but tenuous position between the processes of depression and those of uncomplicated mourning as he maintains his introjects.

Although the patient himself perceives and describes his introject as a representation of part of the deceased, a closer look at it reveals that although it is indeed dominantly an object representation it is also contaminated with self-representation. It is, in fact, a specific kind of differentiated object representation that strives for absorption in the self-representation to achieve identification, and for prime rank among many object representations. Not all object representations are introjects. The introject is functional, being that object representation that is metamorphosing into an identification while yet falling short of it inasmuch as it retains characteristics of an object representation and a separateness — in Schafer's terminology, a specific "inner presence" — apart from other self- and object representations.

The psychotic and established pathological mourner may talk about "inner presences" and treat them as concrete entities, but the analyst should not perceive — or fantasize — as concrete what the patient is describing to him. It is no doubt for this reason that Jacobson (1971) refrains from using the term "introject," preferring "introjection" instead because of its more abstract reference. As I have indicated, the analyst's "maps" of the movement of inner presences serve admirably to communicate situations that are virtually ineffable, but the metaphorical implication of the term "introject" should not be forgotten, however concretely the patient may describe it and however well the concept of the introject as a locus

[76]

upon which identification may be built served theoretical design. The introject remains an abstraction of the patient's perceptions he is struggling to communicate to us. The theoretical nature of the introject is even clearer when we speak of it in early life as a precursor of psychic sinew that will allow identifications and ultimately the formation of ampler psychic structure.

We do know that it is not the internalized replica of another individual (or of any part of him) that promotes that effective identification that will effect structural growth or change. As Kohut (1971) emphasizes, once the psychic apparatus is ready for the formation of structure there occurs a breaking up of those aspects of the object imago that are being internalized. This breaking up comes before the withdrawal of cathexis from the object. A depersonalization of the integrated aspects of the object image then occurs. Emphasis shifts from the total human context of the personality of the object to certain of its specific functions. Thus the internal structure becomes capable of performing those functions for the execution of which the child formerly had to depend on the object itself.

On the therapeutic process

Loewald (1960) relates psychoanalytic treatment to the process of normal personality development. I agree with his assumption that ego development is resumed in the therapeutic processes of psychoanalysis. Loewald explains himself by reference to Erikson's (1956) concept of identity crises in life. Even though there is marked consolidation of ego organization about the time the

[77]

oedipal complex resolves, ego development is a process that continues without a given end point unless psychosis or neurosis intervenes. In the absence of such disturbance, higher integration and differentiation of the psychic apparatus goes on. Other periods of consolidation come, one toward the end of adolescence and others at different phases of the life cycle. Consolidation occurs after a period of ego regression, since relative disorganization ushers in reorganization. Erikson calls this event an identity crisis, and Loewald sees the promotion of transference neurosis in psychoanalysis as an induction to ego disorganization and reorganization — in short, to ego development. The resumption of ego development in psychoanalysis is contingent on the relationship with a "new object," the analyst. His "newness" depends not on his being an object not hitherto encountered, but "the newness consists in the patient's rediscovery of the early paths of the development of object-relations leading to a new way of relating to objects and of being oneself. Through all the transference distortions the patient reveals rudiments at least of that core [of himself and "objects"] which has been distorted. It is this core, rudimentary and vague as it may be, to which the analyst has reference when he interprets transferences and defences, and not some abstract concept of reality or normality, if he is to reach the patient" (Loewald, 1960, p. 20).

The relationship between child and parent provides a model. Loewald reminds us that when he internalizes aspects of his mother the child at the same time is internalizing the parent's image of himself, as the mother sees, feels, smells, hears, and touches him. Thus, early ego identifications are built not only by absorption of what the mother is like but also by absorption of the way the mother regards her infant. "The child begins to experience himself as a centred unit by being centred upon... In analysis, if it is to be a process leading to structural changes, interactions of a comparable nature have to take place" (Loewald, 1960, p. 20).

This kind of thinking appears also in Strachey's (1934) classic paper on the therapeutic action of psychoanalysis and the importance of influencing the superego. It seems likely that the resumption of ego development, the modification of the superego, and the taming of instinctual drives are interdependent processes within the whole psychoanalytic process. Strachey asserted that the superego can be changed by the introduction of the analyst as a new object, designated by Strachey as an auxiliary superego. His concept of mutative interpretations includes two steps, the first of which is a qualitative modification of the patient's superego, the second being the analyst's demonstration to the patient of the discrepancy between the patient's view of the analyst as an archaic object (representation) and his simultaneous perception of him as an external object in the real world:

> The patient's original super-ego is ... a product of the introjection of his archaic objects distorted by the projection of his infantile id-impulses. I have also suggested that our only means of altering the character of this harsh original super-ego is through the mediation of an auxiliary super-ego which is the product of the patient's introjection of the analyst as an object. The process of analysis may

from this point of view be regarded as an infiltration of the rigid and unadaptable original super-ego by the auxiliary super-ego with its greater contact with the ego and with reality. This infiltration is the work of the mutative interpretations; and it consists in a repeated process of introjection of imagos of the analyst—imagos, that is to say, of a real figure and not of an archaic and distorted projection—so that the quality of the original super-ego becomes gradually changed [p. 157].

Later, Heiman (1956) stated: "What really changes the archaic superego and divests it of its demoniacal or godlike character are processes in the ego: its conscious recognition of its impulses, its accepting responsibility for them and withdrawing projections from its external and introjected object.... Alongside the modification of the ego, the superego changes its character" (p. 308).

What Loewald (1960) described—the child-parent relationship that develops in the therapeutic process of borderline and psychotic patients—occurs "on levels relatively close and similar to those of the early child-parent relationship. The further we move away from gross ego defect cases, the more do these integrative processes take place on higher levels of sublimation and by modes of communication which show much more complex stages of organization" (p. 21).

Such observations are made also by other analysts. For example, Cameron (1961) holds that operation on archaic levels, although creating problems, permits such patients as we are discussing here to "use the equivalence of early partial identifications in ways that a more maturely developed psychic system could not. It may even still be possible ... to introject massively with archaic completeness in adulthood and then be able to assimilate the new introject as an infant might, so that it disappears as such, but some of its properties do not" (p. 95). Giovacchini (1972b) uses the term "analytic introject" when the analyst is taken in to provide the patient with an analytical attitude that he may use as a characterological modality of his own.

On becoming an "analytic introject" in the transference psychosis

Strachey (1934) referred to the importance of having the patient come to know his analyst as a "real figure." Anna Freud (1954) states that many analysts have the opinion that a patient's fantasied relationship to his analyst—the transference—is strongest when he enters treatment. He then works through his transference neurosis through interpretations, and only at the end of his treatment does a real relationship come about. Anna Freud agrees that this may be true for psychotic and borderline patients but that the reverse holds for the common neurotic. The patient enters analysis with a reality attitude concerning the analyst, but this becomes secondary as the full-blown transference neurosis develops. When this is worked through the figure of the analyst can emerge once again. But "as far as the patient has a healthy part of his personality, his real relationship to the analyst is never wholly submerged."

Greenson (1969) states that admitting the "real" relationship into psychoanalysis is nonanalytic, but it is not anti-analytic. According to him, it is the "real relationship" rather than positive transference that serves as the core of the working alliance between the patient and his analyst. In fact, Greenson adds, only those patients with the capacity for transference-free (real) reactions are analyzable. If the patient is unable to form transference-free responses he needs preparatory psychotherapy to build object relations based on reliable perceptions. While there is always the danger of misusing the "real" relationship—i.e. it can be a seductive gratification—its importance should not be forgotten, especially with borderline and psychotic patients.

The term "real figure" may be misleading inasmuch as it does not refer to the analyst as a social person with his own name, his own social security number, and a life style of his choice—a model to be carbon-copied by the patient. Kernberg (1972b) takes up the "real person" issue about the treatment of borderline patients:

> If "real person" refers to the therapist's direct and open interventions, his provision of structure and limits, and his active refusal to be forced into regressive countertransference fixations, then the therapist would indeed be a real person. However, if "real person" means that the regressive transference reactions of borderline patients—their inordinate demands for love, attention, protection, and gifts—should be responded to by "giving" beyond what an objective, professional psychotherapist-patient relationship would warrant, objection must be made to the therapist being made a "real person" [p. 273].

The clinical fact is that excessive dependency manifested by this type of patient stems from the reactivation in the transference of primitive internalized object relations. "The working through of the negative transference, the confrontation of the patients with their distress and hatred, as well as with the ways in which that distrust and hatred destroy their capacity to depend on what the psychotherapist can realistically provide better fulfill their needs" (*ibid.*).

One of the clinical manifestations of the reactivation of primitive internalized object relationship is the patient's attempt to merge in the transference process with his therapist, or to include him in his introjective-projective relatedness. While the therapist's inclusion in the patient's introjective relatedness, on one level, can be seen as his (the therapist's) being sucked into the patient's pathology, it is in the repetition of such introjective-projective mechanisms that the introject of the therapist will be formed, transient at first but ultimately stable. It is suggested that at first, because of psychotic transference distortions, object representation and the introject of the analyst will be modeled after archaic object representations or archaic introjects. In fact, the analyst will be taken in at different times in multiple fragmented or split representations. It is the "realness" of the analyst as Kernberg has described it that eventually influences the character of the analyst introject, making it a functional analytic introject the hoped-for assimilation of which will bring structural alteration. Thus any maneuver of the analyst to offer himself to his patient as a model is usually seductive intrusion that will lead to anxiety and reduce the possibilities of ego building. However, techniques that deliberately foster the patient's introjection of and identification with the therapist have been attempted (Rosen, 1953; Scheflen, 1961). These may result from the therapist's mistaken perception of the introjective and projective processes as mechanical, and the introject and object representation as concrete.

It should be noted that internalization that occurs in the transference psychosis may, rather than serve in ego-superego building, indicate an effort to retain a primitive type of relationship. Searles (1951) indicated in an early paper that the "incorporative processes" within the trans-ference-countertransference relationship may, when used as a defense against anxiety, "be at the basis of many long-standing stalemates in psychoanalytic therapy." Similar warnings are given by Kernberg (1972b). The analyst would be forcing the internalization of himself as a "model" should he provide much personal information about himself, or convey in an exchange I could only call anti-psychoanalytic, the way in which he handles his own life. The analyst must try to have a precise understanding of what he represents when he is taken in by his patient; such insight will indicate what kinds of function the analyst-introject will perform at any given time.

What prepares an analyst to help his patient form an analytic introject while working through a transference psychosis? The analyst's ability is based on the experience of his own analysis and the resolution of regressive aspects within it, his supervised and nonsupervised work with neurotic patients, his intellectual knowledge of early psychic development, and his present capacity to maintain the analytic position. Nevertheless, the relationship within the psychotic transference has a certain "newness" for the analyst as well; the level of intensity in the relatedness that the patient strives to reach (modeling it after the intensity of the early mother-child unit), the abrupt shifts in the way his patient perceives him — these are more alien to the analyst's ordinary state of being than the relatedness and problems brought by the neurotic patient for his therapeutic consideration. Moreover, the distance between the therapist's higher-level observation and the regression he experiences in the service of the other (Olinick, 1969) is not only greater than it is vis-à-vis the neurotic patient, but longer-lasting. Until he can achieve a "work ego" (Olinick et al., 1973) for this kind of task, the analyst may find that it takes an enormous amout of energy to deal effectively with the transference manifestations of the patient who reactivates the primitive internalized object relationship as a dominant feature of the long part of his treatment.

CHAPTER IV

INTROJECTION OF AND IDENTIFICATION WITH THE THERAPIST, AND ALTERATION OF THE PATIENT'S PSYCHIC STRUCTURE

This chapter describes the patient who is engaged in a continuing effort toward ego (and superego) formation; his relationship with the therapist is dominated by intro-jective-projective relatedness. As the therapist enters this vicious cycle, the experience yields no therapeutic gains for the patient who manifests transference psychosis, because initially he cannot differentiate the therapist from archaic self- and object representations or archaic introjects. In fact, this cycling may gratify the patient's instinctual needs and thus pose major resistance against therapeutic working through. It is only when the thera-pist is differentiated from the archaic image that the patient's introjection of and identification with the thera-pist's function is seen as operating in the service of altering structures already formed and/or forming new ones.

Clinical material that provides specific illustrations of the internalization of the therapist by patients of this kind is cited; in these examples the process is accompanied by primary-process ideas of incorporation. Internalizations are crudely symbolized as taking in something from the outside world through body orifices. It is hoped that deliberate selection of these examples, rather than those of more sophisticated and complicated instances of introjection and identification, will demonstrate clearly the kind of representation in which the therapist is taken in, and with what results, in a variety of circumstances and in different phases of treatment. The study of primitive identifications in a clinical setting may provide the analyst with tools with which to examine early structure formation and alteration.

Crudely symbolized internalizations

Empirical evidence from psychoanalysis demonstrates that the acceleration of the process of introjection and identification is commonly accompanied by many oral—often cannibalistic—fantasies (Hendrick, 1951). The primary-process ideation of taking the object in through the mouth, other body orifice, or skin expresses either the wish to continue within oneself the relationship to the other (to introject him) or the wish to assimilate (to identify with) some aspects of his being. Clinical experience shows that very primitive identifications are accompanied by incorporative ideas and are experienced as incorporations of object representations. Schafer (1968) reminds us that the situation is different for later identifications, such as those involving superego formation. It is simplistic, for example, to think of the superego as an incorporated paternal phallus image. Schafer notes that in this instance the incorporated object image does not bring with it a set of moral imperatives, and that it does not necessarily acquire, after it is taken in, those self-qualities without which identification cannot be made. In later identifications there occurs depersonalization of the integrated aspects of the object representation, and a shift in emphasis from the human context of the personality of the object to certain of its specific functions (Kohut, 1971).

The study of primitive identifications in a clinical setting may provide the analyst with tools with which to examine early structure formation and alteration. This chapter will deal with those adult patients who are prone to exhibit what must be described as transference psychosis, rather than the transference neurosis that is classic in the analytic process. Moreover, it relates only to aspects of their treatment that appear before significant alteration of their psychotic core. They typically bring to treatment some nonpsychotic parts that respond in the fashion of transference neurosis. Although neurotic symptoms will thus occasionally demand attention (Boyer, 1967), it must be remembered that any attempt to work through the patient's problems by interpreting aspects of the transference neurosis will fall far short of modifying the truly psychotic core which responds to external objects by reactivating primitive internalized object relations.

These patients, schizophrenic or borderline, are

considered here because, unable at times to use symbols in any advanced way, they openly manifest the intro-jective-projective aspect of primitive internalized object relations in association with such bodily functions as eating and spitting out. For these patients, the primitive symbolism of eating the analyst—or part of him—stands not only for the incorporative ideas involving him, but the internalization of the analyst himself. What is brought into play in the simple process of eating or spitting out can provide insight into vastly more subtle processes in which patients take in or eject the analyst image in the course of transference. The use of this physical model to symbolize internalization in its simplest form, however applicable, should not lead to an oversimplified view of a complex psychological process.

The kind of patient under discussion may gain little that is new from his experiences with external objects, since his primitive mode of relating to external objects leads him to regard whatever he internalizes as represen-tations of archaic introjects, themselves originally dis-torted by drives and fantasies. Instead of promoting the establishment of ego integrity and an integrated self-representation by assimilating new introjections, the pa-tient embarks on a cycle of reprojecting and reintroject-ing something little distinguishable from the old.

The analyst himself is included in this cycle, being introjected at first as a representative of the patient's archaic object representations, projected self-representa-tions, or archaic introjects. Thus, the initial introjection of the analyst, his internalized representation, fails to provide the patient with an analytical attitude to use as a characterological modality of his own. In other words, what comes from the analyst to be introjected by the patient is initially not an analytic introject. As he and his patient work through in the treatment, however, the analyst will differentiate himself in piecemeal fashion from archaic object representations and archaic introjects in order to alter the representation of himself that the patient has internalized; thus the patient may in turn alter the nature of his archaic introjects. The primary initial goal of therapy with borderline and psychotic patients is the alteration or replacement of existing archaic ego-superego introjects (Boyer, 1961, 1967, 1971; Volkan, 1968; Volkan and Luttrell, 1971; Giovacchini, 1972a).

Thus it is the analyst's task to appreciate precisely what it is he represents when he is being "taken in" by a patient. Primitive identifications that are accompanied by incorporative ideas help the analyst to observe this process and its rather obvious meanings. In subsequent discussion I shall first illustrate crudely symbolized internalizations and then show how the analytic introject competes with the archaic introject after being differentiated from it, and how differentiated analytic introjects may begin to prevail over the archaic introjects and initiate integration, alteration, and the formation of a new structure.

Clinical illustrations

A young woman, Jane, came to my attention after an acute psychotic episode six months before she was to be graduated from college. (For details of her case see

Chapter VI.) Since completion of her college work was necessary for her self-esteem, she returned to school after nine months of four hours' weekly work with me. During her absence from the city for the required six months, our contact was limited to the one afternoon and one morning hour made possible by an overnight stay at home. She subsequently returned to four hours a week and finally underwent analysis on the couch; this reached successful termination six years after our first encounter.

During her six months at school our sessions were marked by introjective-projective relatedness. She began to introject me during our time together. I sensed this; while I was with her, I felt as if I were posing for a picture. She regarded me with eyes that blinked as though she were using them as a photographic lens. This habit of hers reminded me of a young schizophrenic patient who at times thought of himself as a camera, whose case Luttrell and I have reported (1971). Fox (1957) reported the case of a photographer who used his camera as an organ to control visual intake and to satisfy his incorporative strivings.

The girl came under increased stress at the approach of examinations. Her simulation of photography became markedly exaggerated. She would ask me to smile and to turn my face toward the light. I did not oblige her in this, but neither did I interpret what she was doing. When she brought a snapshot of herself to show me, I commented that I had noticed her "taking pictures of me" for some time. She then spoke of the extreme anxiety she had experienced in school so far away from me, and how she had dealt with it by going into a dark room and summoning me up by mentally "developing my picture." She could then sense my presence and ease her anxiety. (This process had a defensive function also, since she was not introjecting me but my *pictorial image;* I was safe from destruction by internalization.) In this example the analyst was a "good," protective object representation.

In the following case, during one phase of her treatment, the patient externalized aggressive self-object images onto her analyst, and felt the need to defend herself against internalizing him. The daughter of a narcissistic woman and an ineffectual man, this patient was in her late twenties. During her childhood her anxieties had been dealt with by enemas given almost daily by either of her parents or one of her two elder sisters. At the age of 15 she had wrapped a piece of her feces in a tissue and presented it to a sister; after this episode the enemas were discontinued.

After her marriage at the age of 25, however, she persuaded her husband to give her enemas. By then she was addicted to sleeping pills also. Her analysis started a few years after her marriage. In spite of her physical beauty she appeared to me at times to be a little more than a gastrointestinal tube, or an "earthworm" (Suslick, 1963), as she lay on the couch. She could control what went into her mouth and what came out of her rectum. Her experiences with enemas were condensed with her primal scene fantasies. In the transference situation she would try to arouse in me a desire to intrude within her body; at the same time she feared such intrusion. She perceived her analysis as an enema experience, feeling that the analyst would go to work in her entrails. She therefore needed to protect herself from internalizing me as the bad, intrusive object.

In the eighth month of her analysis, just after my holiday during which I had become the noncaring early mother, she came to her session eating "lifesavers," popping one into her mouth whenever she felt anxious, with the fantasy that this would keep me out. Daily, at home, she placed an enema tube in her rectum as reassurance that she was in control of whatever went into or came out of her rectum. Meanwhile she maintained "all good" self- and object representations within herself. The use of lifesavers continued for a few months, after which she brought other candies. I understood that her fear of internalizing me was no longer a matter of life and death to her, and that I was somewhat different from the archaic "bad" self- and object representations. A few months later, *after* I felt that I had made adequate interpretation of her behavior, especially its aggressive aspect—i.e., the notion that my "coming in" might destroy her viscera—when her symptomatic behavior continued in spite of adequate interpretation, I suggested that I could work more effectively with her if she had no candy in her mouth during our sessions. She responded positively and thus developed anxiety, which I hoped to utilize for working through.

Although the analyst acted here to inhibit behavior after what he felt to be adequate interpretations rather than waiting for the patient to modify her behavior herself, this step should not be seen as inconsistent with the analyst's task of being tolerant of the patient's projections long enough to make the necessary connections with their intrapsychic aspects, and long enough for the patient to "take in" a like tolerance in reinternalizing her analyst. A quality acquired in this way may be retained, recalling the suggestion of Giovacchini (1967a) with reference to character disorders: "In the beginning of treatment, interpretations may not involve much in the way of specific content. However, from the very first interview, the patient is making projections, some quite obvious, but others subtle. By constantly interpreting the projection, one causes an internalization of conflict. The analyst's purpose is to focus on the intrapsychic, and when the patient succeeds in doing likewise, he has gained considerable security" (p. 224).

Aspects of interpretation and the "reality base" at the beginning of treatment

Interpretation is the analyst's basic tool in dealing with both neurotic and psychotic patients in psycho-analytic treatment. Boyer (1971) views interpretation in the treatment of schizophrenia as the most important contribution to the structuralization of the ego, but he does not regard it as optimally effective before the cathexis of "maladaptive introjects" has lessened, and healthier introjects have begun to replace them. He emphasizes the great value to the patient of coming face to face with a calm, accepting, objective, incorruptible and essentially optimistic analyst who provides an atti-tudinal model with which he can identify.

Boyer's (1967) "office treatment" of schizophrenic patients "begins with steady but gentle confrontations with distortions, contradictions, and other abandonments of reality, coincident with interpretations which are, as a rule, of the defensive functions of the products of his psychotic thinking" (p. 159). He suggests that the analyst not concentrate at first on any material arising from sexual drives *per se,* unless an erotized transference threatens and seems likely to become unwieldy and to restrict his interpretation of the aggressive aspects of what is being presented. Boyer chooses, moreover, to deal with depressive material rather than to pursue paranoid idea-tion, adding: "Both changes in technique reflect my growing conviction that ego introjects cannot be altered efficiently unless simultaneous changes take place in the superego introjects, in the direction of reducing the archaic, sadistic nature of that psychical structure" (p. 160).

In dealing with the type of patient I describe, analysis of the oedipal conflicts must await resolution of pregenital conflicts. Interpretations should stress the defensive nature of the patient's productions; I concur with Boyer (1971) in suggesting that they should be inter-preted from the standpoint of object relations rather than content. What is initially significant for the psychotic is systematic interpretation that basically provides differen-tiation of the analytic introject from his archaic objects, however piecemeal this process may be. Although inter-pretations are, whenever possible, directed toward the surface, it is at times difficult with some patients to determine the surface (Giovacchini, 1969). During the psychoanalysis of a typical neurotic patient the analyst makes so-called "id interpretations" after long prepara-tory work and after an exploration of surface resistances and other defenses. By the term "id interpretations" or "deep interpretations" I mean those that are directly pointed at id impulses such as the impulse to devour. The analyst may find in treating the psychotic or borderline patient that certain id interpretations *are* surface interpretations (Volkan, 1968).

What lies on the surface of the patient's relatedness to his analyst in full psychotic transference, i.e., cannibalistic fantasies relating to introjection, are manifestations of what we would call "deep material" in the case of a neurotic patient. The analyst should not, I believe, shy away from interpretations about such manifestations from the point of view of object relations, since it is helpful for the patient to have his uncanny fantasies and experiences given a name, and designated as events in a developmental process rather than as grotesque occurrences taking place outside human experience. Such interpretation also assists the patient as he learns how to tame his aggressive impulses, and gives him ideas concerning libidinal involvement.

One of my patients, knowing that I am Turkish, felt panic lest his indulgence in a turkey dinner cost me my life, and it comforted him to hear that his cannibalistic fantasies showed a wish to relate to me, and that, furthermore, my destruction would mean his own. This interpretation clarified his basic fear of self-destruction.

In dealing with patients prone to develop psychotic transference we know that not only is interpretation of vital importance but that the patient's experience of the "newness" and stability of the analyst-object is also. The two aspects are naturally intertwined; the analyst is "new" since he interprets. Nonetheless, with the kind of patient discussed here, I feel it advisable to establish a reality base — and to establish it very early in the treatment. In his fusion with or introjective-projective relatedness to his analyst such a patient will perceive him undifferentiated from his own archaic object images, and will profit from help whereby he may begin at the outset to make some such differentiation. In treating neurotics we try not to interfere with the developing transference neurosis, but with psychotics the establishment of a "reality base" *in advance* of the full development of the transference psychosis may be useful, providing something for him to fall back on as he tries to work through the differentiation of his analyst from his archaic object images. The development of the psychotic transference, and its resolution by means of interpretations and working through, are required if the treatment is to be appropriately called psychoanalytic.

With a neurotic a built-in "reality base" in the analytic relationship can be assumed by the very fact that the neurotic patient *knows* that the analyst is paid by him and thus is clearly not in the parent role. It is over this base of reality that the transference neurosis will be built. In contrast, the psychotic patient who in the psychotic transference may not differentiate the analyst from the parents must have help from the analyst in developing a reality base and taking it into account as he relates to him. Such help may also activate the patient's observing ego. In the following vignette the patient in his third therapeutic hour merged his perception of his therapist with that of his archaic mother representation and became involved in an introjective-projective relatedness with the therapist, now indistinguishable from an archaic object representation. The "interference" offered by the therapist was designed initially to include a representation of reality in his image before allowing the transference psychosis to develop fully.

Eighteen-year-old Ricky was born with unusually small digits on his right hand and right foot. His mother marked each of his birthdays, beginning with the fourth, by the gift of a wedding ring, usually one too large for his deformed fingers. The mother never talked openly to Ricky about his congenital deformity, which, though obvious, became psychologically a secret between mother and son, the latter being reared in the shadow of what we describe as an engulfing mother.

When a girl in high school told Ricky his voice had changed, he interpreted this to mean that he had become a man, whereupon he worried lest girls anticipate, on the basis of his visible deformity, that his penis was abnormal; his overt psychosis appeared soon thereafter. One of his symptoms was his eager reading of books on Nazi Germany and his identification of himself with Goebbels, Hitler's "right arm." He submitted to his tyrannical mother as he felt Goebbels had submitted to Hitler. When Ricky turned sixteen his mother gave him the usual gift of a wedding ring for his birthday, and on the following day his parents committed him to a mental institution. I saw him two years later.

During his third hour with me he suddenly fell silent, relaxed, and made sucking movements with his lips in a gesture of oral introjection, saying that he was drinking

German wine. On this day he had stopped for a moment at my door as he entered my office, deciding that the name on the door was of German origin. This conclusion agreed with his knowledge, conveyed by my accent, that I am a foreigner in this country. He saw me as someone "as strong as Hitler" and projected the Hitlerian image of his archaic mother representation on me, proceeding then to reintroject me as such (Volkan, 1968). My response to him was a simple declaration that I was Turkish, and, in reply to his question about wine, the statement that Turkey produced both sweet and sour wine just as Germany did. Had he been neurotic I would not have interrupted his fantasies about me. With him, I interfered in order to establish the reality base only when a fully developed transference psychosis required appropriate interpretations. The clarification of my national origin arose *naturally* within this situation; my differentiation from the archaic object representation did not include furnishing the gratification of detailed information about myself. In other cases such "interferences" are not necessary for the establishment of a reality base; the analyst's insistence on an analytic attitude from the very beginning is enough.

Rather than providing illustrations of crudely symbolized internalizations as they occur disconnectedly and randomly during therapy hours, I shall refer to them as occurring within a process of the alteration of old, unloving, cold, and maladaptive introjects, and forming new structures. Nevertheless I again choose internalizations that are reported by the patient in crude symbolic form, since the appearance of these crude symbols per-

[100]

mits the analyst to follow easily the process of structure formation. As indicated, such observations give the analyst a tool with which to examine early structure formation and to gain insight into the vastly more subtle and complicated processes involved in the introjection of and identification with the analyst. Aspects of my treatment of a Methodist minister I called Attis will illustrate this point.

Attis

There are at least two versions of the myth of Attis (Erhat, 1972), but both speak of the preservation of part of his body after death, the continued growth of his hair, and the viability of his little finger, which could move of its own accord although attached to a dead body.

As the story is told by Kerényi (1960), the Agdos rock assumed the shape of the Great Mother. Zeus fell asleep on it, and his semen caused the rock to deliver Agdistis, a bisexual being of great savagery. In an effort to tame Agdistis, Dionysos turned water into wine, which the thirsty Agdistis drank until he fell into a deep sleep. Dionysos then tied the male member of the sleeping Agdistis to a tree, so that when he sprang up from his sleep he castrated himself. The earth drank the blood and the torn-off member and from these grew a tree; Nana, the daughter of Sangarios, the river god, placed its fruit in her lap. She conceived a child of it, and Sangarios left the infant out in the open to die, but a he-goat tended him and he survived. His name was Attis and his beauty was such that Agdistis, now without a male member, fell in love with him. Midas, King of Pessinous, sought to

[101]

separate Attis from Agdistis, and to this end gave the boy his own daughter in marriage. Agdistis appeared at the wedding and drove the guests mad with the notes of a syrinx, whereupon Attis castrated himself and died. Repentant, Agdistis besought Zeus to return the boy to life, but all that Fate would allow to do was to grant that his body would never putrefy, his hair would continue to grow, and his smallest finger would remain alive and capable of movement. (For an in-depth psychoanalytic study of various versions of the Attis myth see Weigert, 1938.)

I call my patient Attis because, when he was four years old, an elder brother "accidentally" chopped off part of one of Attis's fingers with an ax. The severed member was kept in a bottle by their mother until her death, a year before Attis, then 38 years old, became my patient. After the mother's death Attis himself kept the finger in his bedroom and sometimes thought of it as living. Although I shall not go into great detail about it, it is evident that other aspects of the Attis myth pertained to his man and his preoccupations. The themes of bisexuality, incest, castration, the domination of a phallic and monstrous mother, death, and rebirth were certainly present.

A finger in a bottle

Attis was the fourth child of a rural family. Family tradition made much of the fact that his birth occurred during a terrible storm, and that the day of his birth was Groundhog Day. As a child and, later, as an adult schizophrenic he felt that the circumstances of his birth pointed to a malign destiny; occasionally he identified himself with a groundhog, and he was often impressed by a sense of doom, which was, in fact, not incompatible with the events of his childhood experience.

When he was two his mother bore twins, a boy and a girl. As luck would have it, two other women in the neighborhood gave birth to twins about the same time, and the three women became highly competitive about their offspring. The mother's preoccupation with the twins and with a deaf girl born a year after the twins arrived served to deprive Attis of adequate mothering in early childhood. For a time he stayed in diapers along with the babies, and between the ages of three and four was involved in several severely traumatic episodes. On two separate occasions there was a fire in his house, once while he was sick in bed with a high fever; his mother rescued him each time. These incidents not only left psychological scars but contributed to his preoccupation with hell, and the choice of a career in which as a religious leader he might hope to have some control over being consumed by fire. He seemed to have no religious calling in the usual sense, and was very much conflicted in relating to the church.

When part of his finger was chopped off, his mother rushed him to a doctor to have the severed piece sewed back in place. Her oft-repeated account of what actually happened indicated that in her excitement she "forgot" to take the severed segment with her, but had she done so the child might have had his finger restored. Instead, the severed piece was preserved in a bottle. Attis felt that in mutilating the finger his brother had been acting as his

[103]

mother's agent. He regarded the object in the bottle as his penis, and perceived his mother as having it in her possession just as she had had his life in her possession when she rescued him from the house fires. She was proud of the grim object, which she kept in the guestroom and often displayed to visitors.

The child's finger stump was not yet healed when he had his first experience with surgery—a tonsillectomy. Related throat surgery was necessary for him much later, once when he was 24 and again at 26. In the same year in which he had his tonsillectomy, he fell off a ladder into a bin of cottonseed. This experience acquainted him with the horror of being buried alive and the sensation was recalled in his adult phobia of being so interred.

In childhood he had been regarded by others in the family as unduly tied to his mother's apron strings, but their "togetherness" was full of tensions and sadistic attacks upon one another rather than being blissful and supportive. As I treated him, I speculated that his mother may have had unconscious guilt over the deficiencies in her mothering of Attis; she would not allow him to individuate, and he came to the oedipal age with unresolved pregenital problems. His sadistic father did nothing to help him come "unglued" from a "crazy" mother. Attis once saw him in a fury forcing a stick up a donkey's anus. The boy felt menace in the environment; for a while he was preoccupied with the account of a neighbor's self-castration, and he sustained a back injury when he was eight that not only left a physical scar on his hips but supported his belief that life is full of danger. When

Attis reached puberty, his father had an appendectomy, and the mother added the appendix, in a bottle like Attis's finger, to her morbid display of body parts. Attis recalled during therapy that he had gazed at them and concluded that the appendix was bigger than the finger segment. He had introjected it as a representation of the paternal phallus. At the age of 20 he was terrified to recognize his inability to repress fully his incestuous desires for his mother. He himself had an appendectomy at this time. Two years later the father died, but Attis, convinced that his parent had been buried alive, expected him to return and punish him.

By the age of 25 he was graduated from divinity school and ordained in the Methodist church. Two years later he went to a mountaintop in emulation of Jesus. When he was discovered three days later, wandering about naked and exhausted, he was hospitalized for the first time, but he was able to leave the hospital within a short time and return to his job.

He soon met a woman his mother approved of, and made plans to marry her, learning just before the marriage took place that she had had an affair with an older man as he suspected his mother had done in her girlhood. He nevertheless went on with the wedding, feeling that events were outside his control. In his later delusional state he identified his wife with his mother. During sexual intercourse with her he felt himself turn into a frog, which in turn became his dead father. He felt the continuing presence of his father after his death, locating it particularly in the closets of his house, which at times he refused to open on that account. He developed rituals to exorcise his father's ghost. When he was 38, his mother died. At her death he took the bottle with the finger in it to his own home and kept it in a dresser drawer. By this time his swings from extreme dependency upon to extreme rage toward his wife had increased. It seemed that he was called upon to perform an unusually large number of funeral services in his capacity as minister, and he became preoccupied with graveyards and the return of his dead parents, sometimes seeing lights moving about the graves at night.

He was unable to leave home without dread of having left something burning inside the house, and went about compulsively checking the stove and all of the locks each time he went out. He had a recurrent dream, reflecting his childhood accident; in it he saw a door drop like a guillotine on a snake and cut it to pieces.

The year after his mother died he could hardly differentiate her from his wife. Although he could not leave his wife he kept longing for his "freedom" from her, and one night as she lay sleeping beside him he had the impulse to kill her. Going into the back yard of their house, he got an ax. He remained outside all night, in what he recalled as a kind of catatonic state that thwarted his impulse. The interpretation of this act was that he aimed to do to his mother/wife what his brother had done to him "under mother's orders."

On the following day he was hospitalized, and my work with him began. The five years of treatment with him before I moved elsewhere was conducted on an outpatient basis except for a few brief intervals in the hospital. During the 11 years since his treatment "terminated" he has visited me at least twice a year in spite of the great distance of my present location from his home.

Aspects of Attis's treatment

In the next section I shall summarize the therapeutic processes undergone by Attis by the end of the fourth year of his treatment. Here I shall highlight what happened before that, in order to provide a perspective.

As I have indicated, at the outset of Attis's hospital stay he was acutely psychotic, a bisexual "monster" like Agdistis. Although he regarded as male members not only his actual penis but his cut finger, his finger-in-a-bottle, and the paternal phallus (which rested in his abdomen by means of internalization), he also had two vaginas—his armpits. Both his outer and his inner world were inhabited by aggressive "monsters" involved in introjective-projective cathexis. He slept hidden beneath a bed sheet in symbolic regression to the womb. In his dreams the blade of the guillotine fell upon the serpent again and again. His self-representations and object representations merged, and various object representations were interchangeable. He could not distinguish me from his dead father, nor his wife from the dead mother. During his interviews he talked openly about incestuous wishes and other aspects of oedipal striving. The defensive function of presenting the therapist so openly with oedipal material was obvious from the start; it served as a screen for his underlying murderous rage. It is a mistake for the therapist faced with a patient like Attis to regard oedipal material as something to deal with as if the

[107]

patient were functioning at the oedipal level. I concur with Rosenfeld (1966) and Boyer (1971) in their belief that interpretation of such apparently oedipal material on a libidinal level, when it is offered by this kind of patient, can promote psychotic excitement; the patient can all too readily see in such interpretation a seductive invitation on the part of the therapist. Boyer (1971) states:

> If I refer to such material, I do so from the standpoint of its aggressive and manipulative aspects, or interpret upwards.... Thus, as an example, if the patient relates that he has open fantasies of intercourse with his mother, I respond that he must love her very much. I believe the patient who suffers from a severe characterological or schizophrenic disorder has massive fears of the vicissitudes of his aggressive impulses and that analysis proceeds smoothest when attention is directed gently but consistently towards the analysis of the protective manoeuvers he employs to defend against his fear that his hostility will result in the analyst's death or his own [p. 70].

Attis's preoccupation with open oedipal striving and his abundant production of brilliant and bizarre fantasies became, in a way, an obsessional defense that permitted him to control, to reject, or to isolate drive derivatives from the conscious ego. Beneath his obsessional defenses, however, lay primitive defenses, such as alternate activation of contradictory ego states. In this kind of situation, as Kernberg (1967) points out: "the lack of interpenetration of libidinal and aggressive drive derivatives interferes with the normal modulation and differentiation of affect dispositions of the ego, and a chronic tendency to eruption of primitive affect states remains" (p. 673).

Attis perceived any reconciliation of the two types of representations as the conquest of "all good" units by "all bad" ones. Their location shifted: when the "all bad" ones were in himself he *was* a monster, dangerous to himself and to objects in the external world. When, on the other hand, the "all bad" units were located outside himself, he had to protect himself from an environment full of menace. When his self-representations lacked differentiation from his object representations he would identify with the object on which the aggression was projected (projective identification). Under stress he produced hallucinations and delusions which gradually disappeared from his repertoire as the third year of treatment reached its close.

Most of the time the therapist was his archaic mother representations in the psychotic transference, and Attis expected him to act accordingly. He himself alternated dramatically on the clinical level between aggressive and passive positions toward the therapist. I shall detail (see Chapter VII) one of his therapeutic sessions that took place toward the end of his fourth year of treatment. This will illustrate how Attis was able to *tolerate* the experience of emotional flooding of an aggressive nature in the transference situation. His expression of this flooding, which stood for his murderous rage toward the therapist, as conceptualized by both of us later, was handled therapeutically, and I feel that this episode marked the crystallization of the differentiation of the therapist (and thus his internalized representation) from the archaic mother representations. The patient had been previously working through in piecemeal fashion the difference between his therapist image and his early mother images, and between the analytic introject and the archaic introjects. When the analytic introject became distinctly other than the archaic introjects, identification with the former became possible, with consequent new structure formation.

Identification with the therapist in the new structure formation

During the fourth year of his treatment, when Attis had become better able to differentiate between me and his archaic object images, he entered my office looking very pale. He opened the hour by saying that he had eaten a *turkey* dinner the night before and had been anxious ever since. He knew that I had come to the United States from Turkey. On this visit he became aware that the suit he was wearing was very much like one of mine, in fact, the one I wore on this occasion. He had had the impulse the day before to visit a clothing store, and while there he had purchased the suit in question, along with a shirt and tie very like my own. His wish to imitate his therapist had become clear to him, and he attributed his anxiety to this as he began this session. Although his awareness of his imitative behavior had been spontaneous, he remained unaware of the meaning of his symbolic oral introjection of me in eating the "turkey dinner." As the hour went on he spoke of his fantasies of destruction directed toward me which he had entertained en route to my office. I was able to interpret to him his wish to resemble me by "eating me up" and his subsequent fear that he had destroyed me by this act. After this exchange he relaxed and asked what I thought about the recent Supreme Court decision about prayer in schools; he speculated about my religion. The tenor of my reply was: "Look, if you want to be like me don't apply the resemblance on an all or nothing basis. To be sure, you received 'bad' things from your parents but you also got 'good' things. You are an altogether different person from me, and in the long run we will continue being two different persons."

He wore the same look-alike clothing to our next session, saying that he had been impelled to do so. Just before we began the hour he broke the usual routine by a trip to the bathroom, where he had a diarrheal stool. I felt that he needed to rid himself of "bad" aspects of the therapist introject, and I made a remark to this effect, in a sense giving him "permission" to get rid of the unwanted aspects of the introject. As the hour went on he fantasied his own death and I interpreted his destructive fantasies regarding the therapist introject, his identification with it, and his fears of his own death. Toward the end of the hour he reported a sensation of getting out of his shell and developing a "new personality." He wanted to take a long vacation trip with it. For all practical purposes his life and movement had been confined within a limited geographical area; until now he had been a "satellite" (Volkan and Corney, 1968) of his church, but now he was determined to have "adventures" with his "new personality," which I felt was his perception of a functional analytic introject. He thought of my coming to the States as a highly adventurous undertaking. He set Pennsylvania as his travel objective; this did in fact involve a considerable journey for him. His associations centered around the Liberty Bell in Philadelphia, and I felt that this indicated a need for symbolic celebration of the birth within himself of a new ego. As we discussed the proposed trip to Philadelphia I mentioned having once made the trip there myself, implying that it was not a journey that involved any danger. In retrospect, I suspect that I sensed in him an anxiety about finding his liberty, and that my remark was in response to this. I needed to protect him — and perhaps myself within him — by such reassurance.

Before long he did take a six weeks' vacation, going to Philadelphia. It was successful, and on his return journey he visited the elder brother who had amputated his finger. "I wanted to show him my new personality," he said, and reported being amused at hearing his brother, only four years his senior, call him "son." When he returned he heard of the birth of a baby girl to my wife; he had not known of her pregnancy and kept referring to my newborn child, calling her "him" in spite of his knowledge of her sex. After the trip he went to a physician for a thorough medical checkup. I felt that he sought the examination for psychological reasons, wanting reassurance that his "new personality" was indeed a healthy one.

In feeling that he had been born again he became anxious about whether the newborn "son" would be treated like the original one who had been under the shadow of the early mother. Again I became the early mother in the transference. Was he playing second fiddle to my new baby? Would I be able to give him my attention now that I had a new baby at home to distract me? I interpreted to him that when the twins and the deaf sister were born he had had to play "second fiddle" in the competition for his mother's attention.

He soon manifested anxiety lest the newborn "son" might face castration as the original one, symbolically castrated at age four, had done. He had recently become president of his district ministerial association but had begun thinking of giving up this position of honor—a self-castration proposed to control the castration he felt I might inflict on him. He ceased having sexual relations with his wife. He owned a flesh-colored car which, during his psychotic days, was included in his body image, its hood being a penis and its exhaust an anus. Once when something went wrong with the exhaust pipe he developed hemorrhoids. New he wanted to sell the car to rid himself of a sexual symbol and his castration fears. I interpreted all these developments to him.

According to Abse and Ewing (1960), "The inevitable introjection of the therapist [by a schizophrenic] is itself partly corrective insofar as this introject competes with the archaic introject of the tyrannical mother" (p. 508). Attis's old unloving and tyrannical mother introject actively competed with the analytic introject, as Attis saw symbolically. He speculated as to which would be victorious. Later he decided that his mother had been like Kruschev, regarded at that time in America as an aggressively invested "bad" object—and that the brother who had "castrated" him resembled Castro. The therapist was from Turkey, which was on the side of America. He reported that although his mother had warned him not to trust strangers (foreigners) he felt that he could trust me.

In a later interview he was able to express gratitude to me for saving him from "fire" — his psychosis. He recalled that when his mother had saved him from the burning house, and, later, when she had "preserved" his penis, the finger-in-a-bottle, obligation to her had necessitated his being in her shadow, unindividuated, i.e. staying ill.

Still later he touched on the same subject when he spoke of the finger-in-a-bottle. It was a link between him and his mother, a kind of shared fetish. She had stolen his penis although at the same time she had preserved it. He was afraid of freedom from her lest she destroy it. In the transference situation he saw me as a homosexual; his associations helped me interpret the mother transference. If I were a homosexual I would emulate his mother in keeping his penis, and I would not permit him to individuate. Once more I helped him differentiate between his mother representations and the analytic introject.

Whatever happened to Attis?

My work with Attis was unfortunately brought to a close after five years by my moving to a new location. Although he followed my suggestion to continue his psychotherapy with another psychiatrist, he found no benefit in it and discontinued treatment within a few months. Although the five years' work he had with me had considerably modified his psychotic core, the work was by no means completed. He had made a new adaptation with his "new personality" which was not fully individuated from me.

He has come to see me at least twice a year during the intervening 11 years, and I came to understand much about his present adaptation. I can say that at no time did his psychosis return, although he did experience transient breaks with reality too brief to justify a diagnosis of psychosis. He was transferred from one church to another in the usual way, remaining in each an average of three years. In each congregation he located an older "bad woman," a "bitch" who he knew represented his early mother. His appreciation of what she represented did not keep him from experiencing her as the early mother. He was afraid of these "bitches" and at times fought bravely against them. His vacillation between dependency upon and hostility toward his wife was no longer so marked, and the vagina was no longer perceived as the mouth of a walrus. He still has his "finger-in-a-bottle," but now he keeps it in the attic rather than in his bedroom, and it has lost some of its magic. His relations with other men improved; he loves golf, and sports competition no longer evokes homosexual fantasies and the anxiety they entailed. At each move from one church to another the separation heightened his obsessional symptoms and hypochondriacal preoccupations. On several occasions he indulged in lively flirtations with different women and thought of having affairs with them. My understanding of this behavior indicated his perception

[115]

of his wife as his mother, and his consequent attempt to accomplish separation from her. In his approach to other women he was like a teenager trying to date for the first time. After kissing and hugging the other women he would be turned away from further pursuit by his anxiety, and go back with hostile submission to his wife. He called on me whenever he was in one of his periods of anxiety. He had become my "satellite."

The satellite state

Greek mythology tells the story of how Daedalus was imprisoned on Crete. Minos prevented his escape, keeping watch himself and offering a large reward for his capture. Finally, in order to escape, Daedalus made a pair of wings of feathers held in place by wax; he made a pair also for his son Icarus, warning him at the moment of escape not to fly too high lest the sun melt the wax — nor too low, lest the sea wet the feathers. Icarus disregarded his father's warning and soared toward the sun until its heat ruined his wings and he fell into the sea and drowned. This tale dramatizes oedipal problems in which there is danger in flying higher than the father.

In 1968 Corney and I investigated the latter part of Daedalus's advice — that Icarus should not swoop too low. This relates to unresolved problems of separation-individuation as described by Mahler (1963, 1968) and Mahler and Furer (1963). Corney and I went on to describe patients like Attis who adopted a life style of orbiting around a center (the early mother representative) in a satellite state. This adaptation, however malignant it may prove to be, is a special compromise solution for problems of separation-individuation. As long as he stays in orbit as one celestial body circles another, he can function without clinical psychosis; the compromise permits certain functions to evolve at the cost of impairing others. Its malignant aspect arises from the fact that what ego does develop is largely engaged in the service of perpetuating the developmental compromise; a move away from orbit in the direction of either "progression" or regression has grave (psychotic) consequences. The church was for Attis a mother substitute as well as a "center" for his orbit as a satellite; he never committed himself as to what it represented to him but, although he complained about his vocation, he was unable to give it up. For such patients a special physical place may represent the early mother; they orbit around it, and sometimes physical separation from this place represents intrapsychic separation and brings about psychosis.

The situation recalls poetic accounts of the moth attracted to a flame. As long as it orbits the flame the moth is safe, but symbiotic union with the flame (a re-fusion of self- and object representations) destroys it. To move out of orbit is to be deprived of all warmth and thus to suffer (a pseudoindependent psychosis) since the satellite lacks sufficient ego identifications. From the standpoint of internalized object relations the satellite patient has differentiated his self-representations from his object representations but not yet integrated them. The center is the locus of "needed" object representations as well as of those that are "all bad" (engulfing). Orbiting, a form of distancing, enables the patient to avoid facing the tensions of ambivalence toward an important object.

[117]

Some patients with an adaptation to life in a satellite position typically have dreams in which they—or representations of themselves—are doomed to move around a central object. Corney and I called such dreams *satellite dreams.* Kohut (1971) later reported identical dreams in his narcissistic patients; he felt that they indicated the narcissistic transference. He saw the patient's failing to shoot off into space from the orbit (psychosis) and his affective pull to the center as the narcissistic transference (toward the center/analyst) that protected against the danger of possible permanent loss of the self. I do not believe that Kohut's interpretation of these dreams necessarily rules out our understanding of them. In any case, satellite patients do develop satellite transferences, and only after the assimilation and integration of further internalized object relations can they move out of the orbit without risking identity loss.

CHAPTER V

PRIMITIVE SPLITTING COMBINED WITH INTROJECTIVE-PROJECTIVE RELATEDNESS

This chapter is designed to show how two conditions, i.e., introjective-projective relatedness and primitive splitting of primitive internalized object relations, are manifested in a clinical setting. A case illustration exemplifies the way in which the mending of primitive splitting begins as a ferociousness of early mother introject is altered.

Adult patients who use primitive splitting as their dominant defense mechanism have a history of extreme frustration and intense primary or secondary aggression during the first years of life. An attempt to mend the primitive splitting threatens the patient with the necessity of facing his primitive emotions as direct derivatives of the drives without the defense the primitive splitting has been providing. In order to get the mending under way he must experience these emotions either in piecemeal fashion or in some dramatic outburst as in the case I report in this chapter. Adequate repair of primitive splitting brings about the taming of drive derivatives, particularly affective aspects of the aggressive drive.

More on primitive splitting

In the two previous chapters I dealt with theoretical and clinical aspects of fusion, and particularly the intro-jective-projective relatedness that involves self- and object representations. I will now refocus on another "condition"—primitive splitting—that justifies calling internalized object relations primitive. I will here examine clinical aspects of primitive splitting coincident with introjective-projective relatedness.

The term "splitting" is applied in various ways; by qualifying it with the adjective "primitive" I limit my reference to specific use. When memory traces of pleasurable-good-rewarding and painful-bad-punishing experiences are organized and allocated to self- and object representations, they provide "all good" and "all bad" self- and object representations. Primitive splitting is a defect in the integration of representations of opposite quality; in the course of normal development the splitting no longer occurs and the representations coalesce; the split is mended. Primitive splitting can be used for defensive purposes, and, in fact, appears as the major defense of psychotic, borderline, or narcissistic patients against primitive anxieties. Lichtenberg and Slap (1973), in their review of the term "splitting," which includes

Freud's many different applications, refer to primitive splitting as the "splitting of representations":

> Splitting of representations differs from both denial and repression. Denial functions through the disavowal of whole percepts and the substitution of a wish-fulfilling fantasy, whereas splitting of representations separates along affective lines the self- and object representations involved in a disturbing percept. Repression acts by the repulsion of a mental content from consciousness in conjunction with a linkage of that content with a conflictual memory; splitting of representations may or may not involve exclusion of contents from conscious awareness. At times, both separated emotional sets are conscious [p. 781].

In Chapter IV I described the patients' inclusion of the analyst in their cycle of introjective-projective relatedness. With this type of patient the analyst representations stood not for one archaic object representation alone, but for many, especially before the establishment of an analytic introject. On the clinical level it is the analyst's task to follow the changing nature of whatever fragments may be projected on him and subsequently reintrojected. Schematically these fragments align themselves with one side or the other of the split representatives—the "all good," or the "all bad." Such alignment is illustrated in Samantha's case, described in Chapter II.

The general idea that the child—or the adult neurotic patient in the transference situation—at the oedipal level is involved in a triangular relationship, whereas at the early pregenital stage he is involved in a dyadic one, is not altogether correct from the standpoint of internalized object relations. One must posit the presence of at least four basic players in the constellation as the transference moves forward in the analyst's office. At the pregenital level, after self- and object representations are differentiated and primitive splitting is fully accomplished, there are "all good" self representations and "all good" object representations as well as "all bad" self representations and "all bad" object representations. These shift location, join, and separate. Patients who come to the oedipal phase still making extensive use of primitive splitting do not accomplish integration of the superego. Two additional players, not unconnected with the first four, may then be more clearly identified in the constellation; these represent respectively the "idealized" self-image that relates the the elaborately idealized image of the parental model, on the one hand, and the fiercely sadistic self-image that reflects fierce parental prohibition and punishment, on the other. These neither coalesce with one another nor with the other four if Stage IV (Kernberg, 1972a) is not reached.

Primitively split representations are involved in introjective-projective cathexis; the following clinical illustration shows the start of mending between the representations during the process of introjective-projective relatedness.

The primitive splitting of the idiot-genius patient
My patient Joseph, in his early twenties, had as a child been diagnosed as autistic or mentally deficient to an

extreme degree. His family had noticed his failure to develop normally when he was little over a year old, and at the age of four he was evaluated at a well-known university center. Extensive records made at that time indicated that he had encopresis, his mother having started bowel training without success when the child was a year and a half. He had difficulty eating, rocked himself a great deal, or sat in a corner in what appeared to be a dream state. Although he would not answer when spoken to, he occasionally ran to a stranger and said "Hi!" His entire vocabulary at age four was hi, mama, dada, candy, bacon, and bye-bye. He used a jargon to talk to himself, and was six before he began speaking normally.

Although his parents were told he was severely limited, the mother never gave up. The family was well able to send him to special schools where he had individualized training. His parents eagerly followed up any news of relevant medical developments such as the "discovery" that glutamic acid can benefit the child with impaired intelligence.

The boy learned to talk and to care for himself in the course of his specialized training, and after some years he was able to return home and to transfer to public school. During puberty and thereafter he studied mathematics, physics, astronomy, and other fields of learning that required no social interaction and lacked emotional content. He began thinking of himself as a genius, and was encouraged to do so by his mother. Nevertheless his self-representation as an idiot persisted, although it was submerged beneath his self-representation as a genius. Corresponding object representations, which at times were not differentiated from self-representations, were likewise seen as shifting between the poles of genius and idiocy. As his treatment proceeded it became clear to me that the polarity of idiot-genius was condensed, and represented primitively split self- and object representations of "all good" and "all bad" constituents.

His Jewish father had fled from Europe as a boy and had made a considerable fortune in this country as an industrialist. In his forties he married a narcissistic woman 20 years his junior. Although he himself had only a very limited education, his wife was a college graduate who thought of herself as a gifted pianist, a selfless humanitarian, and so on. Being very proud of his fine "catch," the father readily acceded to any demands she made.

Joseph and an elder brother were the only children of this marriage. The brother grew up, went to college, married, and became his father's business partner. Although the family had regarded Joseph as normal until the middle of his second year, at this time they were unable to overlook his unresponsive and autistic behavior.

We are now approaching the end of three years of four-times-a-week analytic therapy, and I have been able to reconstruct some aspects of what went wrong in the earliest mother-child unit. Joseph had had three years of treatment with another analyst, an able colleague of mine, before he became my patient, but much was left unanswered. It seems likely that the child had a constitutional deficiency and that his faltering responses to his mother dealt her a narcissistic hurt; she required him to be perfect and made the achievement of this perfection a mission that intruded upon him. During his first year of analysis he often lapsed into withdrawal that resembled sleep, evoking in me a compelling wish to intrude on his detachment (as his mother had so often done), but I refrained. Sometimes he dozed thus all hour; although his breathing was deep and audible this did not seem sleep in the usual sense. He always arose from the couch and left when, at the end of an hour of slumbering inattention, he heard my voice very softly indicate that the session was over.

His mother had been highly intrusive in promoting his bowel training. She gave him an enema at any sign of constipation from the time he was a year and a half old. She wanted him to be clean as an extension of herself, but to him the giving of an enema was a blood-sucking attack. During his first year of treatment he did not pronounce "enema" correctly, calling it instead something like "anemia." The mother tenaciously sought help in her narcissistic struggle to toilet-train her child and to get him to talk; in his analysis Joseph revealed his puzzled conclusion that her crusade to help him was conducted largely for her own benefit, for the removal of a blemish on her narcissistic self-regard. He was, however, grateful for the outlay of so much money for his instruction in talking, reading, and whatever degree of competence he had in relating to others. The special schools he had attended were not psychoanalytically oriented. Some behavior modification had been attempted by means of rewards and punishments, but he had not been punished physically.

[125]

His mother kept the records of his early hospitalization, schooling, and intelligence tests, and these became magical for mother and child. They were symbols of the idiot self-representation that was not integrated with his genius self-representation. When, during his second year with me, he brought these records to show me, he stuffed under his shirt like a shield a book on the life of many geniuses, Christ, Plato, Einstein, and others. He was afraid that when I saw his "magical records" I would think him stupid. Further analysis showed that the collection of records did in fact represent his "all bad" self- and object representations in a magical external way. They were like a "bomb" (bad fecal material) and he needed literally to shield his "all good" self- and object representations within himself. I saw this incident as a remarkably precise illustration of primitive splitting. His basic defense mechanism was not repression; the idiot "bad" self- and object units were known to him but were primitively split off along affective lines.

With parental influence Joseph won a scholarship at the university where I practice and came to me for analysis, leaving his first analyst behind in the city where he had attended college. His strong autistic and symbiotic defenses were directed toward me early in treatment. Outside of the routine daily interaction involved in making purchases and providing for himself, he lived to all intents and purposes a solitary life, and considered himself above the need of or desire for further human exchange. In the classroom he sat apart from all the others. His appearance helped him to distance himself successfully from other people. He was short and rather overweight. He smiled constantly; his walk reminded me of a penguin's. At the approach of others for "social interaction" he either became excessively "sweet" while feeling remote, or abrupt and rude. He had a naive regard for his "friends," who could suddenly change in his view into "all bad" people. He judged others according to his estimate of their I.Q. This was the only dimension they had for him, and he felt emotional response only to those he judged unusually high on the I.Q. scale (genius) or unusually low (idiot), disregarding all that seemed "average" to him. His use of "average" reminded me of Samantha's "bar" (Chapter II). Her bar was the division (split) between her "left" and "right" representations; it offered nothing for her to alight upon. Similarly, Joseph's "average" offered him nothing to stand on; it was a gap between polar opposites that he had to regard as a chasm rather than simply a colorless expanse or "gray area" between two striking extremes.

Sometimes his pants were greasy, and whenever he had a cold he stuffed so much toilet tissue into his shirt pockets that his chest bulged. If he lost a button from his cuff he substituted strings to keep his sleeve tight to the wrist, and let the string ends hang out. In analysis we were able to understand these odd ways of behaving as defensive maneuvers designed to mock others and to avoid anxiety-provoking closeness. Further analysis disclosed primitive splitting in these behaviors in an effort to keep his "all good" units apart from their opposites. The possibility of mending the opposites brought about primitive anxiety. He would rock on the couch as I made interpretations of what he was doing. He lacked any experience of qualified affect; there was no possibility of anything being "somewhat bad"—it must be "all bad."

Initiation of mending of primitive splitting

During his first year of analysis Joseph protected his genius, "all good" self-object representations by making me contemptible—or perfect—as an extension of his own representation. He did not "grieve" in the usual sense over the loss of his first analyst, but selected real or fantasied aspects of me and merged them with similar aspects, real or fantasied, of his first analyst, merging us and keeping the first analyst "alive" in me. Both of us, in fact, could be made his own extension. At other times he grieved in superman style, in cosmic terms, grandly discussing the symbolism of one galaxy moving away from another. His object and self-representations at times during this first year merged and again differentiated, occasionally giving me the feeling that there were four persons in the room when we were alone together.

He revealed more about his intrapsychic processes during the second year when he felt sufficiently secure about my not engulfing him or killing whatever individuality he possessed. Toward the end of this year he noticed a picture of a tropical forest on my office wall; knowing I am Turkish, he insisted that this depicted a Turkish scene. He had once traveled to Israel with his parents and spent a few days in Istanbul on the way home. He remembered quite well that Turkey did not look like the scene in the picture, but he kept insisting that it did and became panicky, talking like a machine gun spitting bullets to kill me. He went on to say that the picture represented an African locale in which cannibals lived. A few days later he came in with his trousers zipper broken, and opened his legs as he lay on the couch as if inviting me to enter his "symbolic" vagina. I told him I had noticed his interest in me, but pointed out that it had led to his seeing me as a representative of those he considered dangerous, and had heightened his fear that I might devour or engulf him. Yet a few days later he was able to tell me about his usual masturbation fantasy, in which he used his penis as a vacuum cleaner that sucked up his mother's image into his chest. I concluded that she was an unassimilated foreign body, an introject with archaic superego characteristics. She would then demand of him behavior that he saw as punitive. He heard his mother's orders as inner auditory hallucinations. I felt that the auditory aspects of this experience related to the formulations of Isakower (1938) and Fliess (1953) concerning spoken words "heard" in dreams, formulations consistent with Freud's (1900) original ideas about the utterance occurring in dreams, and the auditory nucleus of the superego.

In reality Joseph enjoyed shutting himself away in a room to read and to retreat from the world, but his introject demanded that he respond to his fantasies of punishment by opening the door in spite of the extreme discomfort it would cost him to do so. Accordingly he would respond to the command and open the door; he would then discharge by ejaculation the tension this capitulation built up in him. This tension was caused by the reinternalization of the "all bad" demanding maternal representation which was usually kept outside himself. It was created by projection of his own aggressive drive derivatives as well as the externalization of his primitively split-off, dangerous, enema-administering, blood-sucking maternal representation. Joseph obeyed the demands of the maternal image from outside (which had been reintrojected) in order to avoid its internalized rage.

Later I too was sucked up through his penis, being in some degree distinguished from the mother introject but yet endowed with her powerful and primitive characteristics. The introject's ferociousness slowly disappeared when I persistently made the interpretation that in spite of the punitive aspects — as he saw them — of the "orders" he received, the order to open the door was my (the early mother's) way of helping him to alter his glorified but lonely existence, and to provide a *bridge* for him to learn the nature of things outside. I pointed out that he himself might want to open the door; that he might be refraining chiefly because of his fear of being sucked into an enema tube. While he perceived dangers in being sucked up through the tube (penis), it was also a way of relatedness for him. Moreover, my interpretations were directed to the aggressive aspects of his experience — his rage at having his blood sucked by his mother at a time when he was trying to achieve autonomy. My interpretations were aimed at altering the ferociousness of the introject while at the same time enriching its nurturing functions, to make it loving enough to be assimilated with analytic characteristics. When the ferociousness of this introject, i.e., the externalized dangerous mother representation ("all bad" object), disappeared, it would be more compatible with the "good" self- and object representations within. Thus a mending of the primitive split between the "good" self- and object units and the "bad" ones was initiated.

Not long after this interaction Joseph suddenly turned on me physically during an apparently comfortable and routine analytic session. The attack took me by surprise. I defended myself and no one was hurt. Joseph was flooded emotionally for several minutes when he had "contact" with me. He then left the room but soon returned with an apology to take his place on the couch. I report this incident in full realization that some technical mistake or unconscious action of mine may have provoked it. However, I believe that with certain patients whose problems are deeply embedded in the preverbal period, an ideational and verbal understanding of infantile rage and infantile defenses may not be enough, and that Joseph needed to "act in" in an analytic setting what was in effect a first experience for him. It represented the affective component of the contact between "all good" and "all bad" representations. Joseph experienced the primitive anxiety (emotional flooding) at the threat of losing his "all good" units by contact with the "all bad" ones. I believe that the patient needs to tolerate the emotional flooding — hopefully, in less dramatic fashion than in this instance — in order to keep previously primitively split opposing representations together. (I examine emotional flooding further in Chapter VII.)

Joseph's relatedness to the world then changed in ways that were for him drastic indeed. He befriended a student whose blindness reduced the threat Joseph always felt in other human beings, but who nevertheless offered a genuine experience of human interaction. He began attending meetings at "The Bridge," a meeting-place for people to find salvation through religion, and he did find a bridge there whereby to meet others. He began going into court a few times a week, sitting through trials in order "to learn about human beings." A summary of the events that followed will, I believe, show how the altered introject, now an analytic one, promoted further structural change within the patient, including the beginning of processes of identification more sophisticated than those involving crude forms of introjection.

His associations indicated active involvement in the mending of his primitive splitting. "All good," all genius object images were being brought together with the "all bad," all idiot images, and like changes were taking place with the split self-images, thus promoting integration and reality assessment. He was prompted to sit closer to his classmates in the classroom. He dreamed of being in a hallway leading to a cafeteria, a barbershop, a bookstore, and a post office. Associations indicated that the cafeteria represented his mother, the barbershop his father, the bookstore himself, and the post office the analyst. He moved his bowels while in the hallway and felt appropriate embarrassment. In telling this dream he recalled having once soiled his trousers en route to the office of his previous analyst. In the dream he demonstrated *autonomy* in moving his bowels in front of representations of his parents and his analyst.

In the next dream he reported he was in a classroom, somewhere about 1885 in time. He saw himself as a

[132]

bright young man, in a realistic characterization of his real self-representation. Another student was there, a genius like Einstein (a representation of his genius self). This dream followed a visit to Hillel, where he had enjoyed a lecture about Jewry. Although he had been in the habit of going to the Christian resort, "The Bridge," he had seldom gone to Hillel; he was mending his image of his father (all Zionist-all hypocrite), and I felt that he could now allow himself to affirm his Jewish heritage. He connected 1885 with the time when the North and the South of this country (good and bad) were united (mended). In his opinion the President at that time was neither particularly strong or illustrious. In his dream his associations indicated that he was making the President unimportant in order to make room for "new" father figures, seen as immigrants who had come to this country in great number around 1885. The father and the analyst were both immigrants. Perhaps the new father figure was in the service of his genius self, since Einstein, too, had been an immigrant. In associating to the dream, the patient showed insight into his psychic processes, and expressed his desire to learn from the analyst to be "benign" and neither a total genius nor a total idiot, but a functioning human being.

Some technical suggestions

Before primitive splitting can be successfully mended it must be worked through thoroughly in the transference. Primitive splitting causes the patient to see external objects, including the analyst, as "all good" or "all bad." When the analyst is "all good"—or, in Kernberg's (1967) phrase, subject to "primitive idealization" — the patient views him as a bulwark against all "bad" objects. The patient will then identify some external object as diabolical ("all bad") and point it out to his analyst during a therapeutic session. Some patients are highly "sophisticated" in doing this and may persuade the analyst that the object under discussion is in truth evil and that he should in fact be protective towards his patient against this malevolence, and partisan on his behalf. The analyst should be warned against helping his patient devalue and distance the object he describes as "bad." The opposite should also be true. The analyst should refrain from premature interventions by trying to show the patient that the "bad" object is not in reality all that "bad." The patient may very well go on to reverse the roles of the analyst and the object currently described as "bad," and this maneuver, after it is sufficiently repeated and is allowed to develop fully in transference, may indicate the moment for the former to call attention to the mechanism. Since no strong repression is operative the patient is aware of his primitive split, although he may use denial to support it.

The analyst may use some parallel situation as gentle persuasion. For example, a young girl with borderline organization reports to her analyst that her "all bad" boyfriend has broken a date with her or has left town for a few days; she regards him in consequence as uncaring and rejecting. Soon the analyst is obliged to cancel an appointment with the girl, who quickly "excuses" him since she cannot permit the "all good" analyst to be contaminated. This response permits the therapist to compare the two situations and to call the attention of his patient to the inconsistency of her emotional reactions. The analyst should keep in mind, however, that the split transference is the expected essential transference of this type of patient, and that it must be allowed to develop fully without the analyst's premature intervention.

In the above example the analyst represented the "good" analyst and the boyfriend the distanced "bad analyst." There may be in a sense more narrowing of the primitive splitting when the patient sees the analyst as sometimes "good," sometimes "bad" in quick alternations within a single session. Premature confrontation of the primitive splitting precludes the unfolding of the background necessary for an *analytic* working through of this defensive adaptation. It is only when primitively split transference toward the analyst develops fully that the analyst's interpretation of the defensive functions of the primitive splitting will be perceived by the patient as authentic. What is basically needed is this *transference* interpretation. The patient can then grasp what lies behind his sequence of quickly reversed views of his analyst.

At one time Joseph began working through his primitively split transference manifestations by arriving for his appointment half an hour late, thus cutting his time with his analyst in two. He made no explanation but began each session as though he had arrived on time. He was friendly, and his opening remarks were fairly consistent with his discussions in the previous session, which had also been cut in half. I did not interfere with this tardiness for a while; then I gently pressed him to examine this behavior with curiosity. At first he declared in a kind of pseudodenial that he had not been late. Subsequently he was able to disclose what he had done with the first half of his hour without the presence of his analyst; he usually spent the time in the bathroom with my image in his mind, having conversations with me — and being attacked by me. Thus he could experience half of his hour with my split-off "bad" representation and by the time he came to my office he could have an analyst who was "all good." The interpretation and working through of such dramatic manifestations of primitive splitting help the patient to integrate his "good" and "bad" object representations.

It must be remembered that self-representations are also primitively split, and the patient must eventually bring them into the working through of a transference relationship. Primitively split self-representations may present a clinical picture like that of multiple personalities. In hysterical multiple personalities there is an underlying integrated self-concept and internalized representational object world. In hysteria the "personalities" are separated by repression rather than primitive splitting or fragmentation.

The most effective working through occurs when the primitively split representations are involved in introjective-projective relatedness, when they join and separate, and are (re-)projected and (re-)introjected. In these patients the inevitable introjective-projective relatedness refers to a fixation (or regression) and it is a pathological manifestation. The analyst's observation that he is taken into this vicious cycle should not be understood as an aspect of working through, once the cycle repeats, unless the analyst helps his patient to develop an active observing ego. By keeping his observing ego alert and at the same time protective of the patient's, the analyst may be able to follow these shifts of target of drive derivatives as well as different self- and object representations, and help his patient with the process of integration.

The introjective-projective cycle may become a transference acting out. The analyst, in working through, needs to frustrate the patient by interpretations and by behavior at appropriate times, at appropriate levels, in order to deal with introjective-projective mechanisms that the patient employs in acting out in an effort to achieve instinctual gratification. It is essential that the analyst himself remain calm in order to tame the affects involved in the patient's introjective-projective relatedness, since many patients experience derivatives of untamed emotions (see Chapter VII) in the course of the processes I have been considering.

CHAPTER VI

PRIMITIVE SPLITTING DURING TREATMENT AT TERMINATION

This chapter reports on the display of active defensive primitive splitting by a young woman in the course of her six years of treatment. Her attempts during this time to mend the polarization of "all good" and "all bad" self- and object representations and images are described.

Once the opposite constellations of self- and object representations coalesce, the attention to the transference neurosis is increased. However, the work on the mending of the primitive splitting needs to be considered throughout the entire analysis.

The patient with borderline personality is likely to return to his pathological modes of operation when he is at the termination phase. The termination phase of this young woman's analysis is examined, and the contribution of her dreams to an understanding of the return to and final resolution of the early defensive modality of primitive splitting is emphasized.

Mending of primitive splitting in the termination phase of analysis

The person arrested at (or regressed to) the developmental stage in which primitive splitting dominates classifies self- and object units by simple black-or-white differentiation; when primitive splitting mends the person becomes able to make finer discriminations and to establish hierarchies of importance within such classifications. We can expect the patient with borderline personality organization to stop externalizing his aggressively tinged self- and object images at the end of successful treatment, and to stop defensively protecting the good ones that he has kept within himself. Both patient and analyst must work to reinforce the mending process throughout the *entire* analysis, and once mending occurs the transference neurosis will demand more attention. Joseph, described in Chapter V, commented, after great advance in the mending of his primitive splitting, that his analysis had left him with scar tissue which was "solid in the middle." He added, however, that he and his analyst should continue working on the scar tissue to strengthen its periphery. Although "neurotic areas" continuously require attention in the treatment of such patients, the basic focus is the establishment of a new personality structure as mending occurs with help from analytic introjects; new identifications then available serve as grafting tissue.

My experience has shown that in the termination phase of their analyses patients who had once exhibited the dominance of primitive splitting may "revisit" this operative mode, sometimes in an exaggerated way. Such "return" takes place now under the watchful eye of the observing ego. This mechanism was demonstrated by a patient who had entered analysis dominated by attention given to primitive splitting. Her dreams in the termination phase clearly illustrate how mending is (re)accomplished and how it is accompanied by interpenetration and neutralization of aggressive and libidinal drive derivatives.

Jane

I called this patient Jane because of her habit of swinging vigorously back and forth between aggressively and libidinally invested objects, her "all good" and "all bad" objects occupying the polar extremes characteristic of primitive splitting. The process reminded me of Tarzan swinging in great arcs through the jungle as he clung to a vine. When I shared this whimsy with my patient in her third year of treatment, her newly acquired feminine self-representation prompted her to object that she was *not* Tarzan—but she might be Jane, his mate.

She was a 21-year-old art student attending a college within a hundred miles of her home when I first saw her. The college psychiatrist made the diagnosis of acute schizophrenic reaction and sent her to us for hospitalization. He felt that her anxiety had increased as her college graduation approached; she reported seeing bizarre alterations in his office, such as undulations in the walls and ceiling, and changes in colors. She complained of being "empty" and having no identity, and spent hours writing down her thoughts in the hope that the college psychiatrist would read them. Page after page of loose association included self-administered ink-blot tests, pseudophilosophical statements about life, and wishes that she might die and turn into a flower. She described in detail some balance scales, particularly one small machine that performed poorly; this seemed an obvious reference to her appreciation of the fragmentation of her self and her internalized object representations as well as her partial regression to an undifferentiated stage. She wrote:

> Before daybreak she [the little machine] tiptoed away, but one of the big machines awoke. "Where are you going?" "I must go into a vacuum to balance myself," she said. The others awoke in horror. "You are running away!" "Escape!" "You must face reality!" "A vacuum is not for living!" "Immature!" And she cried and crept away in spite of them. In the vacuum, in the dark away from bits and questions and answers, she measured herself in every direction, learning that she was bigger than she thought and smaller than she had thought, and brighter and duller, prettier and uglier, more sensitive and less sensitive; more balanced and less balanced than she had thought. . . .

Jane's father managed an estate whose present and long-time owner had inherited it, along with substantial holdings elsewhere, from her husband, whom she had met when, as a young self-supporting woman, she had nursed him through an illness. She occupied the main house little more than three months a year, and Jane's family had all the resources of a lavishly equipped farm at their disposal much as though Jane's father himself were the owner. The arrangement was one of long standing, since Jane's grandfather had been the manager before his death, and his son had lived on the estate since he was five years old. Jane felt a sense of unreality, however, as she noted the class and role differentials that came into focus when the real owner was in residence and Jane's mother lapsed from being the "queen" into being perforce a "lady-in-waiting" at the beck and call of the owner.

At the time of their marriage Jane's father was in his late twenties, her mother only 17. The couple's first child, a year and a half older than Jane, had a congenital heart-lung deformity and died in her mother's arms on the way to the hospital when Jane was a year and a half. The mother had experienced great anxiety over the frailty of the first child, and was unable to grieve over her death and unable to mother Jane adequately. (She later had two sons, three and seven years younger than Jane, respectively.) Moreover, when she was nursing Jane she had a breast infection. The first dream Jane reported in her treatment was of being fed a huge bowl of oatmeal, falling into it, and starting to choke before anxiety awakened her. Much later in her analysis, just before the termination phase began, Jane recalled a special doll with a china head, plastic hands, and a cloth body. It had been her mother's and when Jane was small it was given to her with the admonition not to play with it lest she break the fragile head. She dropped it and broke the head after all; her father tried to repair it. As we worked her associations to the doll indicated that it represented her crippled sister, her own depleted self-image and, later, her detached penis. In recovering the meaning of the doll Jane re-experienced her early relationship with her grieving mother, and evidenced intense and appropriate emotion. It became evident that after losing her first child the mother had cared for Jane as though she were the "special doll," fragile and "easily broken," as the little dead sister had been. Jane recalled longing for her mother's touch and her warmth, and her frustrations over their absence. She saw how she had identified with her grieving and cautious mother when she herself treated her dolls so carefully, afraid that they would break.

For her part, the mother, while fearing that Jane might be as fragile as the child she had lost, also perceived her as a savior. Jane was in effect a "replacement child." This is a child conceived to replace one who was lost; Poznanski (1972) saw this situation as involving a syndrome; the new child in such cases automatically has a "past history" and inherits a legend of expectations (usually idealized) that were generated by the child who died. Poznanski states: "Replacing a child with another allows the parents partially to deny the first child's death. The replacement child then acts as a barrier to the parental acknowledgment of death, since a real child exists who is a substitute. Thus the first stages of bereavement are prematurely arrested and the process of mourning continues indefinitely with the replacement child acting as the continuing vehicle of parental grief" (p. 1193). In other words, the second child becomes a living "linking object" (Volkan, 1974b).

When Jane was five, her father began to play sexual

[144]

games with her. He would show her his erect penis, make her touch and fondle it, and he would kiss her genital area; there was no actual intercourse. Their "secret" at the oedipal level resulted in Jane's regression, aided the preservation of the earlier symbiotic core, and kept alive the primitive internalized object relations. The incestuous relationship continued until the patient had her first menstrual period at which time Jane's father approached her in her bedroom and kissed her breast so hard that she screamed; her father never sexually touched her again.

As Jane grew she became capable of differentiating self- and object representations in relationships that were not intimate. Nevertheless, a symbiotic core in which Jane/mother differentiation had not fully taken place persisted. In a series of dreams that recurred during her analysis she saw herself in the middle of a circle of chairs that were empty save for one occupied by her mother. Jane convulsed while her mother laughed at her helplessly. In analysis these repeating dreams were understood to represent her unsuccessful attempt to shake herself out of symbiotic relatedness to her mother.

Distinctions among social classes were strongly felt in Jane's family, which lived in a traditional Southern community. As a teenager Jane aspired to a marriage that would bring her wealth and social position; in this goal she was an extension of her mother, and reflected the example of the estate's owner who had married so successfully. Her mother encouraged her to shine socially, but social climbing was hard for her. She was sent to a college traditionally acceptable to wealthy Southern girls, but had to wait on tables to meet her expenses; she raged silently over this necessity. Her acute psychosis appeared a few months before graduation, which represented an intrapsychic independence and individuation for which she was unready.

Summary of the initial phase of Jane's treatment

Jane's treatment lasted for six years and a month, during which time she was seen four times a week except for a six-month period at the end of nine months when she was out of town finishing her requirements for graduation and could come to therapy only twice a week. In Chapter IV, I indicated that this phase of her treatment centered chiefly on her "taking pictures of me" by blinking her eyes and carrying my image away with her, summoning me up mentally whenever she felt the need to do so, and "developing" my image as a protective good object representation. Throughout the first 16 months she was admitted to the hospital from time to time for brief stays. I saw her in my office except for one or two occasions when she was too violent to leave the ward and I saw her there.

After she was graduated from school and we had completed a year and a half of face-to-face work, she switched to the couch; we were able to establish a psychoanalytic relationship and in due course to arrive at termination. For a year at the outset she seemed to live with terror. The inner world revealed by her fantasies and dreams was crowded with fragmented images of threatening animals such as bulls or wolves; body parts such as eyes, faces, detached nipples, or penises; and

[146]

violent acts of mutilation and burning. Sometimes soothing object images suddenly replaced the bloody and
devouring creatures of her fancy. She described all
objects, animate or inanimate, as being either "benign"
or "aggressive," providing in this reference a graphic
illustration of the process of primitive splitting. Self- and
object images within the "good" core as well as those
within the "bad" core were not differentiated (Stage II)
most of the time, and she had difficulty differentiating
the human from the nonhuman. On many occasions she
reminded me of a purring kitten which could suddenly
become a bloody tiger.

After graduation she lived in the home of her
parents. She began going about with a psychotic young
man with transsexual tendencies whom she had met in
the hospital. On one level he represented her own split-
off and degraded self-image; on another she saw herself
as his "savior."

After initially reacting to the couch with increased
helplessness she gave evidence within two months that her
thought processes were becoming better organized and
her primitive splitting more crystallized. The head nurse
of the hospital ward on which she had spent so much time
became an "all good" mother, and I was perceived as the
"all bad" mother, at times being condensed with "the
devil"—the all bad father. At the same time, after the
transsexual left town, she tried to carry out her mother's
unspoken command by dating a young man with "credentials" who took her from one humiliating event to
another. She was able to deny her humiliation in order to

be ready to go out with him again. Her past experiences with him were not integrated with present activities and expectations.

In her repeating dreams her father made sexual attacks on her while the "uncaring," almost paralyzed mother watched without interfering. Then the nature of her dreams underwent subtle alteration; in them she tried to protect herself from attack.

Two years after her treatment began she found employment as secretary to a surgeon.

Interpretations serving to re-establish contact with reality

Although to some degree Jane was still experiencing a gross break with reality, I felt as she switched to the couch that she had established a sufficiently stable analytic introject to help her observe the course and meaning of her irrational attitudes and behavior. When gross breaks with reality occurred I used interpretations of the kind Giovacchini (1969) called *linking interpretations.* These serve to link events in the outer world to intrapsychic phenomena and thus promote the re-establishment of contact with reality. Giovacchini recalls Freud's (1900) concept of the day residue of dreams. A day residue, an extrapsychic stimulus, a seemingly irrelevant event, becomes fused with an id content and acts as stimulus to that content. Giovacchini applied this concept to the analytic setting, especially in dealing with schizophrenics, who do not make sharp distinctions between reality and intrapsychic phenomena. "An interpretation may make a causal connexion by referring to the day residue which may be the stimulus for the flow of

[148]

the patient's associations or for some otherwise unex-
plainable behaviour" (Giovacchini, 1969, p. 180).

Jane's first day on the couch provides an example.
She looked intently at the ceiling in her effort to adjust to
the new situation demanded by the couch, and she saw
blood dripping from the holes in the acoustic tile over-
head. I was able to connect this weird perception with a
remark made earlier that she had just begun her menstrual period; it was possible to interpret her identification of her bleeding body with the bleeding environment and to indicate the causative factor and the process
by which such a stimulus could disrupt one's inner world.

Events in the external world and Jane's cosmic laughter

By the time Jane had been in treatment a little more
than two years primitive splitting and related defense
mechanisms such as introjective-projective relatedness
dominated the clinical picture. External stimuli still
fused so readily with the intrapsychic content that their
origin was lost. For example, Jane complained of pain in
her ear after her mother underwent minor ear surgery;
the pain reflected her merging with the mother image. In
her transference psychosis I became interchangeable with
her early (primitively split) mother as well as with the
primitively split oedipal father. Thus her self-representation could merge easily with the analyst/mother representation. The couch became a swimming pool in which
she swam within me; when she identified with the
mothering element of her therapist she had related breast
sensations. Her bisexual conflicts were not repressed.
Nevertheless the analytic introject that could observe and

initiate integration had to a certain degree established itself, and she was able to appreciate some comparison between the symptoms that marked her behavior and their genetic origins.

At this time an event in the external world had a significant influence on me and on my patient. One of my small children was in an automobile accident and had to be hospitalized for some months because of a leg injury. As luck would have it, he was seen in the emergency room by the surgeon who employed Jane, so she learned of the event in the course of her work. She regressed, and in the psychotic transference I became the grieving mother who was anxious and awaiting the death of her first child when she withdrew her "breast" from Jane herself. Jane became preoccupied with the pictures of cancerous breasts.

In a gesture of saving the early mother/analyst she brought peaches for me to eat. She attempted to put them in my parked car at the hospital, and, finding it locked, broke with reality. She perceived the pavement of the parking lot as brittle like the shell of an egg; she felt that a huge insect was devouring the earth, which was about to collapse; she expected her leg to be injured. (In fact, about this time she did manage to injure her leg, which was treated by the same surgeon who had cared for my child.)

Another external event, a widely publicized and disastrous earthquake in Turkey, made itself felt, fostering a representation of an undependable, shaky, Turkish-grieving-uncaring mother/analyst. She returned to the use of fully primitive splitting as her main defense mechanism. I was the "all bad" object while her boy-friend with "credentials" was idealized as the "all good" one, although in reality he openly humiliated her almost daily. (Chapter II gives details of the content of her sessions during this period of her treatment and illustrates the ways in which the reactivation of primitive internal-ized object relations appears in the clinical setting.) At the time when Jane's idealization of her boyfriend was at its most fervent he unexpectedly married another girl. When Jane tried to report this marriage on the day after learning about it she stuttered and shook her head in violent negation, as though using the first symbolic assertion (Spitz, 1957, 1965; Olinick, 1964) to arrest her overwhelming emotionality. (This type of emotionality and its accompaniment of headshaking are examined in Chapter VII.) She stopped the shaking of her head by pressing her head between her hands and, whimpering like an animal, seemed scarcely human. After her agita-tion subsided she reported her (hallucinated) perception of what had occurred; she called it Cosmic Laughter because of its visual and auditory effects. She had perceived an oyster-colored cloud which represented a breast. It contained a window (nipple) and in drawing what she had seen Jane placed a circle (herself) below the window, like a mouth. Over the window knelt an "om-nipotent," teasing presence, and when relatedness be-tween the mouth/Jane was abruptly broken the presence broke into cosmic laughter that echoed in Jane's mind. In her associations with this experience Jane talked about having had something similar in the first grade when the class had rhythmic singing and she would respond to it by an abrupt plunge into distress after having been in a happy mood.

What Jane experienced in Cosmic Laughter was not limited to response to the young man's rejection or rejection by the bad mother/analyst, or the sudden loss of the idealized "all good" object and the vulnerability to her "all bad" units that this loss entailed. Analysis of the experience showed that what she had perceived was the symbolic representation of the earliest frustration at the mother's infected breast and the sudden transformation of the breast from something "good" to something "bad."

A week before this experience took place Jane accompanied her family to church. When her father told her she was sitting where communion would be given she decided that she would never again take communion. Her report of this during the hour in which the Cosmic Laughter experience had occurred, led her to talk about the feeding habits of certain Indian tribes in which the children are allowed to go hungry, given the breast briefly, and then deprived of it in order to frustrate them and make certain that they will develop into fierce warriors in adult life.

I hypothesized that the Cosmic Laughter experience related to the mother's abrupt removal of her infected breast from Jane's mouth, and the frustration this brought about. It is quite possible that the mother had laughed (as she actually did in later years when faced with a situation in which she was helpless) at these times in an attempt to provide a socially acceptable symbolic disguise for a sudden release of hostility. (It was only in the last year of Jane's analysis that the "phallic" aspect of

Cosmic Laughter was analyzed. Although she feared her father's penis, she was disappointed not to have it; she had perceived that it too had been "jerked away from her"; her primitive relatedness to the breast was condensed with relatedness to the penis.)

The re-establishment of object relations at the nursling level

I have examined elsewhere (Volkan, 1974c) the Cosmic Laughter as it resembled the Isakower phenomenon (Isakower, 1938) and the dream screen (Lewin, 1946, 1948). Because the analyst remained calm and maintained an analytic position Jane's nursing experience on the couch was not a mere repetition of something from the past. Through her identification with the analytical attitude her ego could now *tolerate* the experience of tensions and emotions from which her primitive splitting had previously protected her. The re-establishment of relationship to the nursing mother (her primitively split breast) in the transference thus had a corrective influence and enabled her to begin essential change in her relatedness to external objects. With tolerance of primitive tensions and feelings in analysis came a reduction in the need for the mechanism of primitive splitting, progress toward ambivalent relatedness to objects, and an increased ability to mend contradictory ego states instead of regressing toward autism. Jane's arrival at this improved state occurred in dramatic fashion that enabled me to observe the process clearly. It is more usual, however, for patients like Jane to approach it gradually. In examining similarities among Jane's Cosmic Laughter experience,

[153]

the Isakower phenomenon, and the dream screen I (Volkan, 1974c) noted observation in the psychoanalytic literature (Rycroft, 1951; Boyer, 1960; Van der Heide, 1961) that the appearance of the latter two phenomena at specific times may be an indication of clinical improvement as well as a defense. Boyer (1960) points to these times as being: (1) when the patient has reached the stage of development in which narcissistic identification is giving way to true object relations through transference; (2) when the patient is threatened with the loss of the new object; and (3) when an event in the external world reminds the analysand strongly of some severe childhood trauma that he had perceived as his desertion by the mothering figure. Jane's Cosmic Laughter was quickly followed by her energetic attempt to break her symbiotic ties with the mother/analyst, as evidenced by her actions and her working through of obstacles standing in her way.

Toward Jane's transference neurosis

In Chapter VIII, I describe Jane's utilization of her cat as a transitional object during the severing of symbiotic ties to her mother/analyst. Details of the further unfolding of her transference neurosis are beyond the scope of this presentation, but I should nevertheless like to differentiate the work required by the patient previously involved in a transference psychosis and the use of primitive splitting, introjective-projective and related defenses from that appropriate for the typical neurotic. In the first instance transference neurosis is formed in front of mended and newly found structures; the background situation so recently turbulent must have attention throughout the entire analysis. Moreover in such cases the transference neurosis will include many elements of new structures as they continue to form, i.e., ego structures that can repress. In the analysis of the typical neurotic, however, the analyst is working with previously formed structures. There is a stable self-concept and a stable representational world. The primitive phase of internalized object relations has passed; there is no particular pathology of internalized object relations. In Jane's case primitive splitting remained in the background, sometimes hard to recognize among the shadows and at other times clearly evident in full view, but nevertheless present throughout her analysis. For example, when she found a new boyfriend she was aware of the "gray areas" of character and behavior, but underneath this awareness lay alternating views of him as "all good" or "all bad." When he was "all bad" I was "all good," etc. When her intense penis envy was being analyzed, the background of this interchange, including her use of her fantasied penis as a buffer between good units kept within the self-concept and the "all bad" external object, required close attention.

Jane was living in her own apartment and working as a secretary in the fourth year of her treatment. She was at this time, although easily hurt, responsible at work, but she and a newly acquired boyfriend, a few years her junior, lived like teenagers, exploring the world around them. Later she separated from him with appropriate grief, and expressed a wish to move from a "teenage existence" into what she thought of as "womanhood." She left her job and became a grade-school teacher. This move involved identification with me, inasmuch as I teach in a medical school, and with her maternal grandmother, who taught and who brought "some good sense" into the family. Jane managed her students with amazing maturity, and developed a more integrated self-concept as a woman. However, she still split the male image and developed an intense, fearful, and erotic transference neurosis in which she desired me to be her sexual partner. I was idealized and she wanted to have idealized children by me. Her idea of me as a "perfect man" was finally punctured and, after considerable difficulty, she permitted herself affectionate feelings for a man (her analyst) who was neither idealized nor degraded. This relationship followed her achievement of the ability to relate to men more realistically.

As she entered the termination phase of her analysis aspects of her primitive splitting resurfaced; she referred to them as habits she had had in the days "when I *was* sick." On meeting someone new she would at first, perhaps for no more than a day, put primitive splitting dramatically to use before integrating the image of the new acquaintance. She was very much aware of her visit to her "craziness," and performed exercises in her transference and in actual life situations to (re-)mend her primitive splitting. Sometimes I felt that she was like a happy child playing with a toy that had once been terrifying and difficult to manipulate. The sections that follow will examine in some detail the fate of Jane's primitive splitting during the termination phase.

Fate of primitive splitting at the termination phase

Glover (1955) uses the term "review dreams" to refer to the kind of dream I shall describe. Glover warns against premature termination of analysis because of impatience, boredom, or undue optimism on the part of the analyst, and points to the need for adequate confirmation of termination readiness, to which *dream reactions* may make an important contribution. "From time to time during analysis, the more frequently when a true transference-neurosis has developed, 'review dreams' occur, some of the manifest content of which can be readily interpreted as an assessment of the patient's progress in overcoming his difficulties" (pp. 157-158). I likewise (Volkan, 1971) have used the manifest content of dreams reported by pathological mourners to assess their progress in re-grief therapy. Glover (1955) emphasizes the unique significance of *recurrent dreams* and tells of the review dreams of an impotent patient who dreamed repeatedly of automobiles: "When (he) began to report consistently that he could now engage gears without much difficulty and that the cars no longer shrank to small proportions when he sought to drive them, I decided to terminate the analysis, in spite of the fact that he had not yet had any opportunity of proving his sexual potency" (p. 158).

Throughout her treatment Jane had a series of recurring dreams, to some of which I have already referred. Two others merit consideration here. The first concerned a room that "evolved"; the second dealt with climbing a ladder. The first appeared early in treatment

[157]

during the time when Jane was acutely psychotic. The room of which she dreamt lacked walls, a ceiling, and a floor, but was somehow recognizable to Jane as a room nevertheless. The electric outlets to "suck energy," gradually appeared in this "room," which, as Jane became able to discriminate between self- and object representations as well as between different object representations, took on transparent walls, ceiling, and floor, which became more and more substantial as the analysis progressed. At last it contained furniture in a variety of arrangements.

The second set of dreams began later, in the seventh month of Jane's treatment. She was involved in climbing a ladder that hung in space but she never reached the top of it. Later she reached a kind of plateau in space after ascending the ladder, and felt bewildered about where to go from there.

In the fifth year of her treatment these two dream series were combined in Jane's dreaming. She would find herself at the top of the ladder at the plateau, where the room, now outlined and peopled, appeared across an empty gap in which unknown danger lurked. She wanted to jump from the plateau into the room but was unable to do this without knowing what the danger in the chasm was. Her main concern at this point was this unstructured chasm.

In giving the dream that signaled the termination phase of her analysis I recognize that I place considerable weight on its manifest content and that I am not exploring here the contributory genetic material. Nevertheless I maintain that the events that followed this dream demonstrated that Jane had become able to face and neutralize her aggression and to replace the yawning chasm (her primitive splitting) with adequate structuralization. In it she climbed the ladder and again saw the room awaiting her across a chasm.

> This time I learned there were ways to go into the room. In fact, now I know that it was easy for other people in the room to jump into it from the top of the stairway. The gap between the top of the stairs and the room looked like Hell the first time I saw what was in it — Negro convicts, shooting at the people who jumped over. [She went on to describe a man who jumped the gap without harm. This was obviously her analyst.]
> Then I tried to jump. I ran on the plateau in order to make a long jump, but at the last minute I couldn't do it. Then I realized that there might be another way. I went down several steps. There was a room there, too. I was there with Phillip [one of her grade-school students]. Then a convict appeared; I was now faced with what had been scaring me. The convict had an ice pick. I thought he might hurt Phillip. I asked Phillip if he were hurt, and he said he was not. I thought I could walk on the structure of the gap into the room, looking the convicts straight in the eye.

Jane was teaching at the time, and the dream's day residue came from the European history with which she was dealing in class. She had been reading about aggressive Ottoman Turks and associated them with me because of my national origin, associating herself with the Europeans they conquered. Later she had a fantasy during her school hours in which she thought of me as dangerous; at the same time, however, she felt tender toward me as I offered her hope of being well. She recalled how on occasion I would be totally bad and frightening, but she was unable to sustain this view of me since her present tenderness toward me interfered. As she told me of this Jane recalled once asking me to hug her to tame her aggression. She now acknowledged that she must now recognize my interpretations as having been more useful to her than a hug would have been.

As she went on associating to the dream Jane recalled her recent wish to finish her analysis and my remark that we still had some unfinished business. Now she could understand that her goal of jumping over the dangerous chasm in her dream and entering the room was a desire to short-cut the working-through ways of dealing with the danger. My reference to "unfinished business" now made sense to her. She felt that the black convicts represented "them," as she referred to aggressively tinged externalized self- and object images. They also represented the dangerous phallic father/analyst; the theme of black people having this symbolism had appeared before in her analysis. I had, for example, been Othello (since I was born in Cyprus) and she had been my Desdemona. For some time Jane had been encountering a black man waiting for the bus she took to keep her appointments with me. After she had the dream I have described, she found herself able to greet him in a friendly way as they waited for the bus to arrive; his blackness no longer seemed threatening to her.

[160]

Phillip represented her tenderness, her libidinal drive derivatives. He was a favorite student and she invested him with loving feelings. It became clear that what she had been avoiding all along was combining her loving units with her aggressive ones because she anticipated that the latter would damage the ones she valued. When she could face aggression and realize that Phillip was unharmed by it, a structure replaced the chasm and her splitting was remended.

Whatever happened to Jane?

My first glimpse of Jane after her analysis terminated was four months after its conclusion, when she unexpectedly appeared at the door of my office. She explained that she had come to the hospital to see the surgeon she had worked for, and, if I was available, to see me to say goodbye before leaving to begin life in a metropolitan center elsewhere. We had a few minutes to chat, and she told me of going to her new home a month earlier and obtaining a position as executive secretary to the chairman of a university department. She had a relative in the city who had shown her around, and she had located an apartment of her own. She talked with zest and excitement of the life she anticipated.

I received three letters within a few months after she settled in her new home. The first reflected her excitement over the novelty of life in a big city. The others contained more sober reflections on the solitary struggle to make a life for herself that lay ahead. I responded very briefly with my good wishes.

I did not hear from her again for a year, but then

[161]

received a kind of progress report from her a year and a half after she terminated analysis. She wrote, "Mainly, I'm writing to let you know that I'm happy—at least as happy as I can allow myself to be." She spoke of a relationship begun the previous year with a young Ph.D. candidate in the department where she worked, describing him as "strong and serene," and indicating that they were beginning to talk of marriage.

> I know that I'm no longer afraid of age and am looking forward to my thirties. I still could not say this to you face-to-face (or top of my head to face), but I am fond of you. To this man I can express some of my positive feelings I never dared show you except in neurotic ways.
>
> Now I regard myself as having successfully completed analysis, although at the time of termination it looked as though I had a long way to go, and even now I have to wrestle with my worst self. It helps that I love him and know my capacity for making him unhappy, but very much—because I love him—to make him happy.

I wrote saying that I was glad to hear from her and to see that she was working on her fear of marriage. The next news came six months later when she wrote of her plans to marry. The day before her wedding, four months after that, she telephoned me to say that she was in town for her wedding, which was to take place in the home of her parents, and that she would like to see me but had to be content to talk for a few minutes on the phone on this day so full of activity and excitement. I wished her the best of everything. Two days later I saw her bridal picture in the local paper above an account of her wedding.

A year later—in the fourth year after her analysis terminated—I met Jane as I waited at the airport for the arrival of a friend. She was traveling with her husband. When she saw me she impulsively ran to greet me and, apparently stopping just short of hugging me, shook my hand with a few words about her trip and the occasion for it. Then, suddenly realizing that she had left her husband and waiting relatives, she shook my hand again and left to join them. When I saw her smiling face I knew that the fragmented, bloody images of wolves, bulls, and faces that had terrorized her once were now gone forever.

CHAPTER VII

EMOTIONAL FLOODING AND ACCOMPANYING MOTOR ACTIVITIES

This chapter examines another "condition" that accompanies primitive internalized object relations. Patients in whose treatment the reactivation of primitive internalized object relations dominates are apt to experience eruptions of diffuse primitive affective states. I refer to these as emotional flooding in my effort to differentiate them from other kinds of emotional storms that may appear within the therapeutic process, i.e., abreactions and affectualizations. Clinical illustrations indicate how emotional flooding is customarily accompanied by characteristic motor activity and perceptual change. The mending of the primitive splitting is attended by neutralization of drive derivatives, particularly those of the aggressive drive, lessening the possibility of emotional flooding.

Aggression and primitive splitting

Psychoanalytic investigation of certain clinical pictures shows them to be related to excessive aggression that not only stems from severe early frustrations but also from constitutionally determined factors. Olinick (1964) emphasizes the role of primary aggression in the negative therapeutic reaction; it is his impression from psychoanalytic reconstructions that: "those people who display the negative therapeutic reaction were endowed from birth with greater than average funds of aggressive orality and anality. This in turn made the mothering relationship stressful (as it may later the analytic), by investing it with realistic anxieties about filling an assigned role with these masterful infants and children" (p. 544).

Like Olinick, Kernberg (1967) also refers to constitutionally determined excessive intensity of aggressive drives. He speaks of it as exhibited by psychotic patients and those with borderline personality organization, suggesting that in the latter certain deficiencies in the development of primary ego apparatus and "constitutionally determined lack of anxiety tolerance" may interfere with the phases of synthesis of introjections of opposite quality. Nevertheless, he sees the great intensity of aggressive drives as the main pathological factor.

From the borderline patient one usually elicits a history of actual excessive frustration in infancy and childhood, with consequent heightening of aggressive drives. It is perhaps this secondary aggression that condenses with the constitutionally determined excess of aggression that makes early relationships traumatically stressful and connects severe aggressive strivings with early self- and object images. It is the intensity of aggression with which these have been invested that impairs the ability to bring together aggressively determined and libidinally determined self- and object images.

The person with borderline personality organization deals with the problem of aggression by means of the primitive splitting mechanism. He protects "all good" self- and object units from those that are aggressively determined. Moreover, primitive splitting keeps the ego from experiencing primitive diffuse anxieties; this is accomplished at the cost of impairment of ego function, particularly the ability to synthesize. If the primitive splitting mechanism functions poorly there may be a regression toward an autistic position—or, from the reference point of internalized object relatedness, toward the loss of self- and object images. The normally developing infant or the patient with borderline personality organization who is undergoing psychoanalytic treatment progresses toward repairing what has been separated by primitive splitting. Such advance is accomplished piecemeal as the child or the patient comes to tolerate the synthesis of his aggressively determined units with units that are libidinally determined, and thus accepts the ambivalence, a combination of love and aggression toward the same object. Such advance is accompanied by a reduction in denial of the emotional connection between different ego states.

As stated in Chapter II, one of the characteristics of *primitive* internalized object relations is the possibility that emotional storms may appear. Patients with borderline personality retain a chronic tendency to eruptions of primitive affective states because of the failure of libidinal and aggressive drive derivatives to interpenetrate;

[167]

by this failure they remain obstructions to normal modulation and differentiation of affect dispositions of the ego (Kernberg, 1967). This chapter will be devoted primarily to a study of these primitive affect states as they appear — usually accompanied by seemingly aimless motor activities — *within* the therapeutic process.

Types of emotionality occurring within the treatment situation

Psychoanalytic writers have paid relatively little attention to the description and classification of types of emotionality occurring *within* the treatment process. As Valenstein (1962) points out, psychoanalytic work requires the appropriate blending of the intellectual and emotional at the appropriate time. Only when the blending is suitable and the timing favorable can the material brought into consciousness be made dynamically accessible to interpretation; only then do the consequent psychoanalytic insights feel authentic and immediately applicable to the inner and the outer life. Without emotional experience psychoanalytic treatment would be but intellectual gymnastics.

In any attempt to classify the emotionality that appears within the treatment the first classification would be "blending emotionality" — emotions which blend appropriately with the ideational and the actional aspects of such treatment. Other types of emotionality may appear in the treatment situation, however, in ways which either indicate a high intensity or the failure of blending with ideational and actional aspects. Abreactions and affectualizations would be examples of the latter type. I designate the eruption of primitive diffuse affective states in the treatment of the borderline or psychotic patient as "emotional flooding," a "condition" that accompanies primitive internalized object relations. One should remember that blending emotions, abreactions, affectualization, and emotional flooding may overlap; in order to elucidate the latter I propose a review of abreaction and affectualization.

Abreaction

Bibring (1954) included abreaction, which was originally considered curative, among his five therapeutic principles. It is employed as a technical tool for the acquisition of insight through interpretations, with all of the related consequences. Bibring wrote: "Abreaction, now in the sense of 'emotional reliving,' came to be thought of as offering evidence and establishing conviction in the patient as to the actuality of his repressed impulses, etc." (p. 749). This definition of abreaction is very much like the definition of emotion in the psychoanalytic process which blends with the ideational aspects of the psychoanalytic process in a timely and appropriate manner. I believe that abreaction also does occur in the classical sense, i.e., discharge in the psychoanalytic or psychotherapeutic process of "strangulated affects" attached to the previously repressed experience.

To distinguish it from emotional flooding, my classification holds that an emotional storm occurring in the therapeutic process is an abreaction when the patient himself (spontaneously and authentically, or readily with help from the analyst) can form a sustained connection between the emotion and ideational and/or actional fields. This definition of abreaction calls for an ego sufficiently differentiated to sustain, through readily available secondary-process thinking, a relation between the emotion and the idea or action. Accordingly, the emotional storm seen in therapy is an abreaction when the ego is not entirely overwhelmed by the emotion but retains observational and integrative function. However dramatic this emotional storm may be, it still has a signal quality and communicates to the patient something about the nature of his dynamic conflict.

A woman patient of mine in her mid-twenties had had a criminal abortion at the age of 15. At the start of her analysis years later she was able to describe the horrifying details of this without appropriate emotionality. After a year and a half in analysis, she ceased to have menses and symbolically became pregnant; at one time, by shrinking in size in her fantasy, I represented her fetus to her. An actual separation — a previously planned one-week interval for my vacation — represented an abortion, and she went into an emotional storm which was, by my definition, an abreaction. The emotion did have maximum outpouring, but with a little help from me she was able to use the observational function of her ego effectively throughout the experience. Although somewhat shaken, she was able to return to her work at the end of the abreaction and the end of the hour.

Affectualization

Here the emotionality within the treatment hours is

basically in the service of the defensive function of the ego. Its purpose is to keep the patient from understanding his mental conflict. Affectualization was described in a paper by Bibring et al. (1961) as, "the overemphasis on and the excessive use of the emotional aspects of issues in order to avoid the rational understanding and appreciation of them. Feeling is unconsciously intensified for purposes of defense" (p. 64). This special defense mechanism built out of affects was further described by Valenstein (1962):

> A superfluity of affects is unconsciously utilized for defensive purposes, often in association with instinctual derivatives and their discharge; and this overdoing of affects is habitual enough in certain patients, and possibly specific enough to justify its designation as a mechanism of defense [p. 318].

Affectualization usually occurs in hysterics "who not only have a strong propensity for fantasy life and acting out, but also are prone to powerful and relatively primitive affect responses" (p. 317). An example is provided by an unmarried hysterical patient in the middle phase of psychoanalysis who used every excuse to display emotional storms of anger as a screen against talking about having had sexual intercourse without contraceptive precautions—and especially against associations evoked by this incident which pertained to her oedipal wishes directed toward the analyst in her transference neurosis.

[171]

Before Valenstein, Seigman (1954) described the production of a profusion of affect in hysterics for both the onlooker and the "internalized observer." Greenson (1958) defined the "screen affect" as a similar phenomenon. Sperling (1948) described patients who fear excess emotion and whose affects are subdivided and spread; he went on to speak of the opposite state of affairs—emotional crowding—which, he said, usually appears in psychopathic personalities, with the crowded emotions reaching one simultaneous climax. He compared crowding emotions with counterphobic attitudes. Here, too, emotionality becomes a defense mechanism similar to acting out—"feeling out." Valenstein (1962) noted the similarities between affectualization, acting out, and intellectualization, making it clear that defenses evolve from three different modes of drive discharge. Like intellectualization in obsessive persons, affectualization usually is a habitual, chronic defense, and thus a character trait. Once the analyst knows the patient, he can predict the appearance of emotional storms as defenses. The patient with affectualizations may respond to suggestion when it is warranted, by "snapping out" of his emotionality (Peto, 1968).

Emotional flooding

Because of the introjective-projective cycle and the occasional fusion of self- and object images in intimate relationships, the borderline patient who activates primitive internalized object relations in treatment does not successfully project his aggression, nor can he successfully externalize "all bad" self- and object images. Whatever externalization is possible does not adequately distance the "all bad" self- and object images; they persist and haunt their counterparts with which the person attempts to furnish his inner world. This impasse demands a kind of illusory global control to come into play against the threatening object, a representation on which aggression is projected, and "all bad" self- and object images or representations are externalized. When the patient fears that his "control" is breaking down, he may attack the threatening object before it attacks him. Without interpretations and the benefit of working through in the treatment situation, such repeated attacks are unlikely to have curative value, even though, in a theoretical sense, they provide "contacts" between the "all good" and "all bad" counterparts. To be useful, they have to be a component of working through. Joseph's case in Chapter V provides an example of this.

Only the coming together of the "all good" and "all bad" units that have been primitively split asunder — under the gaze of the observing ego — will work toward repair in a curative way. Before such mending is accomplished, however, the impulse to attack will erupt in the transference, accompanied by primitive emotions and seemingly diffuse motor activity. I refer to such primitive emotions as emotional flooding, with the implication that their function is more that of drive discharge than of a signal. Clinical observations suggest that emotional flooding and some of the accompanying motor activities are not simple discharges but probably involve interaction between self- and object representations that have already been formed. Mahler (1968) suggests a similar formula for the autoaggression seen in psychotic children, stating that it: "is probably directed at an already formed self and object representation that, for various reasons, may be connected in the child's mind with a particular part of the body. The autoaggressive activity, like some autoerotic activities, is probably also an attempt on the child's part at defining the body-self boundaries, an attempt to feel alive, even if at the price of enduring pain" (p. 215). It should be remembered that the affective channeling of libidinal drive derivatives also occurs in the type of patient we describe, and that his basic difficulties relate to the channeling of drive derivatives that are aggressive.

I believe that although emotional flooding represents the eruption of diffuse primitive affects, with accompanying motor activity, in adult patients it provides a rather characteristic clinical picture which may differ, even on a descriptive level, from affective forms of abreaction and affectualization. In the treatment situation, however, there are gray areas between the different forms of emotionality displayed. Emotional flooding, as a discharge against early self- or object representations, may be defensive, but in a primitive way. One may think of abreaction as appearing on a spectrum at the upper end of which the observational power of the ego is evident early in the emotional storm. The higher the abreaction is on the spectrum, the more usual it is for the patient to experience a sense of achievement from it, the reliving of an event, or of being able for the first time to live through the event with feelings. The emotional experience more closely approximates the kind necessary in analytic work and blends appropriately with ideational and actional fields. In the lower range of the spectrum, the ego's observational functions are primitive; what is observed seems like the symbolic representation of primal affects, as will be illustrated, and no sufficient secondary-process connection can be made between affect and event.

The question of phenomenology

In psychoanalytic theory the concept of affect (the subjective aspect of feelings) and emotion (their outward display) (Darwin, 1872) as an experience of the ego evolved as interest shifted from the instinctual drives to the ego; the ego theory of affects supplemented those formulated earlier. A phenomenological question remains as to how "tamed" emotions (Fenichel, 1945) may be distinguished from primal emotions connected with discharge phenomena.

Although the history of psychoanalytic theories of affect and attempts to clarify and classify the emotions has been studied by many (Brierly, 1937; Glover, 1939; Fenichel, 1941; Rapaport, 1942, 1953; Jacobson, 1953; Novey, 1961; Valenstein, 1962; Smith, 1970; and others) we are forced "to agree that we do not yet have a full or complete theory of affects" (Rangell, 1967). In the early days of psychoanalysis affect played a leading role in theory and practice; the oldest psychoanalytic theory equated affect with the amount of psychic energy. Affect was later viewed as a process through which psychic energy of instinctual origin was discharged (the id theory of affect). Rapaport's (1953) essay indicates that even in *The Interpretation of Dreams* Freud (1900) recognized

[175]

that one of the concomitants of the development of secondary process and reality testing is the "taming" of affects to the point of changing them into signals. Freud also realized that this process is never completely successful. In *Inhibitions, Symptoms and Anxiety* he (Freud, 1926) stated, anxiety (an affect) could be experienced only by the ego, in which it arises as a signal response warning of internal danger. This new formulation of anxiety significantly indicated that affects are a means for the subject to communicate not only intrapsychically but, in an extended sense, at the interpersonal level (Valenstein, 1962). "Tamed" affects are not only signals and communicators; they are also contributors to cognition (McDougall, 1936) and integration, defense, tension reduction, and reality testing (Alexander and Isaacs, 1964).

In making the distinction between what he designated as "id emotions" and "ego emotions" Eissler (1954) pointed out that the first accompany instinctual drives and have limited signal power whereas the latter are so tamed that they do function as signals and contribute to the organization of mental activity and behavior within the requirements of both the inner and outer worlds. The phenomenology of "id emotions" is somewhat unsatisfactory inasmuch as Eissler himself stated that, "the ego is the only province of the human personality in which emotions have their being." One can theorize that, from a structural point of view, we can trace the ontogenesis of affects to the id, or, in modern terms, to the undifferentiated id-ego matrix; but since affects (felt emotions) are subject to experience, they must be within conscious awareness. Eissler's classification is, however, clearly meaningful and useful in actual practice.

Touching on the same subject, Engel (1962) stated that as affects become more highly differentiated some are notably characterized by signal and scanning properties, and others display more discharge qualities. The two classes of affect are interrelated. Engel gives as examples of the signal or scanning affects anxiety, shame, guilt, sadness, joy. His examples of the drive or discharge affects are anger or rage (associated with the aggressive drive), love, tenderness, sexual excitement (associated with libidinal drive). Valenstein (1962) similarly refers to affects which are closer to the drive and drive discharges and, in a sense, consonant with primary process and, in structural terms, the id (primal affects). These kinds of affect are thus differentiated from those that are tamed and brought within the ego sphere with adaptive value for signal and communication. Rapaport (1953) described a hierarchy of affects based on closeness to instinctual or ego sources. Hartmann (1950) described the same phenomena with reference to the degree of neutralization. Peto (1968) suggested the terms *intrasystemic* and *intersystemic*, the former referring to affect that operates an ego signal proper, the latter to an affect complex that is more of a drive-derivative with the nature of a discharge.

Fenichel (1945) described an early stage of development in which the ego is weak and affect is dominant. This is followed by a second phase in which the ego is strong and has learned to use the affect for its purposes by taming it. Fenichel continues, however, to a third pos-

[177]

sible stage in which once more an elemental affect can overwhelm the organism. Emotional flooding refers to the appearance of primal affects and their ascendancy over tamer ones. As our knowledge of the metabolization of internalized object relations increases we can redefine "ego weakness" or "ego strength" in order to understand the appearance of emotional flooding or tamer emotions. Kernberg (1972a) holds that it is an inadequate explanation of the situation to conceptualize ego weakness as frailty of the ego barrier which, when assaulted by id derivatives, cannot prevent them from "breaking through" or "flooding." He indicates that in borderline personality organization underneath ego "weakness" are extremely strong, rigid, primitive, and pathological ego structures. The formulation of Hartmann, Kris, and Loewenstein (1946) as well as that of Rapaport (1957) shows the ego as an over-all structure within which substructures determine specific function: "the ego weakness should be conceptualized not simply as the absence or weakness of such structures, but as the replacement of higher-level by lower-level structures" (Kernberg, 1972a, p. 263). Patients prone to exhibit emotional flooding and a lack of motor impulse control during their therapeutic hours do have lower-level ego structures of which the basic defensive mechanism is primitive splitting and related defenses, such as denial and illusory global control of the external object. The "all good" and "all bad" structures are not integrated, so the affective ties between them are not neutralized; thus the eruption of primal emotions and accompanying motor activity remains a constant possibility.

[178]

Emotional flooding and accompanying motor activities

Patients who experience emotional flooding are usually prone to develop transference psychosis; their inability to distinguish the source of affects in different events is very marked. Affects then seem to combine without neutralization. The first manifestation of emotional flooding, although neither always observable or a necessary prerequisite, is usually an accumulation of memories and fantasies (flooding in the ideational field) that support the same emotion. The patient can refer to the contents of these memories or fantasies only in a kind of "shorthand" — fragmentary sentences, or a single word. He may then begin stuttering and lose the power of intelligible speech altogether. It is impossible at this point to distinguish between flooding in the emotional, actional, or ideational field. The patient may scream and exhibit diffuse motor activity; he may seem to have lost his human identity.

Observing a patient with defective ego structure, Eissler (1954) noted that an emotion accumulated new energy by activating all closely related memories that can feed it. He suggests that this phenomenon can be seen in normal persons, too, but that in the case of his patient once an emotion was activated it always reached maximum limits, and she could experience no more than one emotion at a time. Her ego could not support a full assortment of highly divergent, often mutually contradictory emotions as can the normal ego. Peto (1968) illustrated a related phenomenon in the case of a patient whose different shades of a dominant affect (in his case sadness) arising from different events merged during a therapy hour.

At the height of emotional flooding motor activity is diffuse and seems to be aimless, but before this stage is reached the patient usually shakes his head in what I see as a representation of the gesture of negation. I believe that this motor behavior is purposive although not consciously so, and that it refers to the first symbolic assertion, brought into play to stem the overwhelming emotionality.

Spitz (1957, 1965) has shown how the rooting reflex — a rotary motion of the head used by the sucking infant as he seeks the nipple — is affirmative behavior in the neonate. In the objectless state this behavior is without intention signal or communicative quality, and it disappears as the infant becomes more mature. When the infant is six months old, however, the same motion reappears with a change of function; at this stage rotation of the head is used in refusing food by a gesture not directed toward any special object. Spitz further proposed the outline of a comprehensive explanation as to how the motor pattern of head rotation becomes the matrix of the semantic gesture of negative headshaking when the child is between 15 and 18 months old.

When the infant becomes capable of locomotion, communication between mother and child suddenly changes to the frequent use of the word "No" as an expression of prohibition or reproach with a headshaking accompaniment; the mother behaving so prevents her child from carrying out his intentions. But more than an imitation of the mother is involved in the acquisition of the concept of "no." Spitz saw it connected with the biological urge to replace passivity with activity, since a child will not tolerate without resistance being forced back into passivity. It is also connected with an aggressive thrust from the id when every "no" of the mother represents emotional frustration for the child, and with the use by the end of the first year and throughout the second, in practically every situation requiring mastery of defense, of the mechanism of identification, especially identification with the frustrator (or aggressor). The ability to express "no" by word or gesture marks a milestone in the child's development, presupposing as it does the capacity for judgment and negation.

The gesture of "no," appearing before the peak of the emotional flooding, relates the activation and identification with the mother representation as a frustrator; the patient uses it in an attempt to cut off the primal emotions that threaten to overwhelm him. When the patient was an infant the mother, his "external ego," performed this function for him. As the child internalized this maternal function he learned to take action to protect himself against strong stimuli. This explanation of the learning of the concept of "no" assumes that the child's biological urge to progress from passivity to activity met with no obstruction.

In a study of negativism as it appears in human development, Olinick (1964) suggests that the child's "no" may have been at first a means of resisting excessive stimulation, an aggressive warding off of excessive stim-

[181]

ulation: "At this point, the anxiety-signal leading to the 'No' might be conceptualized as 'Too much to be safe'—that is, too much excitation to be assimilated. Later, when additional external forces are introjected as part of the superego system, ordinarily gratifying experiences will evoke negativistic responses, as being 'Too good to be true' or, as one patient quoted her envious mother, 'More than the law allows' " (p. 544).

Clinical observation of the patient who is going into emotional flooding shows him trying to recapture this early identification with the frustrator in a last-ditch effort to resist the flooding. One of my patients (Volkan, 1974c) as she went into emotional flooding shook her head violently, clenched her fists in the manner of an infant, and placed them on either side of her head in an effort to stop its motion. She seemed tormented in body and mewed like an animal. She finally released her introjects of ferocious early frustrators and gave them tongue in her voice, crying "Shut up! Shut up!" and gave them action in her own hands that slapped her face until the emotional flooding ebbed away. Sometimes the body as well as the head will shake in negation. It is quite possible that the rhythmic discharge of aggression, along with a motor recreation of the rocking and soothing object, may be condensed in such bodily movements.

It is usual for the patient to fall into a state of diffuse primal emotionality accompanied by random motor activity once the headshaking or bodyshaking that appears so purposeful to the therapist is arrested. The motor activity that seems so aimless at this point is in fact in the service of defending the self against the threatening object. In

[182]

this situation there is danger of physical harm to either the therapist or his patient, and it is up to the former to prevent it.

Perceptual changes

Patients capable of reporting their experience of emotional flooding after the event usually indicate that strange perceptual changes took place. They underwent a "metamorphosis" during the experience, becoming monstrous and diabolical when signal affects were replaced by primal affects closely related to the aggressive drive. If the primal affect was close to the libidinal drive, however, there was another kind of change, the kind reflected in poetry or romantic prose when a lover tells his beloved, "I love you so much that I am a new person." What the ego close to the state of id-ego matrix — and the ego with split and fragmented structures at a lower organization level — perceives during emotional flooding seems like the representation of the self and object images *saturated* with affect and kept within. In this state the representation of the affect becomes the patient's perceived self, as Werner (1948) suggested about situations in which "primitivization" of mental activity takes place. He pointed out that when the schizophrenic cries, "The door is devouring me!" the affect "has once more become a factor in the configuration of the surrounding world as in the case of a genuinely primitive mind. And this occurs not in the sense that the world of things becomes invested with an especially strong overtone of emotion, but rather in the sense that affect actually forms the world itself" (p. 81).

The unintegrated ego seems able to symbolize the

representation of the overwhelming emotionality and self- and object images tied to them; the symbols themselves are primitive and openly associated with bodily functions. The patient's perception of having turned into a bursting balloon is a case in point. The feeling of bursting or falling into fragments, and the dread of the helpless state recall the "aphanisis" described by Jones (1927). Jones suggested that this is a tension reaction due to the unavoidable absence of efferent discharge of erotic excitement. Glover (1939) wrote about the feeling of "mental bursting" and "flying into fragments." Like Jones, he used oedipal terms to describe the "bursting," but he also mentioned its possible association with pregenital aspects of sexuality — delivery by bursting through the abdominal wall, and the pressure of anal or urethral retention. And Arlow (1963) suggested that powerful affects may unconsciously represent the loss of control over urinary or anal sphincters, and the discharge of some aggressive or erotic wish.

One recalls Searles' (1962) term "desymbolization" with reference to the patient's report of being, at a time of emotional flooding, "a balloon ready to burst": "By this term I refer to a process, seemingly at work in the schizophrenic patient, whereby the illness causes once-*attained* metaphorical meanings to become 'desymbolized,' and in the grip of the illness, the individual reacts to them as being literal meanings which he finds most puzzling indeed. This would seem to be one of the important respects in which the thinking of the regressed schizophrenic adult differs from that of the normal child"

[184]

(p. 43). Searles states that the so-called "concrete" thinking of schizophrenic patients is indeed undifferentiated
thinking—there is a lack of differentiation between the
concrete and the metaphorical. Thus when the patient
says he is turned into a balloon he is unable to think in
effective, consensually validated metaphor. But Searles'
studies remind us too that the patient is also unable to
think in terms that are genuinely concrete, "free from an
animistic kind of so-called metaphorical overlay."

Spitz (1965) dealt with the interplay between the
phenomena of affect and perception and between their
undifferentiated precursors in the newborn. After a
reference to experimental work in this field he stated
that, "Affect colors perception, it makes perception
important or unimportant. . . . Ultimately affects determine the relation between perception and cognition" (p.
85). It appears that overwhelming affect changes differentiated perception of reality; the perceptual field is
filled with the primitive symbolic representations of the
affect itself, and cognition is altered accordingly.

Attis turns into a monster and a groundhog

I will turn again to the patient Attis, of whom I
spoke in Chapter IV, to give a clinical illustration of
issues involved in emotional flooding. There I followed
the clinical process of Attis's introjection of and identification with his therapist after he became able to distinguish his therapist as being different from his external
representation of the introjected archaic mother. I
emphasized that it takes some time in treatment for

the patient to make this distinction, which is crystallized only after much working through within the transference-countertransference relationship.

The events described in Chapter IV had not yet taken place when, in his fourth year of treatment, Attis experienced emotional flooding. We were subsequently to reconstruct this occurrence as a consequence of the confrontation of his "all good" self- and object units by the "all bad" ones, and the danger this represented. Attis had moved beyond the need to meet such a threat by regressing toward autism; he could now bring secondary-process functioning to bear on his situation soon *after* the emotional flooding overtook him. Using secondary process, he was able to understand what was happening, to try to integrate what had until now been primitively split, and to neutralize related affects.

What follows illustrates that affect about to erupt in emotional flooding can be considered an amorphous force in which there is no degree of shading. Just before the flooding takes over it is usual for the patient to recall many memories that support the same emotion; many different events seem to be remembered, the affective content of each adding force to what soon becomes overwhelming emotionality, just as tributaries of a destructive force can join in a river that thereby attains raging power. The vignette that follows exemplifies perceptual changes that are typical of emotional flooding. It must be remembered that the hour described here came only after much work on the patient's understanding of the distinction between the therapist and Attis's archaic object representations, and after he had become aware of the manifestations of his repetition compulsion. In short, considerable work with the transference psychosis preceded the events I am about to relate, although this patient would still in some circumstances regress into transference psychosis with the possibility of emotional eruption.

Attis lived more than 150 miles away from my office, and during the winter in question he canceled a number of his hours with me on the ground that the bad weather we were having at the time made the trip a dangerous one; he offered as an additional reason the need to officiate at an unusual number of funerals among his parishioners. The cancellations represented his wish to separate from the early mother/therapist; the winter weather helped him to materialize as well as defend this wish. He felt that if he came to me I might engulf him — and feared also that he might kill me (and thus himself, or part of himself, at the same time.) I believe the rather extended separation between us helped him to keep me in the role of the "all bad" entity from which he must remain distant to be safe, since by not actually seeing me he had more chance for reality distortions.

Finally he was questioned by a new secretary about his reason for cancelling an appointment, and felt great resentment over what he regarded as her aggressive curiosity. He saw her as an extension of me, the "bad mother" representation, and at his next hour with me he opened the session with complaint, albeit calm complaint, about her pointed questions. He then began to tell of a quarrel that had taken place in his home town. The owner of a funeral home there had discontinued his ambulance service because it was unprofitable. The townspeople were sharply critical of this curtailment of service. As he talked about this Attis became angry; he spoke of what had happened as unjust persecution. He felt involved in it himself inasmuch as he had been called by a community leader who suggested that the financial affairs of the mortuary needed investigation. Attis wanted to give a sermon in support of the funeral director, although this would endanger his own image in the community. In following his opening complaint about inquisitive interference over the telephone by another episode involving telephone pressure Attis did not seem to see the parallel between them — how in each a persecuting "bad" object tried to intrude on a "good" one. I did not interrupt him.

He went on to say that he had recently been upset. He had fallen into the habit of looking in closets for his dead father. Although he had in the past hallucinated his father's presence, his search now referred to a certain temper tantrum his father had had that he connected with his own murderous rage. He now sought to see one particular aspect of his father — his punitive and taunting grin. As I indicated in Chapter IV, Attis had arrived at the oedipal age with many pregenital problems still unresolved. His superego could not be appropriately integrated into his psychic system, which contained untamed projections of his earlier "bad" self- and object images; the superego was not depersonified. At the time I now refer to, Attis felt the need to defend himself from attacking the "bad" externalized objects that threatened him, and mobilized in his hallucinations ferocious, forbidding, and extremely aggressive superego images with which to control the defensive rage within.

When he reported having been unwilling to keep this appointment I understood that he was afraid of being unable to control his temper; he had thought of turning around and going back home. He had been angered further by something that had happened as he parked his car outside my office; he had located an empty spot in the crowded parking lot but had been "tricked out of it" by a "big guy" although he had found it first. This incident triggered the anger which supported the emotions that had attended other episodes he told about during the hour. He recalled the brother who had cut off his finger; he was angry because the brother had been his mother's favorite and had pushed him into second place. He had been reminded at a basketball game the previous week of his boyhood prowess in athletics, which he had given up because of his mother's disapproval. There had been two brothers in the game he saw; the younger was the better player but he had refrained "for psychological reasons" from shooting the ball into the basket. Although these incidents contained aspects of the oedipal struggle as it involved a sibling in a triangle, Attis emphasized the dyad of himself and his mother within the triangle.

Attis grew more and more angry as he poured out these memories. He was not at this point conscious that they all were serving to support his anger, and he could not separate one event, with its accompanying feeling, from another. Suddenly he went into emotional flooding. Motor activity accompanied this, and he moved toward me to attack. When he later recapitulated this incident in secondary-process thinking he was briefly aware of feeling "rage." This feeling state was soon diffused without being identified, and he felt paralyzed as his motor activity lapsed. When we tried later to understand this feeling of paralysis, he recalled the events of the night in which he had left the house in search of an ax with which to kill his wife (see Chapter IV). Although on one level his "paralysis" might seem a highly sophisticated defense mechanism directed by a highly developed superego, the patient's associations to it pointed to it as a global defense like a primitive state of shock, a maneuver of "playing possum" before an overwhelming affect. I have noted how Attis would try to invoke ferocious early introjects such as his father's face with a savage grin on it, to arrest his defensive aggression; he was unable to employ a functional superego that would be more depersonified for this purpose.

Since Attis had by now identified himself to some extent with his therapist's observing functions, the "paralysis" that overtook him in the transference was transient, and to a degree brought under his observing ego. Nevertheless, his capacity to bring reality testing to bear on himself was absent. He thought of himself as a swollen, balloonlike monster of indeterminate sex, and vaguely imagined bursting and destroying everything around him. What did Attis really perceive at the time of his emotional flooding? It is likely that the swollen balloonlike monster represented his self-image when it was saturated with defensive rage; it seemed to be a symbol of the fear of anal explosion, supporting Arlow's (1963) view

[190]

that powerful affects may unconsciously be perceived as the loss of control over the sphincter.

Those mental processes under the sway of affect clearly prevailed over the conative and cognitive at the time of emotional flooding and gave direction to them. As the flooding subsided, Attis's perception of himself as a monster gave way to a perception of himself as a groundhog, and he adhered to this throughout what was left of the hour. It will be remembered that he had been born on Groundhog Day, a day marred by storms, rains, and mists, and that his mother had frequently reminded him of this "bad day" and its foreboding weather. Certainly the groundhog image is tamer than that of the monster. Perhaps it represented the core primary affective relationship between the mother and child upon which the first but undifferentiated self- and object representation accumulated.

A light in the dark

The following account of a patient's abreaction will serve to differentiate this clinical manifestation from emotional flooding. The practical as well as theoretical differences between the two kinds of emotional storms will be evident.

A man in his late thirties came into analysis at a time when he was legally separated from his wife. He was obsessional in character and gripped by fear at the thought of having to speak before any group of people. He claimed to love his wife and their three children, and to be mystified at what had happened to his marriage. As his story unfolded it became clear that he had to be the subordinate to his business partner, an older man whose wishes he obeyed without question, repressing any hostility they might evoke. He looked to his partner for his initiation into manhood. The partner had in fact initiated him into the Masonic rites, and he was grateful for this. Rumors of an affair between his partner and his wife reached his ears; he occasionally saw his wife holding hands with the man he regarded as his father and knew that they lunched together from time to time, but could not believe they were guilty of any misconduct. Nevertheless, he felt bedeviled and had occasional emotional outbursts against his wife. He was by then no longer dependent on the business partnership and would have been more prosperous had he gone into business for himself. The continued use of the partner's name was an expense to him, and it became clear that his acceptance of the situation that so distressed him was a reactivation of his oedipal struggles.

His parents had come to this country from Germany before World War II, settling in an urban Jewish neighborhood. Although they were anti-Semitic they had developed a reaction formation and were courteous toward the Jews in the community. The father, who had been in the German Army during the first World War, had stories of bravery and cruelty to tell, always in a kind of odd secrecy. Mementos of his military days were locked away in a trunk. The child grew up associating his German family name with aggression; he longed to change it. This circumstance seemed to account in part for his placing such a high value on the later use of his partner's name in business. He felt that a typical German name would alienate others.

His parents were in their early forties when he was born, their only child. They had to work in a store and leave the patient alone much of the time. The mother taught the little boy where the hands of the clock would be at the time when he might expect their return home, and this exercise remained strongly in his memory. Although he thought that he was happy as a child, he recalled in adult life that he had wanted his father to be more assertive.

As his analysis progressed an incident was reported that seemed to have initiated his neurosis. When he was at the pubertal age of 12 his parents moved from their home and for some months occupied an apartment so small that the family members all slept in the same room. The child slept in his bed alongside that of his parents, and one night when the father unexpectedly turned on the light he saw his mother preparing for intercourse by putting vaseline on her vagina. The light was quickly extinguished, but as his repression began to lift in his analysis he gradually recognized the incestuous wishes and fears that were mobilized. He recalled that in the nights that followed this incident he lay in his bed listening intently for any sound from the parental bed, measuring in his mind the distance between his bed and that of his parents. As an adult he became an engineer-surveyor, measuring distances: he entertained fantasies of discovering some device that would bring sunlight to the dark side of the earth during the night hours.

The move to the new location did not work out for

the family, and they returned to the city a few months after the above incident. While in his city school the patient manifested obsessional neurosis after hearing schoolmates call one another "mother fuckers." Some years later he had an electroshock treatment for obsessional thoughts centered around the possibility of his being a homosexual, or crazy. When some of his friends broke into a theater and caused the owner to have a fatal heart attack, he assumed the blame for the old man's death. Once when he saw a newspaper account of the murder of a young girl he had obsessional thoughts about having been the murderer himself.

He married in his twenties. He was dependent on his wife, and always found an older man who would "take him under his wing." He could not tolerate too much success. When his marriage broke up, the obsessional neurosis of his teen years returned in full force, accompanied by phobic symptoms; he sought psychoanalysis.

The treatment hour in which an emotional storm occurred came at the end of 15 months of psychoanalysis. It can be compared with a similar hour of Attis's. Like Attis, this patient cancelled some of his appointments; he claimed that a proposed visit out of town made it impossible to come. He called my office on Monday morning after the weekend away, saying he was unable to get a plane connection and would have to cancel; at his hour on Tuesday he reported having sat in the airline terminal for eight hours waiting for a plane that he knew intellectually was not due for that length of time, with his eyes on the clock and feeling overwhelmed by anxiety and discomfort. After telling of this behavior he had a genuine flash of insight, understanding that he had perceived me as the rejecting mother and himself as the child left alone to watch the clock. He was now able to experience separation anxiety.

During the next hour he told how, on a recent visit, he and his friends had been drinking; he found himself climbing into bed beside his sleeping friend and his woman. He perceived something peculiar about being in bed with another man and another man's woman, but wanted to have intercourse with the woman. The pair, awakened by his intrusion, left the room. On the following day he was embarrassed and pretended that he had been too drunk the night before to be aware of what he was doing.

The next day he reported having had a "flood" of dreams on the night just past. He had previously reported dreams very seldom. The "flood" concerned "triangle situations" like the one he had tried to experience in his friend's bed. He remembered especially vividly the involvement of two men and a woman in the following dream.

> My wife was having intercourse with a man. I don't know who he was. I could not see his face. Then I saw myself riding my bicycle. I went through a park and then through a building that was a whorehouse.

He exhibited some emotionality as he reported this dream, and spontaneously gave associations to it. Although he had always previously been controlled on the couch, speaking in a monotonous voice, his voice now quivered and there was a tremor of the hand. He nevertheless remained in control of his emotionality.

He spoke of having been blind to the relationship that had existed between his now divorced wife and his former partner. Many years earlier he had ridden his bicycle through a park in which a young woman had been murdered, and for some time thereafter he had been obsessed with the idea that he had committed the murder. Now he realized that he had a murderous rage toward his ex-wife and his former partner whom he had expected to care for him.

The whorehouse reminded him of his uncle whom he had visited as a young man. The uncle had taken him to a whorehouse and invited him to go to bed with one of the girls. He had refused, but the uncle, who was married, did take one of the whores. My patient had been shocked at the idea that a married man would have intercourse with a woman not his wife. He referred to this behavior as "incest," but could not explain how it was like incest when I asked him to elaborate on this idea. He later reported other memories of incidents in which a "triangular situation" was the main theme with its concomitant anxiety; I felt such anxiety building up in him and noticed the flushing of his face. He was like Attis as he reported memories with the same emotional base.

Suddenly he told me that his vivid dream might have been triggered by his having gone to a club where he parked his car in what turned out to be the space assigned to his ex-partner, who appeared simultaneously and demanded an explanation. My patient was obliged to move elsewhere, not unlike Attis, who had been ousted from his parking spot at the hospital by a "big guy." Realizing that he had lost in the competition with his ex-partner for the parking place (and the same woman), my patient became angry. He recalled more of his dream, and explained, "My wife was wearing a black dress. There was something peculiar about it. Oh-oh! I know! I know! There were stripes on the dress of fluorescent material shining like lights." At this point he experienced overwhelming emotionality; he shook and wailed "Oh! Yea! Yea! Yea!" as if griefstricken.

At the peak of his emotional flooding Attis perceived the affect that saturated his self-representation. However, he did not use secondary-process thinking to connect this perception with its supporting genetic-dynamic constellations that supported it. My obsessional patient, on the other hand, was able to hold on to his own identity during and after his abreaction, and to explain that the "light" on his mother's dress stood for the visual trauma he had experienced at age 12. Although the original oedipal childhood wishes were still greatly repressed, he was able in recalling the incident to feel the emotions it had evoked, and to connect them with his incestuous wishes and fear of his father's retaliation. Moreover, he understood that he wanted to call his mother a "whore" and that he had regarded his uncle's visit to the brothel as an occasion of incestuous behavior. It is highly significant that in abreaction—or at least soon after the emotionality

[197]

subsides — the patient can name the emotions that have been awakened. This is not the case in emotional flooding.

Naming and taming emotions

A. Katan (1961) has observed that parents usually name the components of his physical environment for a child some time before acquainting him with words for the various kinds of affect. Noting that verbalization leads to integration, she stated, "Verbalization leads to an increase of the controlling function of the ego over affects and drives" (p. 185). This concept has been used on a therapeutic-educational level at the Hanna Perkins School, a therapeutic nursery school she directed (Archer and Hosley, 1969).

When the patient seems overwhelmed by emotional flooding the situation may tax the therapist's ability to maintain free-floating attention, and he may resort to action in counterresponse. Although he must protect both himself and his patient should the latter's motor accompaniment to the flooding promise danger, he will do well to stay calm and attentive, maintaining a certain remoteness from the dramatic situation. It may be useful to name the overwhelming emotion. One of my patients, Margaret (See "Fuzzballs" in Chapter VIII) would experience emotional flooding while on the couch as a derivative of her aggressive drives. On occasion I pointed out to her, "This is rage! What you feel is anger!" At a later time as she was working through intrapsychic separation from a symbiotic mother/analyst she was using her pet cat as a variation of transitional objects that represented a link between herself and her mother/analyst, a link that also contained aspects of them both. One morning at home she found herself flooded with feelings and while in this state kicked the cat savagely. As she did so she said to herself, "This is anger!" and by doing so stopped her raging. It was her identification with the already established analytic introject that named the emotion and thereby tamed it (Volkan and Kavanaugh, 1974).

In another case a schizophrenic patient seized with emotional flooding was helped by being called by name and so identified. Much later she spoke gratefully of the way in which I had *calmly* called out her full name in the midst of her disturbance. She felt that my verbalization of her name at that moment was the best impetus I could have provided for her to begin some degree of reorganization. I recalled having started to tell her something, commencing with the use of her full name in spite of the fact that I was not in the habit of so addressing her. Perhaps my doing so was a spontaneous counterresponse to what was going on. It turned out that my calm and my spontaneous use of her name provided a focal moment in which she started to undertake a more mature reorganization and to recover the identity she had lost.

CHAPTER VIII

THE TRANSITIONAL OBJECT AND THE GLOBAL CONTROL OF THE EXTERNAL OBJECT

Patients who, during their treatment, reactivate primitive internalized object relations exhibit a need to control the external object, which may be tinged with "all bad" qualities—or idealized and clung to. This chapter provides illustrations of the impressive extent to which these patients use concrete nonhuman objects as buffers between themselves and others. On closer examination these concrete objects are Januslike, providing a control of either distance from or a linking to the other. The lantern has one opaque and one transparent side; when the opaque side is turned toward the outside world the outside world is wiped out in darkness; but the other side illuminates it so that it can be known.

The concept of the transitional object as expanded is reviewed, and the concrete object is referred to as a reactivated transitional object or a variation on the theme of the transitional object. By endowing some object in the external world with magic qualities the child creates the transitional object proper, which links the not-me with the mother (object)-me. It is suggested that the magical concrete object of patients with primitive internalized object relations—although perhaps condensed with higher-level symbolism, i.e., sharing certain qualities with the fetish—may be utilized basically as a variation of the transitional object. The illusion of control over the transitional object reassures the patient that he has absolute control over external objects. In two cases reported, cats became special transitional objects during the working through of severance of symbiotic (transitional object) relatedness to the analyst/mother, and it became necessary for the patient to "kill" them in order to achieve intrapsychic separation. It is concluded that not all transitional objects need be concrete; they may be represented by such intangible manifestations as "transitional fantasies," as described.

Control of external objects

Patients who during their treatment reactivate primitive internalized object relations exhibit a need to control external objects. Because the introjective-projective process cycles, the patient is threatened by the reinternalization of what he had externalized. When self- and object images are fused (internalized object relation Stage II [Kernberg, 1972a]), projection and externalization of aggressively tinged impulses or units onto the object simultaneously make the object appear to be attacking the person (projective identification). It should be understood that my term "external object" here refers to an object tinged with the patient's own projections and externalizations rather than to anything demonstrably present and uncontaminated in the external world.

While some external objects are tinged with "all bad" qualities and evoke fear, others may be idealized and capable of being marshaled against the dreaded ones. The patient needs to maintain global and absolute, although illusionary, control of the psychological distance between himself and the aggressively tinged object as well as that between the "all bad" or "all good" objects. Such controls can be observed in behavioral patterns that appear in the treatment setting, in specific types of fantasies I have called "transitional fantasies," of which I will subsequently provide examples. They may include references to the fusion of self-images or -representations with the ideal self- and ideal object images and representations in an effort to eliminate any dependence on (frustrating) external objects (Volkan, 1973). Giovacchini (1967b) writes about an adaptive but nevertheless primitive maneuver that shows the other side of the coin. This time the patient creates a frustrating environment which is highlighted in the transference since the consistent reliability of the analytic situation denies him frustration. Such patients, I believe, also control the environment; what is created and controlled is traumatic but familiar. Giovacchini refers to a personal communication from Van der Heide, who states, "insofar as a defense is ego-dystonic the ego changes the environment in order to justify the defense." Giovacchini continues, "persons with character disorders do more by their externalization than merely make the environment compatible with their defenses. Their basic identity is involved. The environment has to be constructed so that their total ego organization is maintained" (p. 579).

Such persons are the patients Socarides (1971) perceives as wanting to remain perniciously disappointed and disillusioned. Unlike depression, disillusionment involves externalized aggression and, often, self-aggrandizement. As Socarides shows, disillusionment can be used defensively by persons who cannot allow themselves to entertain hope because they are unable to endure frustration or the painful affect of depression. Although such people cling to the memory of earlier expectations they devalue them at the same time.

Patients who activate primitive internalized object relations often tend to make extensive use of concrete nonhuman objects, animate or inanimate, to establish a buffer zone over which they feel in absolute control between themselves and the external object. They may become nonhuman objects themselves, or adopt the behavior of one in a fashion that symbolizes control over attacking external objects. The following vignette will illustrate this.

The "turtle man"

A young man hospitalized after an acute schizophrenic episode underwent many months of treatment in a hospital setting, and subsequent outpatient treatment of many years' duration. During the early months of his treatment he evidenced extreme panic when anyone, even the therapist, entered his room. Screaming "Don't kill me!" he would pull the bedsheets over his body and try to cover his head. When he acquired a pet turtle, he gained, by displacement, more adequate control over his efforts to protect himself and became able to face the therapist. Moreover, he could still identify with the turtle. The early fantasies of this "turtle man" featured testudinal behavior. For example, he fantasied himself to be omnipotent, not unlike the "little man" described in Chapter I, as he lived in his fantasied glass dome. The dome kept out dangerous insects; should any find their way inside he had electric traps waiting for them.

Global control of psychic distancing between the patient (who tries to hold claim to the "all good" and idealized elements) and the feared external object by means of a buffer promotes continuation of the basic defense mechanism of primitive splitting and protects the patient from such diffuse emotional and actional flooding as the preceding chapter describes. Although some patients develop rather stabilized controls toward the same external objects, other patients are inadequately stabilized and are prone to have quick cathectic shifts between themselves and their objects; they seem to want closeness to an object at one moment and great distance from it at another. The patient has as great a need to control his distance from the "all bad" object as he has to cling to his protective, idealized objects, and this dual need complicates his situation. Thus global control of the psychological distancing involves lengthening as well as shortening the distance between the object and what is kept within the self.

The need-fear dilemma

Schizophrenics have "need for and fear of support" from the therapist in the treatment situation (Abse and Ewing, 1960). Burnham, speaking of the "object need-fear dilemma" of such patients, explains that the schizophrenic has an inordinate need for external structure and control because he himself lacks internal structure and autonomous control systems. He is an "object addict" (Fenichel, 1945, p. 436). Burnham (1969) writes:

> The very excessiveness of his need for objects also makes them inordinately dangerous and fearsome since they can destroy him through abandonment.... They can make or break him.... This threat may be further understood if we consider that his precariously balanced inner structure is extraordinarily vulnerable to external influence in its most literal sense, "flowing into." He lacks adequate insulation from others. This is due not so much to a hyperpermeable stimulus barrier or "thin skin" as to his lack of reliable internal structure. Like a ship at sea without adequate navigational equipment, he requires directions from external sources [p. 28].

Burnham suggests three basic forms of reaction to the need-fear dilemma that may appear in combination: (a) The patient gives way to need and clings to the object, abandons efforts at differentiation and independence; (b) he avoids the object, perhaps by withdrawal; (c) he redefines the object, treating it in various roles in a drama of his own creation, contriving thereby a "temporary pseudoconstancy" for the object, which may, for example, be idealized (p. 37). Burnham suggests, "A more complex form of redefinition is the splitting of the object field into good and bad actors containing principal hero and principal villain roles" (p. 38). It appears that Burnham sees splitting of the object as a reaction to the schizophrenic's need-fear dilemma; I see it as a basic defensive constellation that stems from the inability to integrate and modify libidinally and aggressively tinged internalized representations of self and object and gives rise to the need-fear dilemma.

Substitute objects

What is interesting here is Burnham's observation, shared by many others including myself, concerning what he (p. 35) and Fenichel (1945, p. 436) call "substitutes for objects," or, more briefly, substitute objects. By means of the substitute object the patient may maintain or regain a semblance of object contact. It is agreed that such substitute objects need not be concrete but may be ideas—religious ideas, for example. Substitute objects themselves may, however, like human objects, become sources of either fear or security, and may be similarly clung to or avoided.

Burnham briefly notes a similarity between the substitute object and the transitional object. Agreeing that there is a likeness between them, a significant likeness, I examine it in some detail in the sections to follow.

Although it is true that the patient gains some degree of contact with the other (the person important to him) by clinging to or avoiding a substitute object, closer examination shows a more complicated situation than this statement indicates. The substitute object not only provides control; it supplies a bridge between the self and the other. It is Januslike. Its selection, as the following examples will demonstrate, is made as carefully from among many possibilities as the child's choice of transitional object. Although it exists in the world of reality, in the patient's eyes its purpose is "the perceptual human task of keeping inner and outer reality separate yet interrelated" (Winnicott, 1953). The patient can retain the illusion of having absolute control over this type of (reactivated) transitional object—or, in Fintzy's (1971) term, the "variation on the theme of the transitional object"—and thus maintain the illusion that he has like control over the real environment (Fintzy, 1971; Volkan, 1973). Not all of these "variations" are concrete, but I can better illustrate the meaning of our clinical observations and theoretical constructs, and justify my demonstration later in this chapter of how they have been used to control distance between the self and the other—and bridge it—if I begin with an examination of examples that are concrete.

Expansion of the concept of transitional objects and phenomena

Winnicott (1953) wrote:

I have introduced the terms 'transitional object' and 'transitional phenomena' for designation of the intermediate area of experience, between the thumb and the teddy bear, between the oral erotism and true object-relationship, between primary creative activity and projection of what has already been introjected, between primary unawareness of indebtedness and the acknowledgment of indebtedness ('say: ta!').

By this definition an infant's babbling or the way an older child goes over a repertory of songs and tunes while preparing for sleep come within the intermediate area as transitional phenomena, along with the use made of objects that are not part of the infant's body yet are not fully recognized as belonging to external reality [p. 89].

The transitional object becomes vitally important to the child, almost an inseparable part of him. The main function of this object and this phenomenon is to cause the infant to develop, in response to the ministrations of the "good-enough" mother, "the *illusion* that there is an external reality that corresponds to [his] own capacity to create" (p. 95). A "not-me" possession is created. The transitional object is the first not-me but it is never totally not-me since it links not-me with mother-me (Greenacre, 1969). Chosen on the basis of texture, odor, visibility, and movability from whatever is available to the infant in the first year of his life, it is a consolation for the separation involved in going to sleep. It absorbs neglect, even abuse, as well as the most loving closeness. If the baby loses it he usually finds as a replacement some new object that resembles it. Winnicott states that the transitional object is not internalized but fades away through permeation of the "cultural field." The child's memory of it is not subject to active repression.

Winnicott considered the transitional object and phenomena universally present in normal emotional development. Differing, Sperling (1963) suggested that the transitional objects described by Winnicott were pathological manifestations (childhood fetishes) of a specific disturbance in object relations. Before he is two the child becomes attached to an inanimate object, something concrete, using it as a part of his own body, a replaceable feature like his fingernails. The child does not accept weaning but replaces the mother's breast with a fetish, the symbolic function of which concerns separation anxiety during the weaning period; at the height of the anal phase (in connection with retention or release of feces — the mother equivalent); and during the oedipal phase when the mother is renounced as the sexually gratifying object. To summarize, the childhood fetish represents a pathological defense against separation from the mother on the preoedipal level, and may or may not lead to the adoption of adult fetishes.

Their observation of psychotic children brought to the attention of Speers and Lansing (1965) a phenomenon that resembles Sperling's childhood fetish in its dynamic meaning. These children created "instant mothers" by using movable inanimate objects. Mahler (1968) has given clinical examples of the "psychotic preoccupations" of children with an inanimate object (the "psychotic fetish") such as a fan, record-player, a jar — even a thread to wind around the finger. She describes these, however, as a form of transitional object.

[210]

Kavanaugh and I (1974) do not agree with Sperling that the transitional object is a pathological manifestation. We see it, as well as the childhood fetish that originates in it, as marking a point on a spectrum that ranges from normalcy to pathology. In a paper published in 1972 I described the transitional object, the childhood fetish, and the adult fetish, as well as the linking object of the pathological mourner (see also Chapter III of this volume) and pointed out the differences of one from another. Greenacre compared the transitional object to the fetish in a series of papers, acknowledging that while "there are . . . fetishistic phenomena in which the differences from the transitional object are not so clear-cut" [Greenacre, 1969, p. 144]), "the transitional object is almost ubiquitous and does not generally forecast an abnormal development" (p. 149). Greenacre (1970) sees the fetish as a product of marked disturbance in infancy which has led to a need for reparation because of the persistence of an illusion of defect in the body. On the other hand, transitional objects are the "tangible symbol of a relationship undergoing change," and an aid to early growth. Modell (1963) suggested that the object relationships of the borderline patient are arrested at the stage of the transitional object. He later (1968, 1970) emphasized that the transitional object has both regressive and progressive sides (in a watershed concept). The opposite sides correlate with acceptance or nonacceptance of external objects. Fintzy (1971) raised the question as to whether a fixation may not occasion a gradual transformation of transitional objects over a lifetime; he hypothesized that it is the *covert* existence of a transi-

[211]

tional object that has a progressive front and that this circumstance permits the borderline person to maintain a normal facade outside of therapy.

The rationale I (1973) propose is like Fintzy's; I see the patient attaining absolute global control over his transitional object (which may be a reactivated one). He keeps it between himself and his environment; thus he can believe that he enjoys similar sovereignty over the environment itself, and entertain the illusory privilege of being able to acknowledge or disavow the existence of external objects according to the pressure of his anxieties and wishes. He has the illusion that the transitional object is under his absolute control, just as the infant has the breast under magical control because immediately after birth the mother made herself available to him in a way that fosters the illusion of her breast's belonging to his own body (Winnicott, 1953). "The transitional object may be viewed as riding on a two-way street, a pathway from internal to external, as well as vice versa. While the infant turns from mother to a transitional object, the borderline patient, fixated as he is on the level of the transitional object, might be able to relate to a new individual more meaningfully via the route of the inanimate object" (Fintzy, 1971, p. 112).

The "turtle man" briefly mentioned at the beginning of this chapter named his pet turtle "Chastity." His psychotic break had occurred at the time he was associating with a "loose" girl his parents disapproved of, and he feared he had impregnated her. Warts (a shell?) appeared on his body and had to be removed by his surgeon father. I connected the selection of the name

"Chastity" with these events, but it was clear from his treatment that the name also reflected his notion of keeping his dome kingdom pure and available only to his "all good" units, which he was then able to protect from external danger.

Another schizophrenic patient on the same hospital ward had a pet turtle also. She named it "Hope." The two patients and their turtles "merged." The selection of the name "Hope" is interesting; the events of this patient's therapy demonstrated that the buffer the "turtle man" used to control psychological distancing between himself and the intimate other did become a *bridge of hope* between the two. It is this dual possibility of the variations of the transitional object that interests us here. It was true that the dome within which this patient retreated in his fantasy separated him from the world outside, but it was transparent and he could gaze out from it upon his enemies, the insects, becoming acquainted with them under controlled circumstances as he protected himself from their encroachment. In this he was like the turtle that can thrust out its head and view the world from the safety of its carapace.

Closer examination of the "substitute objects" used by schizophrenic and borderline patients may reveal elements of "mother-me" and "not-me" as well as a link between the two, a link under the patient's illusory global control. Searles also shows the mother-directed aspect of the nonhuman environment, although at the outset, in his major work on the subject (Searles, 1960), he suggested that to the normal child (and to the schizophrenic adult) the nonhuman aspects of the environment itself, over and beyond the influence of any person, are of singular importance. Later, he revised this, proposing that the nonhuman realm represents by displacement some increment of the child's essentially mother-directed feelings of love, dependency, and so on: "It is, I have come to see, in this phase (of therapeutic symbiosis) that the whole of the patient's former 'reality,' including the whole non-human realm in aggregate, is as it were poured into the symbiosis with the therapist, and it is out of this symbiosis that the patient's 'reality' becomes more deeply cathected with feelings and with therefore, a genuine sense of reality, and he correspondingly becomes more deeply able to distinguish among such realms as human and nonhuman, animate and inanimate, through rediscovering them in the therapist-mother" (Searles, 1963, p. 50).

Later on, Searles stated that the mother ideally "humanizes" the whole of the inner and outer reality of the infant and young child. Noting that child-rearing practices are seldom ideal, he suggested that every child confronts in some degree the struggle to differentiate human from nonhuman, and animate from inanimate: "every child will have to engage . . . in this struggle which the schizophrenic patient found to be overwhelming in its difficulty. Moreover, if the mother were somehow capable of doing all this differentiating *for* the child, he presumably would never achieve individuality, for the unceasing struggle to make such differentiations may well be essential to the achievement and maintenance of human individuality" (Searles, 1965, p. 30).

Influenced by Kohut's (1971) work on narcissism (see

Chapter IX for a comparison of contrasting views of the narcissistic personality), Tolpin (1972) changed the concept of the transitional object somewhat by suggesting, in opposition to Winnicott's views, that certain aspects of the transitional object "go inside" as mental structure. Writing about the fate of the transitional object, she stated that it is precisely because its soothing functions do "go inside" as mental structure that the treasured object is not missed, mourned, repressed, nor forgotten; it is simply no longer needed. Tolpin further suggested that the transitional object is heir to a part of the infant's original narcissism that is preserved when it is assigned to the idealized parent imago. "Transference" of narcissistic cathexis from the lost soothing functions of the idealized maternal imagos to the transitional object creates a "transitional self-object imago" that serves as a detour to transmuting internalizations of maternal functions that promote cohesiveness of the self, as described by Kohut.

> If the child, however, suffers severe narcissistic trauma, then the grandiose self does not merge into the relevant ego content but is retained in its unaltered form and strives for the fulfillment of its archaic aims. And if the child experiences traumatic disappointments in the admired adult, then the idealized parent imago, too, is retained in its unaltered form, is not transformed into tension-regulating psychic structure, does not attain the status of an accessible introject, but remains an archaic, transitional self-object that is required for the maintenance of narcissistic homeostasis [Kohut, 1971, p. 28].

According to Tolpin, the transitional object (and phenomenon) should be included among psychic organizers (as
described by Spitz, 1950): "As a psychic 'preserve' of an
older form of (self-object, need-satisfying) mental organization and an additional pathway for the acquisition of
new (self-sustaining) structure, the transitional object
assists the infant in the work of the separation process [p.
348] . . . When the soothing functions of the mother and
the blanket [the transitional object] are effectively internalized, a normal phase of relative structural insuffi-
ciency has passed" (Tolpin, 1972, p. 333).

*Differentiation of transitional object, fetish, and linking
object*

Not all the animate or inanimate nonhuman objects
with which an adult patient becomes preoccupied are
reactivated transitional objects; they may indeed be
connected with higher-level symbolism. For example, the
dominant meaning of the shoe with which the adult
fetishist is preoccupied is that it represents the female
penis. However, it is possible that when the nonpsychotic
parts of a schizophrenic or borderline patient use such
objects as higher-level symbols, his psychotic parts simultaneously utilize them as presymbolic (transitional) objects in a kind of Januslike link between "mother-me" and
"not-me" (Volkan and Kavanaugh, 1974). Berman
(1972) cites an example in a patient's use of diet pills as
both fetish and transitional object. I suggest that in a
general way childhood fetishes, adult fetishes, and linking objects used by pathological mourners can be included among variations on the theme of transitional

[216]

objects. Each obviously has a dominant role to play other than that of the transitional object proper. The determination as to which of the condensed factors will *dominate* is made by the patient's position on the spectrum that ranges from the competence of the ego to use the concrete object invested with higher-level symbolism to regression in which it is used as a link between "mother-me" and "not-me." A brief review of the characteristics of these different yet not totally dissimilar kinds of important inanimate objects is indicated.

I see "gray areas" between the transitional object and the childhood fetish and view them as existing on a spectrum that ranges from normalcy to pathology. When the child's development is normal, the transitional object helps the infant to separate from the mother, but when the mother-child relationship is disturbed, the transitional object may become a childhood fetish used to repair the illusion of body defect that stems from incomplete individuation from the mother. The individual who adopts a childhood fetish may or may not become an adult fetishist.

The adult fetish, in the classical sense, represents the illusory penis of the mother, and it may represent the last moment in which the woman could be regarded as phallic (Freud, 1927). Thus it provides a special solution to the castration threat. According to Winnicott (1953), the "*fetish* can be described in terms of a persistence of a specific object or type of object dating from infantile experience in the transitional field, linked with the delusion of a maternal phallus" (p. 97). Recent work on fetishism describes the fetish as a compromise between separation and castration. Bak (1953) states that it reflects: (1) the wish to give up the penis in order to identify with the mother who has no penis, and to avoid the danger of separation from her; and (2) the alternative danger of castration. As indicated in his report of one of his cases, the anxiety over being abandoned can mobilize fetishistic ceremonies. The response to a threat of loss can clearly be seen in this instance.

The main function of the linking object (Volkan, 1972) of pathological mourners is a response to loss (in our study, loss by death). Paraphrasing Freud, I (1970) have suggested that the linking object is a "token of triumph" over loss by death among certain adults.

The child holds, sees, and smells his transitional object. The adult pervert needs at least the sight of the fetish in order to achieve sexual potency. Pathological mourners must know at all times where their linking objects are, but they find it important to keep them at a distance rather then embracing them. The typical (adult) fetish is likely to be an article of clothing, often a shoe that is black (in a representation of pubic hair), and the odor is important. It is symbolically bisexual. The linking object, on the other hand, may have no characteristic easily associated with a body part but derives its power from ideation that has established symbolic connections between the mourner and the dead. As Greenacre (1969) indicated, the fetish contains congealed anger born of castration panic. The linking object also contains anger; it is an instrument with which to control the expression of anger engendered by separation panic. I suggest further

[218]

that the linking object is more significantly invested with the aggressive drive than is the typical fetish, and that this investment accounts for the common need to distance and avoid it. Certainly anxieties over separation and castration are on the same spectrum, and the function of the typical fetish blurs with that of the typical linking object. Significant differences can, however, be noted. Whereas the linking object represents the last moment when the dead person was felt to be living, the fetish used in adult perversion represents the last moment when women were perceived as having penises.

The linking object provides a means for object relationship with a dead person to be maintained externally. The ambivalent wish to have the dead return and to have him disappear altogether is condensed in it so that the painful work of mourning has an external reference and thus escapes resolution.

A mechanical boy

In this brief review of the transitional object and "variations on the theme of the transitional object" it becomes clear that they serve the schizophrenic or borderline patient at the most basic level, beneath higher-level symbolic uses, as a means of perpetuating the illusion that he can control his psychological distance from external objects while at the same time retaining a link with them. Other inanimate objects not descriptively identical with either the classical fetish or the linking object are used to handle separation anxiety in general; at a lower level they may have basic functions

[219]

not unlike those of the transitional object. The case of a "mechanical boy" (Volkan and Lutrell, 1971) illustrates this process.

The patient was 18-year-old Jim, who made and used a number of mechanical devices, at times "merging" with them in such a way that he gave the impression of being himself a machine. On entering a room he seemed to be a camera taking snapshots of its contents; his eyes blinked and focused on one thing after another rather than sweeping over the environment. We nicknamed him the "mechanical boy" after a patient so described by Bettelheim (1959). Since the details of his case and treatment appear elsewhere, I refer here only to those of his creations that were under his absolute control, being placed between himself and other persons for the sake of providing psychological distance as well as a link.

For the first eight months of his therapy, Jim was seen in a hospital setting; subsequently he became an outpatient. The initial sessions were largely taken up by his description of electrical instruments, since he was highly preoccupied with "scientific things" and their technology. This intellectualization or "mechanization," as it were, set the pace for his therapeutic sessions. Within two weeks of his hospital admission Jim began using a tape recorder as if it had a life of its own. He held the machine between himself and external objects (members of the hospital staff and other patients). It permitted him to keep his therapist and others at a distance while at the same time relating to them. Ekstein (1966) tells of Tommy, the "space child," who used the defense mechanism of distancing in much the same way. Meaningful relationships can be maintained by such people only when the distance from others is satisfactory and the control over it assured.

Shortly after his second month of hospitalization, Jim created a machine he called the "sonic anesthesia machine," by which the sound of an electric shaver, tape-recorded, was transmitted to his ears through a stethoscope. The addition of earphones and a special device to produce white sound of varying intensity were later refinements. Jim was able with this device, as he had been with the tape-recorder, to admit or shut off the outside world and to bring about changes in an omnipotent way. This recalls the behavior of the patient in Chapter IV who popped "lifesavers" into her mouth to prevent her analyst (the frightening external object) from entering, thus maintaining control over the illusion that only lifesaving elements could go into her. Jim alleged that the machine could induce sleep; he spent most of his time in the hospital sleeping. He seemed autistic in his withdrawal, but we felt that he was not altogether "alone" in it since he used the stethoscope of his sonic anesthesia machine to "collect" heartbeats of his fellow patients and others in a gesture that we believed symbolic of his effort to fuse with his "good mother" image.

Jim created nine machines within a year; some were introjective, some projective, since he was, as might have been expected, involved in introjective-projective relatedness as well as in primitive splitting. The tape recorder, cameras, and the sonic anesthesia machine were introjective. A later invention, the "hypnosis machine," was projective; an amplified version of his sonic anesthesia machine, it transmitted white sound to several persons at once, in a shift from the earlier pattern of transmitting white sound inward only. In his eighteenth month of treatment, after coming to the end of his machine-making, Jim found a job that included sublimated elements while at the same time it met his need to project; he was actually employed as a projectionist in a movie theater.

Although the machines he invented, particularly the first two, were concrete examples of his control over his distance from external objects, they nevertheless had a progressive aspect and linked him to them. For Jim his machines, like the gadgets in the two cases reported by Giovacchini (1959), "enhanced secondary processes, thereby re-enforcing the integrative and synthetic functions of the ego." It is in this dual role — in the watershed situation — that I see similarities between Jim's machines and the transitional object proper.

Technical considerations

Fintzy (1971) asks whether it is actually possible to introduce a transitional object (or a variation on the theme of the transitional object) into the therapy of a borderline patient as the first step in bridging the chasm between patient and therapist. His speculation may refer only to the treatment of borderline children, but in a sense Jim, who was not a child, introduced his own inanimate objects into therapy. Fintzy finds support in Bettelheim's (1967) deliberate and successful introduction of a transitional object into therapy of an 11-year-old autistic child. I introduced "linking objects" into so-called "re-

grief therapy" to help established pathological mourners to unlock their frozen mourning process (Volkan,
1971; Volkan, Cilluffo, and Sarvay, 1974). Fintzy's patient, Alfred, a five-and-a-half-year-old borderline child,
had the habit of bringing from home something he
considered endowed with omnipotent properties, showing
it to his therapist, and relating to him in so doing, only to
take flight into play immediately thereafter. Since the
therapist wanted to transfer his patient's interest from
inanimate to animate objects, when the child during his
twenty-fourth hour introduced a toy truck as "a friend,"
he countered by stating that he preferred meeting a real
friend, one who could feel, talk, and respond.

Another technical question arises when a patient
uses a concrete object as both fetish and transitional
object, and the therapist must determine which manifestation needs initial consideration. The well-trained and
experienced therapist will follow the dictum of working
from the surface into the depths, but it must be emphasized that, among borderline patients for example, the
deeper meaning of the patient's concrete object (its use as
a transitional object) may be on the surface so that
attention given at this time to higher-level symbolism
connected with the same object (in its function as a fetish)
will not induce therapeutic movement. Moreover, I have
observed patients changing the emphasis on one aspect of
the condensation of meaning in the nonhuman object
when they experience anxiety about working on another
aspect of condensation in the same object. The analyst
must follow such defensive change of emphasis and deal
with it properly.

[223]

In what follows I provide examples of work with patients whose activation of primitive internalized object relations dominated the picture as they used nonhuman objects as variations of the transitional object. For instance, two patients used pet cats as transitional objects as they attempted intrapsychic separation from their analyst/mother. With these patients, if the analyst had focused on the fetishistic aspects of the cats and offered related interpretations, he would have missed the target. I refer, for the sake of comparison, to an analytic case beautifully described by Berman (1972) in which a young woman's use of amphetamine pills first as a fetish and later, the fetishistic use having been worked through, as a transitional object, was analyzed. Then the central *dominant* movement of the analytic process was in the direction of understanding oral elements, the phallic elements having had earlier attention; such a sequence can be reversed with schizophrenic or borderline patients. Berman's patient was unmarried, in her early twenties, and came into analysis because of guilt feelings about her sexual promiscuity and frequent episodes of anxiety and depression. After a year and a half of analysis the patient confessed a dependency on amphetamine pills since puberty, and this became a focal issue in the analysis. The pills made her vivacious and defended her against intolerable feelings of weakness and femininity. Menstruation represented the essence of everything undesirable about being feminine, and at the time of her periods she increased the dosage of amphetamines. She perceived her genitalia as leaky, mushy, hairy, and nasty, and her analysis revealed that the pill symbolized objective masculinity, her illusory penis, in addition to providing a pharmacological "lift."

As her analysis progressed she reduced her amphetamine dosage, but she continued to carry around with her a minute particle of the pill until it was understood that she had originally embarked on amphetamines to defend against the re-emergence of childhood feelings of being genitally damaged and therefore unlovable. This understanding led her to burn her prescription ceremoniously.

Berman describes and documents deep-seated oral fixations that underlay the patient's florid phallic symptoms, and how the phallic and oral elements came together. The pharmacologic effects of the pill reinforced the patient's phallic impulses, relieved her menstrual cramps, and counteracted obesity and unattractive femininity. Pills also represented "emergency food supplies" and defended against primitive fears of oral abandonment. "As a substance that was eaten to prevent eating, the diet pill could symbolize both the feeding mother and the depriving mother." Berman states that the feelings of warmth, well-being, and security the pharmacologic effects of the amphetamine provided were more closely associated with the transitional object than the fetish.

Margaret, a borderline patient of mine, was "addicted" to pills, especially as they were connected with stealing. When she visited in the home of others she would find an excuse to go to the bathroom, where she would look into the medicine cabinet and take for her own use pills she found there, especially those prescribed for use by the women of the household. She also "stole" pills from her mother. Although we learned during her analysis that the pills represented female penises, it was necessary initially and for a long time thereafter to focus on the *dominant* meaning of the pills as transitional objects; the movement here was the reverse of what Berman reported in his patient. In what follows I refer to Margaret's case and to her "fuzz balls" to give a clinical illustration of how transitional objects and transitional object relatedness can dominate the clinical picture.

Fuzz balls

The persistent use of the transitional object from infancy well into adult life is illustrated by Margaret. In her case I believe that the objects she used were predominantly transitional in function although their fetishistic aspects deserve attention. She was fixated in a transitional object-*relatedness*. Her self- and object representations could merge, especially in her relationships with significant others in intimate situations. However, she was able to differentiate between her self-images and object images in other relationships. Her ultimate abandonment of her transitional objects during treatment in an effort to progress from the type of relationship involved in it is significant.

Margaret came into analysis at the age of 19 after a bad LSD trip which had been followed by unsure reality testing. She was the third child of middle-class Southern parents. Her father was employed in the public relations department of a food-processing plant, and since her childhood had been often away from home on business. Her mother had an identical twin, and although the twins' mother survived their birth by ten years, the family always maintained that her death was to be blamed on obstetrical damage suffered in the multiple childbirth. Margaret's mother never fully accepted the death of her own mother and endlessly sought her return. She always felt "incomplete" without her twin sister, and lived near her even after they both married. Margaret was conceived during an interval in which her mother was for a time living far away from her twin. At this time the mother was suffering from a depression that continued throughout the first year of Margaret's life. When Margaret was born her mother unconsciously thought of her not only as a link to her lost mother but also as a link to her "lost" sister. The mother's inability to achieve true individuation—in spite of the many interests and achievements in her life—accounted in no small degree for Margaret's fixation at a symbiotic and early separation-individuation level. Subsequently Margaret's four siblings —two older and two younger than she—paired off, leaving Margaret paired with her mother. They were so close that when Margaret was ill they often rested side by side on the bed with their bodies curved reciprocally together as though they were the halves of a fused whole. At the time Margaret became a psychoanalytic patient she felt able to communicate with her mother and her analyst by means of "waves," "osmosis," or a "third eye."

A behavioral peculiarity Margaret adopted in childhood and continued into adult life with a kind of addiction was her habit of collecting bits of lint and rolling it between her fingers into "fuzz balls" while she sniffed at her soiled panties and chewed gum. She carried a red blanket about with her until she was four or five; the fuzz balls were clearly a compensation for the disappearance of the blanket. As a child, and even occasionally as an adult, Margaret stole things from other people. Winnicott (1953) has noted that "*thieving* can be described in terms of an individual's unconscious urge to bridge a gap in continuity of experience in respect of a transitional object" (p. 97). Analysis of Margaret's stealing made while she was in treatment revealed that under stress she felt the need to create an "instant mother," to use the terminology of Speers and Lansing (1965), and that the objects she "needed" and summarily appropriated were the equivalent of a generous and responsive mother to whose benefactions she was entitled without having to feel guilty.

A few months before her analysis she was traveling in her car when she saw a child with a pet cat and appropriated it for herself. It was a female cat, but she named it after her father, linking it with bisexual fetishistic qualities. In the second year of her five-times-weekly analysis she tried to individuate and to stop relating to the analyst/mother at the level of transitional object relatedness. At this time she became preoccupied with her cat, which became a special "fuzz ball." The cat became important to her as a transitional object that linked her to her childhood treasure, the red blanket. When she was alone she took the cat to bed with her in order to feel "complete." She had to love and cherish her pet—or, on occasion, to hate it—to sleep.

Her working through of the effort to cut the symbiotic tie to the analyst/early mother was dramatic. There was a hypertrophy of introjective-projective relatedness between Margaret and me which I felt, at this time in her analysis, to be in the service of our understanding the earliest mother-child relatedness. The mother had been depressed during Margaret's infancy. Now, in the transference, Margaret would perceive me on one day depressed to the point where she fantasied sending me to a state hospital. On the following day she would instead be depressed herself, as if dejection had flowed into her from the depressed mother/analyst. I interpreted the perception and sensation of affective shifts as connected with her infantile relatedness to her mother. The peak of observing and working through this relatedness was accompanied by her heightened interest in the cat. She felt anxious when the cat was at large, and uncomfortable until it returned home. According to her, the pet developed human characteristics—it became "neurotic" in human terms. Its moods were changeable; it alternated between being "all good" and "all bad." She had to have her pet in bed with her to fall asleep. One morning she was flooded with feelings and found herself kicking the cat as if to kill it. As she did so she said to herself, "This is anger," and her emotional storm subsided.

Her attempt to kill the cat was followed by two dreams reported during the same session. In the first she dreamed of her mother's death, and in the second she was thumbing a dictionary looking for a definition of integrity and integration. She connected these dreams with her wish to separate herself from her early mother/analyst and to find her own integrity. After reporting them she had the sensation of "floating in the air" over the couch

[229]

until the couch itself floated into position beneath her. This experience was further indication that she wanted to move away from the mother/analyst but at the same time to remain connected with her. Subsequent dreams had a peculiar quality; she could not remember their content, but felt that she was "connected to them by an umbilical cord."

From the beginning of her analysis Margaret brought fuzz balls to the sessions, not unlike Fintzy's patient who always brought something with him from home. As she lay on the couch she usually rolled her fuzz balls between her fingers, sometimes openly and sometimes furtively. After trying to kill that special fuzz ball, her cat, she began leaving behind her the fuzz ball she had toyed with during her hour. She did not realize she was doing this, but I began collecting them in an ashtray placed near the couch. She failed to notice them for a month. One day when she said to me, "I don't want to bring my chaotic little balls into your organized life," I called her attention to the growing pile of fuzz balls in the ash tray. Embarrassed, and laughing nervously, she became aware of having left them behind. She then acknowledged that they no longer soothed her anxiety, and I considered the possibility that the soothing functions of the fuzz balls had disappeared because these functions had now been internalized. It was obvious to me that Margaret had acquired a new inner structure and her need of transitional soothing elements was disappearing. I interpreted to her the way she had used fuzz balls as transitional objects. A month later she tried to relax by rolling a fuzz ball and masturbating, but she wound up by collecting all the fuzz balls and flushing them down the toilet. Three months later she gave her cat away; she took it back as analysis progressed, but it no longer had magical qualities, although on rare occasions it became a fuzz ball once again. A remnant of the fuzz ball appeared one week before the termination date of her analysis when she "accidentally" cut her finger, bandaged it, and while on the couch rubbed the bandage as she had earlier rolled the fuzz balls. In the middle of the hour she herself interpreted this behavior as an effort to revisit her fuzz ball relatedness because separation from her analyst lay ahead.

Cats as a variation of the transitional object

The phenomenon of a cat serving as a variation of the transitional object and as an object for identification appeared in the case of Margaret and of Samantha (Chapter II). My patient, Jane, a 21-year-old college student at the start of her six years of therapy, whose case and dreams I described in Chapter VI, also found a cat especially suitable as a representation of the me, not-me, and the link between them. At the borderline level, because of primitive splitting, external objects are separated into "all good" or "all bad" categories. There are indications that across cultures and throughout history cats have been seen as "all bad" or "all good" — even divine, possibly on the basis of their being both dependent and independent, and softly seductive in spite of the awesome weaponry of swift claws. As a household pet the cat, quite unlike the dog, is fickle in mood and companionability. At the level of functioning we are talking about, the child (or the adult borderline patient) alternates between submissive, clinging attitudes and transient grandiose positions in which he demonstrates "independence" of those in authority. Thus the cat may symbolize the link between the patient and the therapist/mother — and for the patient's psychotic parts may even *become* this link.

Jane, like Margaret, did not constantly refer to her pet cat, but focused on it as she worked through the severing of symbiotic relatedness. The behavior of these young women resembles that of Shengold's (1967, 1971) Rat People, who did not talk constantly of mice and rats, but when, during their treatment, the derivatives of cannibalistic impulses were activated, not only spoke of rodents but ground and gnashed their teeth. As children, they had been overstimulated, seduced, or beaten.

Miss Kitty

When Jane was engaged in breaking her symbiotic ties with the analyst/mother during the third year of her treatment, important changes in her relatedness to her immediate environment took place. She began to think of leaving her parental home, and finally did find an apartment for herself. At this point the family cat became her most important object, and she filled her therapeutic sessions with talk about Miss Kitty. She feared being poisoned by her mother as she tried to work out physical and intrapsychic separation from her, and saw the analyst as also dangerous. At times the cat became a total representation of herself, one that she feared was also subject, like herself, to being poisoned by her mother.

[232]

Most of the time, however, it represented—or, as the following events will show—*became* her symbiotic tie with the analyst/mother, or—in what is perhaps more precise terminology, a variation of the transitional object. She herself spoke of the cat as being "a root into my mother."

When she finally moved into her own apartment she wanted to give the cat to her analyst. On one level this represented an offering of her "pussy" to the father/analyst, but her associations showed that the "hot" aspect of this gesture referred to the mother transference. Her transference to the analyst of her relatedness to her early mother was interpreted and worked through. After considerable inner struggle lasting several months she took Miss Kitty to her apartment. Then she was no longer alone since part of the analyst/early mother and the part of herself that "rooted" into her analyst/mother came into her new home with her. At night she took the cat into bed to sleep with her; as in Margaret's case, the presence of the pet was necessary for sleep.

As she worked through her attempt to differentiate herself further from the analyst/mother and individuate herself, she became convinced that Miss Kitty—that root into her mother—was ailing. She took it to a veterinarian and talked him into performing a hysterectomy, in spite of the fact that she knew, even without his warning, that the old cat could not survive it. Her associations to the cat at this time were reduced to an association with breasts and nipples. An artist, she drew a picture of Miss Kitty lying on her back displaying conspicuous udders with large teats. As expected, the cat died from the surgery she

[233]

had arranged; the following day Jane asked me, "Did you know that part of me wanted Miss Kitty to die?" She then experienced sadness but did not undergo mourning in the adult sense.

Some months later Jane acquired another cat in an obvious maneuver to repeat the archaic relatedness represented by Miss Kitty. She had developed intimacy with a young man, and when they lay down together she fantasized biting his nipples, and placed the cat between their bodies. In this behavior she knew that the cat was a symbol, and she recalled its previous existence as a pre-symbolic transitional object. Nevertheless this pet still had magical characteristics. Her magical investment in the cat gradually disappeared as her analysis progressed. In the last hour of the analysis, which she compared to Alice's trip to Wonderland, she had an image of the grin of the Cheshire Cat slowly fading away.

Transitional fantasies

Psychoanalytic interest in transitional objects has concerned itself chiefly with the concrete objects infants select from what is available to be seen, smelled, felt, or tasted, but it has been noted that this phenomenon may appear in intangible form as well. I refer in Chapter II to McDonald's (1970) treatment of certain lullabies and cradle songs as "transitional tunes," and I have called specific recurrent fantasies of one of my patients "transitional fantasies" (Volkan, 1973).

Greenacre (1970) noted two ways in which the transitional object may be relinquished; the infant either "uses it up" until nothing but a scrap remains as a kind of obsolescent memento, converts it into a toy, or "into a *workable coherent fantasy which serves as an intangible bedtime comfort* [*italics added*] or [it] is incorporated into daytime play. Or it may seek objective representation in some other creative form. These changes are only possible around the age of four or later when the ego development is such that the child has become aware of his own thinking as belonging to himself and subject in some appreciable measure to his own control" (p. 352).

Some patients select specific fantasies from all those they have and resort to them over and over. The ones they select to use and re-use include aspects of wishes for and defenses against issues from different psychosexual phases. Appropriate interpretation of these aspects does not cause them to disappear, and soon both the analyst and his patient become aware that the latter is *addicted* to them as a child is addicted to his transitional object. I see such fantasies as intangible representations of transitional objects. They often have such clarity and reality that the patient identifies them by name; their themes undergo only superficial change. Although they are triggered by something in the external world, the patient does not identify them as his own creations but sees them as actually existing "out there." The interpenetration of the actual and the inner worlds is reflected in them. They sometimes have the power to provide sensory stimulation, offering something to the senses. of sight, smell, taste, hearing, and touch. Since they bring solace and sleep, they are beloved, and like a battered teddy bear, they take a beating in the course of their useful service. One of my patients (whose case I shall detail in Chapter X) would begin one of his favorite transitional fantasies and complete it straight to the end, only to "replay" it with slight variation here and there in its unfolding, going through the process over and over again as though he felt the zest of pulling and pummeling it like a pillow until it felt familiar and comforting.

Winnicott (1953) wrote that the infant passes from omnipotent control to manipulative control by use of the transitional object; muscle erotism and pleasure in coordination are involved. The individual may similarly bring the intangible representation of a transitional object under his control; his fantasies are subject to a kind of thought process which he commands. One patient referred to his transitional fantasies as "pillows around me." They both buffered him against and linked him with the external world, enabling him to either accept or deny its nature, according to Modell's "watershed" concept. As long as he controls his transitional fantasy the individual can protect himself from being disillusioned by the cost of relating to real objects in the real world — frustration and separation — since control over the fantasy gives him the illusion of being able to control what is external to him also. The appearance of transitional fantasies during the analysis of a narcissistic patient will be dealt with in Chapter X. This patient had an unusual capacity to transfer affect-laden ideational responses to visual or other perceptual spheres. I felt that in his own way he was creative, and that his transitional fantasies were the source of his creativity. The details and perceptual aspects of these fantasies assumed lifelike proportions for him. Referring to my work with this patient,

Hamilton (1974) explored the ties between transitional fantasies and the creative process, showing with illustrative examples from the work of O'Neill, Ingmar Bergman, and Picasso, among others, that the transitional fantasy is a means of mastering conflicts related to separation-individuation.

CHAPTER IX

PRIMITIVE INTERNALIZED OBJECT RELATIONS IN THE NARCISSISTIC PERSONALITY

The pathology of primitive internalized object relations in the narcissistic patient is exemplified by a case in which aspects of the patient's analysis are described.

The narcissistic personality's inflated self-concept includes a defensive fusion of ideal self, ideal object, and actual self-images. The individual concomitantly devalues object images and external objects. The clinical picture of the narcissistic personality centers around a failure to integrate ego ideal and superego, but behind this failure one sees primitive splitting of "all good" from "all bad" self-images, object images, and their affective links, along with accompanying defense mechanisms. Although such a person is superficially protected by his inflated self-concept, on a deeper level there appears the image of a deprived, hungry infant at the mercy of tension that stems from oral-aggressive conflicts. Such a view of the pathologically inflated self-concept is con-

trasted with the view of it as merely an evidence of developmental arrest.

Narcissism

The term "narcissism" and "narcissistic" have been used in several ways in the psychoanalytic literature, as summarized by Pulver (1970). This chapter will focus mainly on clinical aspects of the narcissistic personality without any attempt to review the literature for formulations of narcissism, which Hartmann (1950) called a "many-faceted and still puzzling problem." Hartmann acknowledged that many analysts of that day were still referring in the psychoanalytic literature to the equivalence of narcissism and libidinal cathexes of the ego, in spite of the fact that, as Hartmann suggested, Freud also referred to narcissism as cathexis of one's own person, body, or self after his paper "On Narcissism" (1914), which was written when only the bare outline of structural theory had been formulated. We owe to Hartmann the emphasis on the difference between the concept of ego (as a psychic system) and self (one's own person). He states that we actually find narcissism in all three psychic systems: the id, the ego, and the superego. He writes:

> It therefore will be clarifying if we define narcissism as the libidinal cathexis not of the ego but of the self. (It might also be useful to apply the term self-representation as opposed to object representation.) Often, in speaking of ego libido, what we do mean is not that this form of energy cathects the ego, but that it cathects one's own person rather than an ob-

[240]

ject representation.... However, the opposite of object cathexis is not ego cathexis, but cathexis of one's own person, that is, self-cathexis; in speaking of self-cathexis we do not imply whether this cathexis is situated in the id, ego, or superego [Hartmann, 1950, p. 127].

This chapter will focus on the analysis of a narcissistic patient with an inflated self-concept accompanied by defenses characteristic of primitive internalized object relations. I shall take up first the view of a narcissistic self-concept as pathological, a view shared by Kernberg (1970a, 1970b), and then Kohut's (1966, 1971, 1973) conception of the inflated self-concept (grandiose self) as evidence of developmental arrest.

The last Renaissance man

George, "the last Renaissance man" mentioned briefly at the beginning of Chapter II, had been involved in an automobile accident before coming into analysis. After the wreck he had been taken to a hospital emergency room where he made light of his injuries, acted like a superman, and succeeded in being sent home. That night, before going to sleep, he made love to his girl friend in spite of considerable pain. When the girl awakened in the morning she found George near death and had him rushed to a hospital, where it was discovered that he had a ruptured spleen and required emergency surgery. The surgeon told him of the gravity of his condition and asked permission to take him to the operating room at once. George was fully aware of the possibility of death, but was even more impressed by the horror of having scars on his body. He bargained with the surgeon, withholding operative permission until the surgeon promised a virtual absence of visible postoperative scars.

George was young and handsome, and thought of himself as a Greek god. He spent hours before the mirror combing and admiring his curly hair, and posed for the admiration of all beholders. Unmarried, he had countless female admirers whom he idealized at first, later deciding that none was good enough for him. This one had wrinkles, that one had thick ankles, and the breasts of another were too big. He would think of each of his girls, "Suppose I marry this one. Since she has thick ankles [or a big nose, or whatever] her children would probably be imperfect too, and I want perfect children. So I can't marry her!" He would date three girls simultaneously; he would take one to his home and, telling her to busy herself there for a while, he would then slip away to take a second girl to a movie, only to leave her there with some excuse and pick up a third girl and have intercourse with her while the other two awaited his return.

George wrote poetry and considered himself an excellent athlete and a connoisseur of the arts. He felt able to "save" his friends by the sagacity of his counsel, and was quite willing to travel long distances to see any one of his friends who was in trouble and in need of his superior insight. He was an accomplished name-dropper. On one of his good will trips, he had to have a particle removed from his eye in a hospital; he was careful to indicate that he had been in the hospital where the famous Senator So-and-So had his checkups. He spoke of

[242]

"unbelievably" beautiful and brilliant people with whom he was acquainted, and was firm in his belief that no girl could fail to surrender to his charms. His friends actually placed bets on whether or not this girl or that at a party would make a move to talk to him since he could usually attract a girl by looking at her with interest.

De Saussure (1971) writes about the narcissistic patient's belief in the power of vision. George had such a belief, and for a long time he insisted when he was with a girl privately that she undress before him in a leisurely strip-tease, but he turned off the lights before removing his own clothes. In analysis I learned that this maneuver not only reflected castration anxiety, but was a precaution against the girl's "stealing" his beauty away by taking it in visually. His beauty was something for his own enjoyment; it was not to be shared.

De Saussure (1971) points out that patients such as this react to any self-image which is not the ideal image much as infants at a certain stage, having substituted for the mother's face the perfect self-image, react to the sight of any face other than hers. She says of the ideal image:

> This image, though an internal representation created by the ego, must coincide with the image of themselves which they believe to be reflected back to them by the object. An essential part of the fantasy underlying this aspect of self-esteem regulation is the illusion that the sight of the perfect self-image will produce a perfect experience. In a way these patients have idealized a state of being which is similar to that of a nursing infant who sees the mother's face while feeling her breast in his mouth. . . . In

their fantasies of fusion between what is seen and what is felt, the controlling power seems to be attributed to vision [p. 95].

I could detail many other aspects of George's superman self-image, his self-adoration, and his feelings of superiority. Others had to be "unbelievably good" to be fit for his company. Clearly, George presented what is usually called a narcissistic personality. He lacked empathy, was self-centered, and had an insatiable need for admiration. His relations with women had one goal — more admiration — in spite of the fact that he was capable of making each girl believe in his devotion to her. He always made his narcissistic conquests easily because of his good looks, creativity, and real intelligence. In addition, it could be said that his narcissistic demands themselves found an echo in the real world. His surface functioning was good, certainly much better than that of the average borderline patient. He had what Kernberg (1970a) described as a "pseudo sublimating potential," being able to function in his daily life, to work out some of his responsibilities, and to achieve his ambitions at least in part. Kernberg suggests that some patients possess socially effective narcissistic personality structures, and that the analytic approach might be more helpful to them in middle or adult life than during their youth, since such gifted individuals secure secondary gains from normal life gratifications in their early adult years (Wylie, 1973). George had certainly obtained secondary gains from his life style. He came into analysis only because of a traumatic event that brought about considerable disorganization. As I reported earlier (Chapter II; see *Another grandfather dies*), George's "omnipotent" grandfather was brutally murdered when George was a college freshman. I believe, however, that what really bewildered this young man was the fact that in the university he was expected to spend many hours in study and to master vast amounts of material by rote, whereas in the past his natural endowment had permitted him to succeed with very little work and no structuring of his time toward success in school. His narcissistic personality had had no experience in dealing with such matters, which he considered necessary only for "average" men. As a result he got into difficulty academically and suffered a loss of self-esteem.

I do not mean to indicate that George was functioning well before he came to the university simply because he was able to get answers in life for his narcissistic demands. He had in fact had rather a tragic life and overwhelming psychological stress. His mother had had inflamed breasts at the time she undertook his breast feeding, and the pain made nursing very difficult in spite of the fact that she dripped milk. According to family memory, the infant had soon been put on a formula. The parents quarreled violently and finally divorced when George was in the sixth grade. Handsome and narcissistic people, they expected their child to be perfect, and reacted to even a transitory blemish on his face with great alarm. The mother, although artistic, was cold in her mothering; George held to the belief that she had never kissed him before he was 17.

The general feeling state of his early childhood was

that of a child who bangs his head against the bars of his crib, or forces his head between the bars until he feels pain. Remnants of autoaggressive behavior were carried over into adulthood. The aggression failed to change direction in the absence of appropriate protective mothering in his early environment. Failing to obtain gratification of his narcissistic demands, he directed aggression against his body in a pattern that eventuated in a series of self-induced accidents. He rode his motorcycle recklessly, for example, with the aim of hurting himself. During the first months of his analysis such reckless behavior was understood as helping him to "feel alive" (Mahler, 1968, p. 215). Another version of this pattern was his addiction to emotional and physical crises, particularly when he suffered a blow to his self-esteem. He was capably of creating an actual crisis for himself during the short journey from his nearby apartment to my office, and he would point out to me that it was only through the "pain" evoked by such a crisis that he felt alive and fully aware of a self-boundary.

It was only after long work in analysis that George would admit that, although his grandfather's interest in him had been "life-saving," the man's own narcissism precluded his acquainting the boy with reality, but fostered instead the illusion that he was a superman. Rich and well-dressed, the grandfather took the boy to the best restaurants, clubs, and hotels, where the genuinely gifted and attractive youngster had no difficulty in evoking positive responses to his narcissistic wishes from the real world.

George saw his "unbelievably" beautiful and seductive mother as a "murderess" when she was angry, and he was unable to integrate the opposing images of her nature. Before she divorced George's father she took a lover, a doctor George called "THE doctor," whom he saw as representing all the doctors in the world and all the men he feared. Although he continued as her lover, the physician never married her. He was involved in shady deals and gave professional care to members of a criminal syndicate. To George, he became the symbol of his unintegrated and externalized superego. George's father drank heavily and became "weak." Earlier, while he was still living in the family home, he would beat his wife in the course of his angry outbursts or literally put his fist through a wall. George's original fears of him were transferred to "THE doctor," who could not be idealized. A sister five years George's junior and a brother six years younger—"the kids," as he called them—accepted their mother's lover more readily than George did. As a result, he gave them gifts and left George feeling envious and neglected. This situation drew George closer to his grandfather, who also disliked "THE doctor."

After his grandfather's death, George tried the drug scene, and during several of his LSD trips he saw a monster in the mirror when he looked into it. Familiar faces of others changed into fearful visages, and George himself felt at times that he was split into "three autonomous systems"—body, voice, and mind. He hallucinated and saw his mother in a murderous fury. He dreamed that she hunted him down through a darkened house, knife in hand. He felt hopeless and without refuge as he had felt in childhood when, it appeared, she actually had come after him with a knife and left him feeling guilty for making his mother "bad." In another set of dreams he beat people as hard as he could, but they would not fall before him. He sought psychiatric help, and received supportive therapy for two years until his therapist felt he was ready for analysis and referred him to me with a clinical diagnosis of narcissistic personality.

The contradictions in George's personality makeup

Once George was in analysis it became possible to see beneath the cover of his narcissistic personality. As might have been expected, I found contradictory elements. Behind the narcissistic armor was a "hungry infant" busy collecting narcissistic supplies which at times he feared to use lest no more could be found. Thus we could understand his peculiar habit of putting any candy he got into the refrigerator "for a rainy day" rather than eating it at once, and leaving it there for so long that it spoiled. The "good" would then turn into something "bad" in a way that vindicated his distrust. Similarly, in his analysis, he would put my correct interpretations "on ice" where they were of no benefit to him. He kept an oversupply of canned goods in his apartment because he felt anxious over any reduction of his stores. He would resolve not to drink alcoholic beverages, but the thought of such deprivation always led him to finish up whatever liquor he had on hand in preparation for thirsty hours ahead. He drank this way when he was alone; he actually felt "hungry" and saw himself as incarcerated, deprived, and liable to "attacks" from someone hostile to him.

[248]

The most striking contradiction in this man was that under his surface of overweening superiority, he was intensely afraid of other people. He feared being intimate with a woman for any length of time lest she smother him. His fear of men was jelled in his fear of his mother's lover as a basically devouring figure, an abortionist who punctured and slashed his victims. Oedipal-castrating elements were condensed in this image. In spite of his great pride in his "masculine" achievements, George had homosexual thoughts and craved adoration from men as well as from women.

All his external objects were either "unbelievably good" or "unbelievably bad." In his early masturbation fantasies this type of primitive splitting played a role in his seeing women as alternately prostitute and madonna, and he was incapable of erotic feelings toward the idealized madonna.

Primitive internalized object relations in the narcissistic personality

From this account of George's symptoms and behavioral peculiarities it is evident that he was using defense mechanisms — primitive splitting, denial, control of the external object either through devaluation or idealization, projective identification, omnipotence — as accompaniments to existent primitive internalized object relations. Thus the defense mechanisms seen in this narcissistic personality are like those of the borderline personality. Narcissistic patients such as George also show the intense oral-aggressive conflicts characteristic of

[249]

borderline individuals (Kernberg, 1970a). I will give further examples of this when I examine his dream of the "middle-sized mint."

What was included in his inflated self-concept? I have described events at the circus that symbolized the crystallization of his narcissistic character structure, the fusion of his idealized self with the idealized object (see Chapter II). When he saw his idolized movie star he had an "aha" experience of belonging himself to that breed of men. When he became my patient he considered himself almost identical in appearance to a certain famous actor, and while watching this handsome man on the screen he felt he was watching himself. As his analysis progressed and he began differentiating himself from the idealized object, watching the same actor made him anxious, and fearful that he fell short of the image on the screen. It took two years of psychoanalysis for him to be able to see the actor on the screen as someone *really* apart from himself. His ideal self-image could not be differentiated from his actual self-image or his ideal object images. Unintegrated, aggressively tinged primitive superego forerunners were excluded from the inflated self-concept by mechanisms of externalization. "THE doctor" was the focus of such externalization. George once found himself in the position of having to give an injection to another person. This "identification" with his externalized primitive superego part sent him into a panic; he had the fantasy that the injection would literally disintegrate the recipient. The narcissistic personality, although better organized than the borderline personality, does not attain Kernberg's Stage IV of internalized object relatedness, so that superego and ego ideal are not integrated. Further elaboration is called for here.

Lampl-De Groot (1962) speculates about Freud's reasons for using the terms ego ideal and superego interchangeably. She believes that he does so because at the outset of latency the establishment of both is centered around the same object representatives — the parental images. She notes that their functions serve opposite ends, however. Although the ego ideal serves wish fulfillment and is a gratifying agency, the superego prohibits and is a restricting agency. Nevertheless both agencies unite into one substructure. "The ego ideal's content, 'I am like my parents,' can acquire an imperative compulsive character. 'I must be like my parents.' Later on high ideals in general may be experienced as demands" (p. 100). She further suggests that in certain pathological circumstances, regression to primitive levels causes a "disintegration" of one agency from the other. Certainly the failure of superego and ego ideal to integrate needs consideration in assessing fixations also.

A. Reich (1953) also clearly points to the dissimilarity that exists between the ego ideal and the superego before they fuse. She writes:

> The superego represents a taking over of the parental do's and don't's. In spite of childish misunderstandings, the formation of the superego is based upon acceptance of reality; in fact, it represents the most powerful attempt to adjust to reality. The ego ideal, on the other hand, is based upon the desire to cling in some form or another to a denial of the ego's as well as of the parent's limitations

[251]

and to regain infantile omnipotence by identifying
with the idealized parent (pp. 188-189).

... In cases of insufficient acceptance of reality, the differentiation between ego and ego ideal
may remain diffuse, and under certain conditions
magic identification with the glorified parent ...
may replace the wish to be like him (p. 188).

What we detect in George's case are the similarities between the defense mechanisms of such patients and
those of borderline patients, similarities emphasized by
Kernberg (1970a). The basic difference in the clinical
picture lies in the narcissistic patient's failure to integrate
ego ideal with superego. As George's analysis continued
and he began to see and feel the unreality of his expectations of his ego ideal (which were included in his self-
concept) he asked me from time to time to smash his head
in order to make him stop indulging himself in unrealistic
but idealized issues. This put me in the position of an
unidealized, harsh superego struggling against the unreality of his ego ideal.

The mechanism of primitive splitting used by such
a person makes it difficult to integrate elements of
superego with elements of the ego ideal. The "all good"
self- and object image unit fosters the creation of an all-
powerful ego ideal, while the primitively split "all bad"
self- and object image unit contributes to the qualities of
the nonintegrated superego. The clinical picture of the
patient with borderline personality organization reflects
more clearly the features of the "all good" and "all bad"
dichotomy, as I have emphasized by examples throughout this book. Kernberg (1970a) proposes that refusion of

the internalized self- and object images does occur in the narcissistic personality at a level of development in which ego boundaries have already become stable. "At this point, there is a fusion of ideal self, ideal object, and actual self-images as a defense against an intolerable reality in the interpersonal realm, with a concomitant devaluation and destruction of object images as well as of external objects" (p. 55). Thus the tension between the actual self, the ideal self, and the ideal object is eliminated by building up an inflated self-concept. Remnants of the unacceptable self-images are repressed and projected on the devalued external objects. Kernberg continues: "One result of the defensive fusion of ideal self, ideal object, and actual self-images is the devaluation and destruction not only of external objects but also of internalized object images. Actually, this process never goes so far that there are no internal representations of external objects: it would probably be impossible to live under such conditions. To want to be admired and loved by others requires that others should appear at least somewhat 'alive,' internally as well as externally" (p. 57).

In my effort to understand George's narcissistic personality I found it most workable to approach his inflated self-concept as representing a pathological constellation. Clinical findings supported the interpretation of George's inflated concept of himself as his way of trying to protect himself from the tensions that arose from his deeply held image of a fearful world seen through the eyes of a "hungry" infant. His failure to integrate "all bad" and "all good" units, and his externalization of the former had created at the deeper level an "unbelievably" dangerous world. The need to cope with such a world awakened in his "hungry self" an impotent rage. This was reflected in the dreams in which he fought with people who would not fall—and who did not even feel the impact of his blows since his hands passed right through their vaporous forms.

George in analysis

Once George's analysis was under way I was an "unbelievably good" analyst for him. I soon realized that I had been "chosen" by him as "Number One." He had heard something favorable about my work in professional circles, exaggerated it greatly, and sought analysis with me for that reason. But I shared the fate of his girl friends whose ankles were too thick or whose breasts were too large as I would suddenly become the object of his scorn, "unbelievably incompetent," good enough for the average patient, no doubt, but incapable of understanding *him*. He began his analytic sessions by providing me with a detailed history of his life and a summation of his problem as he understood it. I felt that after that he came simply to be admired. He had once walked on the beach in Greece, with sandals on his feet and shells in his hair and felt that he was Christ. He had posed in the nude for a painter and had felt that people came to see him posing because of his "unbelievable" beauty. His women friends were also "unbelievably beautiful," according to him, and I was faced with the choice of accepting all he told me or being devalued like all the others for whom he had scorn. He "analyzed" his own dreams and decided which were important and which were not. I allowed this narcissistic self-concept to be fully expressed and did not interfere with the development of a narcissistic transference. As I asked about the repeated use of the word "unbelievable," genetic material began coming to the surface.

His childhood environment was "unbelievably" traumatic. As a child he had been beset by overwhelming stimuli coming from his fighting parents and from a seductive but cold mother. He had "unbelievable" fears, and his achievement of a "superman" role was lifesaving to him. The idealized image of the beautiful mother was not integrated with that of the cold mother. His innumerable affairs with girl friends demonstrated the same integrative incapacity. At first he idealized each new girl, and his association with her inflated his self-esteem. Within a few months, however, she would become to him a replica of his "crazy, hysterical mother" and it would be necessary for him to discard her. This process was naturally repeated in his transference with me. At one point he began skipping his appointments with the explanation that he had many more important things to do. I interpreted the similarities between the way he was treating his analyst and the way he was in the habit of treating his girl friends. He acknowledged the aptness of the comparison, but declared that it was entirely possible that I really was not competent enough to understand him. I responded by stating that I could see nothing more important than his hours and that I insisted on his keeping his appointments. After this, when

[255]

he came to my office, he was in a sense facing his "cold" mother. He developed paranoid ideation which disappeared after we made genetic reconstructions.

I shall summarize the first months of George's analysis without going into any great detail. The dominant transference was a narcissistic one: he glorified himself and saw me as an extension of this glory—or, he devalued and discarded me as someone far beneath him. The genetic reconstructions we made during this time had little effect on his clinical picture. When I left for my vacation eight months after the start of his analysis, he collected his dreams, but by the time I returned they were as "spoiled" as the candy he collected in the refrigerator. Shortly after my return I sensed that he felt secure in my presence, and he became able to express the effect my absence had had on him. He had fallen into an "unbelievable" depression as exaggerated as his triumphant assumption of superman status had been. When he said he felt suicidal I calmly managed to pique his curiosity about the connection between my recent absence and his depression, and his childhood memories of traumatic rejection by his mother poured out. He responded at first to the rejection of the mother/analyst (my vacation) by a narcissistic withdrawal, but after he understood this he started to seek out "surrogates" of other persons important to him in his childhood in order for them to save him from the rejecting mother/analyst. For example, he posed for a male artist, a homosexual of the same ethnic background as his father's, and he allowed this man to perform fellatio on him for a fee, using as an excuse for his first homosexual experience the fact that he was "hungry" and without money to buy food. His associations indicated that his mother/analyst had taken away his oral supplies (due to my vacation) and that he had turned to the father (the artist), having to feed him first (with the "unbelievable" semen) in order to be fed himself. George then turned to his grandfather's image, in what I called his African bead venture (see Chapter II), and identification with it pulled him out of his depression. The grandfather had saved him when he needed rescue from the "unbelievable" trauma at home, and his image saved the day now.

After recovering from his "unbelievable" depression, instead of tightening his grasp on his narcissistic self-concept, George would lapse into depression when faced with "rejection" by me or others, but it was now a briefer and less severe depression. In the past, whenever a girl refused to bed with him on their first date he would quickly find some flaw in her and then dream of himself as a Greek god. Now such an incident led to "depression." As similar incidents occurred within the transference I began slowly to interpret his narcissistic personality as a pathological defensive constellation built to oppose early conflicts and to deal with impotent rage. Whereas formerly George had always glorified the image of his grandfather and refrained from any hint of criticism of him, he began examining his grandfather's role in "saving" him, to look more closely at the method (narcissistic) he had used when he introduced the boy to the world that never was.

The grandfather had been thrown down a stair by his murderer, and George now dreamed of falling down stairs. He knew he was identifying with the dead man, and felt angry toward him. He blamed him for continuing to conduct his business in a part of the city where violence could be expected, and meeting his death there although he had been warned of such danger. George's anger was part of his grief reaction, which developed fully and which was interpreted. I felt that this mourning was related to the loosening of his hold on his narcissistic self-concept, that George was in effect letting the omnipotent grandfather go, and that this was a major milestone in his analysis. The dreams that followed not only referred to this milestone but provided further grounds for the formulation that the inflated narcissistic self-concept was a pathological formation to defend against early oral-aggressive issues, and that George needed to work through them in order to be able to surrender his narcissism.

A series of dreams

Two dreams from the same night were reported together:

1. I saw this fantastic, unbelievable wave, real strong and powerful. I wanted to go in and surf. When I started to walk toward the wave the ocean seemed to be drawing away from me. I was walking on the sands and saw many lizards.

2. I was in the hospital [where the analyst's office is located]. I went to the Pink Ladies' shop to buy Mounds [a candy]. I was given a mint candy. It was an unusual size. In reality these mints come in two sizes, large and small, but the mint given to me was middle-sized.

I refrain from comment on aspects of the oedipal transference neurosis condensed in these dreams; also, in his
own associations to them, George emphasized the pregenital aspects involved as well as his working through of
his narcissistic problems.

George is a good surfer, and he had expatiated at
considerable length on his "unbelievable" conquest of
"unbelievably" powerful and beautiful waves. He saw
himself as a champion, tamer of the waves. Associations
indicated that the waves were his mother. For the first
time he spoke of a phobia; he was always extremely
anxious at entering the water, afraid of being sucked in,
and imagining a myriad of slimy substances beneath the
surface. The lizards represented his "primitivization" and
his cannibalistic impulses. In his associations he talked of
the pet iguana he had had as a child and how he had
collected live insects for its food, growing excited as he
described how the reptile had snatched and devoured
them. The candy Mounds were his mother's breasts,
inflamed when he was a nursling. The mint he had been
given in his dream reminded him of money; the word
mint is connected with money. He talked about his childhood fantasy of confusing a rectum with a vagina. In
cunnilingus, his favorite form of sexual foreplay, he
fantasied absorbing powerful anal qualities, and in his
associations he spoke of "to eat and to be eaten," and
displayed anxiety about the idea of eating his mother or
being eaten by her. When the mother was in one of her
"crazy" moods her wild gaze seemed to run him through
and make him afraid of being devoured. He felt guilt
about his anger toward her and terror at the impotence of

[259]

his rage. He associated his current fear of going to sleep with the fear he had felt with reference to his first dream about entering the water, a fear of being engulfed by his mother. This understanding evoked fear and anger. It occurred to him that the "middle-sized mint" he had been given in his dream was a good omen inasmuch as at this point of his analysis he was trying to accept a view of things that was not grotesquely skewed either toward grandiosity or dejection. The analysis of "middle-sized" brought forth his attempt to accept his early mother more realistically (less subject to primitive splitting).

The hour during which George reported these dreams came just before a weekend, and over the holiday George was gripped with tremendous anxiety, traveling about frantically "saving" friends as if his new awareness of his oral conflicts had turned him to his narcissistic defenses. This time his narcissism failed to protect him from anxiety, however. He felt "crazy" and "spaced out." Before his next session with me on Monday he had another dream in which he lay on my couch:

> You were wearing a sari and there was another man in your office [He identified a colleague of mine who has written on reincarnation, as George knew.] I was terrified of you but you put your sari aside and identified yourself.

This dream suggested that I was his "reincarnated" mother (the mother in transference). Although I was still the "bad" devouring mother, he was to some extent differentiating me from the "original" one. During this hour he reported another dream:

[260]

I was in a Japanese prison camp with my mother. She was wearing a black and white dress. An old friend was there and together we saw a World-War-II-type airplane. There were mean-looking Japanese soldiers around. My friend and I got in the airplane, leaving my mother behind. We started to fly; the soldiers shouted at us. We almost crashed. We flew over them but then we noticed a storm coming. My friend piloted the plane. Then suddenly I saw a sunny spot and directed him toward it.

As he finished reporting this dream an unusual thing happened—for the first time in his analysis George was comfortably wrapped in silence. When he spoke it was to say that he felt as though he had come to a stopping point, and that he had a sense of "birth." He felt that the dream had something to do with his separating from his mother (being born). He recalled having been told that he had "torn" his mother at his birth. The day residue in this dream had arisen from his accidentally having seen an essay of mine about the psychological adjustment of Cypriot Turks forced to live for years in enclaves surrounded by their enemies. The mother's black and white garment reflected George's alternating view of her as "all bad" or "all good." Once again George had an opportunity to work on his primitive splitting of his early mother representatives. His friend, who was in real life a user of LSD, was George's "crazy" self-representation still piloting him dangerously, although the real self-representation wanted to take over and at least direct the plane toward safety.

[261]

Not long after reporting this dream George brought another one that I felt summarized the state of affairs at that point in his analysis:

> I was in the living room of my apartment. Clark Kent [the Superman of the comic books] and another man came in. The second man could have been my grandfather—or you. I didn't want them there but I felt I couldn't fight against them. I went into my kitchen. A hole appeared in the wall. I went through the hole but I was just in another kitchen. This one had a hole in the wall, too. I went through the hole but again I was in a kitchen with a hole in one of its walls. When I came to the last kitchen I saw my maternal grandmother holding a carrot and sticking it in front of me. I didn't want to stay there either so I went back to my living room. By this time Clark Kent and his friend were tearing down my furniture. I got angry and started hitting them. I could feel the impact of my fist on their bodies. I could really hit them. I kicked them out.

Before this dream took place George and I had been discussing his inability to differentiate one girl friend from another, and any one of the multitude from the early mother. I had said something about his feeling that one girl's "hole" was the same as another to him. He felt that the "community kitchens" represented his inability to differentiate among women and his connecting them with his "archaic mother" (grandmother) who teased him. He felt that she had used him as her own phallus and that, in turn, he had to stay under her thumb. The dream suggested his differentiation of the image of his actual self from that of a superman. As he compared the early fighting dreams in which his blows made no impact with this last dream in which he felt the blows drive home, he concluded that his anger was no longer impotent. He felt delight in recalling the impact of his fist on the body of Superman. There was a definite boundary between him and the Superman who could now be driven out of his self-concept.

Whatever happened to George?

The period during which he reported these dreams came toward the end of his first year in analysis. It was a time of drastic changes in his life style, which became less narcissistic. I do not suggest that his narcissism vanished after the first major round in the battle, but I do maintain that psychoanalysis won the first round. After this his transference neurosis needed considerable attention, as will be explained later in this chapter. At present George is in the last half of his third year of analysis, with much more work still necessary before we terminate.

Contrasting views of the narcissistic personality

Kohut (1966, 1971, 1973) adds to the view that the developmental line of narcissism moves from autoeroticism to object love via narcissism a second concept positing an independent line of development from autoeroticism via narcissism to a higher form of the same, which is adaptive and culturally valuable. Weigert

(1967), without seeing a new developmental line for narcissism, had already placed "benign" and "malignant" forms of narcissism on a continuum. She wrote:

> In my practice, I see not a sharp division between benign and malignant narcissism but a continuum from benign narcissism or ego strength, with flexible defenses against disorganizing and anxieties, to a malignant narcissism or ego weakness, with the defenses against emergency increasingly breaking down.
>
> A healthy narcissism holds the balance between self-esteem growing out of phase-adequate mastery of dangers, and dependency on auxiliary supplies of parental or other authoritative support. ... The self-esteem approximates the objective state of ego development in a positive narcissism. The child loves himself not only when he feels loved by his family; in growing independence, he loves himself in spite of rejection by others. But such firmness of self-esteem is hard to reach, because of the power of human interdependence and solidarity. This solidarity is threatened by invidious comparisons, the injustice of fate that metes out unequal frustrations to the young and the old, the males and the females, the rich and the poor [p. 128-129].

Kohut (1971) describes a group of patients as having "narcissistic personality disorders," and states that it is the disturbance of the second line of development that makes the narcissistic patient unable to achieve adequate transformation of infantile narcissism. He differentiates such persons from borderline as well as from psychotic patients, holding that those with narcissistic personality disorder:

> have ... attained a cohesive self and have con- structed cohesive idealized archaic objects. And, unlike the conditions which prevail in the psychoses and borderline states, these patients are not serious- ly threatened by the possibility of an irreversible disintegration of the archaic self or of the narcissis- tically cathected archaic objects. In consequence of the attainment of these cohesive and stable psychic configurations these patients are able to establish specific, stable narcissistic transferences, which allow the therapeutic reactivation of the archaic structures without the danger of their fragmentation through further regression: they are thus analyz- able [p. 4].

Kohut emphasizes that the most intense narcissistic experiences relate to objects which are either used in the service of the self and of the maintenance of its instinctual investment, or objects which are themselves experienced as part of the self—self-objects. The perfection of pri- mary narcissism, disturbed by the mother's unavoidable shortcomings, is replaced by (a) establishing a grandiose and exhibitionistic self-image, which Kohut calls the *grandiose self*; and (b) conveying the original perfection to an admired, omnipotent, transitional self-object—the *idealized parent* image. Here Kohut uses the term "tran- sitional" to do more than reflect the child's inner atti- tudes, and explains these phenomena in metapsycho- logical terms. These two images are activated in narcissistic patients in the transference situation (narcissistic transference). Kohut uses the term *idealizing transference* for the transference which arises from the therapeutic mobilization of the idealized parent image. He uses the term *mirror transference* to refer to those that arise from the mobilization of the grandiose self.

If the material shortcomings are not too great the grandiose self is transformed into a self with mature ambitions and self-esteem. A developmental arrest caused by deprivation and trauma experienced in childhood accounts for the development of a grandiose self-image or an idealized parent image in narcissistic disorders. Kohut advises the analyst to accept the grandiose self-image of his narcissistic patient and his admiration of his analyst, helping thus to foster a full-blown narcissistic transference that will naturally induce narcissism of a higher level; this will in turn usher in a realistic self-esteem. A "transmuting internalization" is an essential curative factor during this process. The withdrawal of narcissistic as well as object-instinctual cathexes from object imagoes (in the analytic situation from the analyst) promotes new structure formation within the patient. Repeated breaks in the patient's attempt to unite with the idealized analyst are understood not to be traumatic, because the patient has been shown what precipitated them and has been given genetic reconstructions. As they occur, some degree of idealizing libido is withdrawn from the self-object-analyst to contribute to the process of new structure formation. "The internal structure ... now performs the functions which the object used to perform for the child — The well-functioning structure, however, has largely been divested of the personality features of the object" (Kohut, 1971, p. 50).

Kernberg's (1970a, 1970b) views about the narcissistic personality challenges Kohut's concept of it as a developmental arrest. As stated earlier, Kernberg demonstrates how an inflated self-concept (corresponding to Kohut's "grandiose self") arises from an early formation of pathological narcissism to protect against conflicts concerned with unbearable rage and envy. George's case has been described from this point of view.

Although he is also in favor of a full-blown narcissistic transference, Kernberg suggests that the working through of such transference requires, in addition to its acceptance, systematic interpretation of its negative as well as its positive aspects. From the standpoint of primitive internalized object relations the patient idealizes the analyst when he externalizes the *pathological* grandiose self onto him. But since this constellation is defensively used to cover up the "hungry" self and its link to a compelling impotent rage, this deeper image also is externalized onto the analyst. Thus one can sense a generalized contempt for and devaluation of the analyst behind his idealization. Sometimes these two aspects alternate, one surfacing after the other, as in George's analysis, and the analysis of Brown (to be described in Chapter X).

Kohut (1970) relies in his monograph almost exclusively on the maturation of libidinal cathexes in the analysis of narcissistic personalities. Later, however, he focuses on aggression in such patients. His understanding of aggression in the narcissistic personality is unlike that of Kernberg, who sees aggression as derived from aggressive drives and displayed by his patients in the form of oral rage and envy. These aggressive drive derivatives are attached to "all bad" self- and object representations in an introjective-projective relatedness. Kohut (1973), on the other hand, talks about "narcissistic rage" when aggressive drive derivatives arise: "when self or object fail to live up to the absolutarian expectations which are directed at their function—whether by the child who, more or less phase-appropriately, insists on the grandiosity and omnipotence of the self and the self-object or by the narcissistically fixated adult whose archaic narcissistic structures have remained unmodified because they became isolated from the rest of the growing psyche after the phase-appropriate narcissistic demands of childhood had been traumatically frustrated" (p. 386). Kohut then suggests that narcissistic rage can be tamed when it is transferred into "mature aggression," when the narcissistic matrix in which the narcissistic rage arises develops into higher-level narcissism.

From narcissistic transference to transference neurosis

As I understand Kohut, his notion of a separate developmental line for narcissism disregards the transference neurosis in the analysis of the narcissistic personality. His position may be stated in his own words:

> In the transference neuroses defenses are removed, object-instinctual investments are given access to the ego, and the result is an improved arrangement of psychological structures.... An analogous process also takes place as a first step in the working-

through process of the analysis of narcissistic personality disorders as the split-off and/or repressed narcissistic cathexes and the narcissistically cathected prestructural self-object are given access to the reality ego. The essential working-through process, however, aims at the gradual withdrawal of the narcissistic libido from the narcissistically invested, archaic, object; it leads to the acquisition of new psychological structures and functions as the cathexes shift from the representation of the object and its activities to the psychic apparatus and its functions [Kohut, 1971, p. 96].

Kernberg's (1970a) view implies that once the pathological narcissistic self-structure is resolved in analysis (when the patient becomes aware that his ideal concept is a fantasy structure), the narcissistic transference gives way to a transference neurosis. At the crucial point, "the deep admiration and love for the ideal mother" and "the hatred for the the distorted dangerous mother" meet in the transference. This is followed by a depression and suicidal thoughts in the patient "because he has mistreated the analyst and all the significant persons in his life, and he may feel that he has actually destroyed those whom he could have loved and who might have loved him" (Kernberg, 1970a, p. 81).

After this phase is worked through the patient acknowledges the analyst as an independent being toward whom he can feel love and gratitude. What Kernberg describes then is a movement from the utilization of primitive splitting to an ambivalent relatedness and, hopefully, an eventual postambivalent one. What I have

[269]

said about the primitively split transference (see *Toward Jane's transference neurosis*, Chapter VI) applies to the narcissistic transference.

In the narcissistic personality it is usual for a narcissistic transference and a transference neurosis to appear simultaneously, one alternately overlying the other. It would be useless to analyze the transference neurosis, however, without having first analyzed the full-blown narcissistic transference. Once the latter has been adequately analyzed, the transference neurosis will require attention. The narcissistic transference will, however, return again and again until it is fully worked through before the analysis terminates. I am aware that its reappearance may on occasion offer resistance to analysis of the transference neurosis — and that the reverse may also be true.

I have given attention to the structure-building aspect of introjective-projective relatedness (see Chapters III and IV) in dealing with psychotic and borderline patients. The role of introjective and projective relatedness and identification with the analytic introject should be recognized in narcissistic patients (although these processes may be less evident on the surface in narcissistic personalities than in psychosis or borderline personalities) and their defensive aspects taken into account. Unlike Kernberg, Kohut does consider this process, but only within his own frame of reference. He says: "The essential therapeutic progress in the analysis of the archaic investments of the idealized object imago . . . occurs in consequence of the transmuting internalization of the narcissistic energies as the idealized self-object is relinquished. It leads to the redistribution of the narcissistic energies in the personality itself (Kohut, 1971, p. 101).

In the following chapter, I shall summarize the entire analysis of a narcissistic personality to highlight the appearance of the narcissistic transference, its alternation with the neurotic transference, and the internalization process that took place during the patient's analysis.

CHAPTER X

TRANSITIONAL FANTASIES
IN THE ANALYSIS OF
A NARCISSISTIC PERSONALITY

This chapter will serve two purposes in summarizing the entire analysis of a patient with a narcissistic personality and at the same time offering evidence to support the thesis that this patient used specific fantasies as though they were intangible representations of transitional objects.

The function of transitional fantasies in a narcissistic personality

The patient who employed what I came to call *transitional fantasies* (see Chapter VIII) was a man in his thirties who underwent four and a half years of analysis. A narcissistic personality structure like that of George's

---

This chapter is based on a paper by the same title, first published in the *J. Amer. Psychoanal. Assn.*, 21:351-376, 1973.

(Chapter IX) underlay his neurotic symptoms and obsessional characteristics. The core of his problems was his view of himself as the center of the world, a belief that he was "Number One," existing for all to admire. In analysis he disclosed himself as a lonely being who was glorified within a kingdom, an "iron ball" that surrounded him, from which his analyst was banned. Behind his narcissism was the image of a deprived and hungry infant, and in analysis he oscillated between adherence to the role of "the most admired one" and the display of paranoid trends.

He functioned well on the surface in spite of his narcissistic structure, and held a responsible job from which he sought to gain admiration. His reality testing in intimate relationships was so blurred, however, by his protection of the belief that he had precedence over all others, that one must ask what kept him from exhibiting generalized psychotic behavior. The answer seems to lie in his use of specific fantasies in a way that suggested my term, transitional fantasies. He employed them as intangible representations of transitional objects, regarding them as though they had lives of their own and behaving as though he were addicted to them, although they were at the same time subject to his absolute control, whereby he could maintain the illusion that he had similar control over the real environment.

Who was Brown?

At the time his psychoanalysis began, Brown was a 30-year-old lawyer, married, and the father of girls seven and five years of age and a boy of four. One of his maternal ancestors had been a Colonial leader, and he took a fierce pride in his family history. He was reared in a home of extreme formality and respect for tradition. His father, the head of an important law firm, was aloof and conventional, although before marrying he had been "wild" and known for his escapades, his fast car, and his athletic feats. Brown's mother, a lawyer's daughter, "had practical answers for everything," and was interested in gourmet cooking, although she delegated most of the care of her children to maids. Brown remembered his own nursemaid only by her wall eyes and her German name; these were representations of fear-inducing archaic objects at a time when Americans were fighting the Germans in World War II. A brother, two years Brown's junior, had apparently adopted the life style of his father's earlier years; he was athletic, happily married, and the operator of a luxurious sports resort. A sister, four years younger than the patient, had many neurotic problems.

Kernberg's (1970a) narcissistic patients often came from families of "chronically cold parental figures with covert but intense aggression." Usually the mother functioned well within a superficially well organized home, but with a degree of callousness, indifference, and non-verbalized and spiteful aggression. This was the case in Brown's family. Life in his home had revolved around a rigid schedule of social amenities. The children were permitted to join their parents during the cocktail hour. Dinner had a special focus each night, with a night when only French was spoken, another when spelling competition took place, and another for special games. The patient had no remembrance of any overt expression of emotion in this stylized family togetherness.

At the time of his birth, Brown's parents were living in the country with the paternal grandparents. Legend had it that when the mother was pregnant she ate so much corn that she was fat and full of milk. When the baby was a year old the family moved to the city apartment where the second child was conceived, and a later move took them all to a permanent home in a substantial neighborhood, where the boy had few playmates. When he was five, his father became a reserve military officer and was periodically absent from home over a period of a year and a half. Later, interest in fishing frequently kept the father away from home.

The patient did well in school. He recalls daydreaming a great deal, even as a child, and at night he was preoccupied with shadowy figures behind his bed, haunting him. At puberty he developed the habit of tying a rope around his thighs and legs at night, fantasying his own execution, and finally masturbating. As a teenager he felt inferior among adults, but concealed this feeling well. A cousin encouraged him, teaching him to dance, but he continued to feel "shy," although when he dated he was in the habit of demanding sex at once. He was 16 when he first heard his parents shouting at one another, and felt relief to learn that they could express themselves. He felt that, in view of the sterile environment in which he had grown up, it was too late for him to learn to express feeling. He was interested in mathematics, but had to follow the family tradition and go to law school.

He developed phobias of high places, especially in connection with climbing ladders.

At 22 he took a trip with a schoolmate (with his mother's permission), and on this trip met his future wife. She was not socially prominent, nor was her background compatible with his. He made her pregnant and married her four months later. After graduation he joined his father's law firm, specializing in a kind of practice that involved little interaction with other people. It was while he was with his father's firm that his wife gave birth to their third child, a boy, about whose physical endowment there was some question at birth, and who came to be considered frail and sickly by his parents.

Soon after his son's birth, Brown seduced a secretary, who was the daughter of a judge, and made her pregnant. She had an abortion, and the affair ended. (The patient's perception of this affair and its eerie promotion of his narcissistic fantasies will be discussed later in this chapter.) Its termination dealt the patient a narcissistic blow and, along with the possibility of a break in his marriage and dismay over his newborn son's imperfections, disturbed his self-esteem sufficiently to lead him to seek professional help. He visited a psychiatrist a few times, but was afraid of him. Moving to another city with his family, he continued to have difficulty and to seek professional advice. Still another move brought him to the city in which he undertook psychoanalysis. Here he held a position consistent with his legal training. Again, it was one with minimal interpersonal involvement.

[277]

The narcissistic personality and the obsessive personality

At the outset of his analysis, Brown appeared to be obsessional, with mixed neuroses, i.e., phobias. One should note the difficulty of distinguishing the patient with a narcissistic personality structure from one who is obsessional and embarking on his analysis with strong narcissistic defenses against oedipal fears or sadomasochistic impulses. Kernberg suggests heeding the kind of transference that appears when narcissistic transference resistance is interpreted. He points out that, unlike the obsessional patient, the narcissistic patient *does not* change his narcissistic defenses into other transference paradigms.

Here the characteristics of the transference involvement oscillate between narcissistic grandiosity and aloofness on the one hand, and primitive, predominantly paranoid trends on the other. The patient's complete incapacity, maintained over many months and years of analytic work, to experience the analyst as an independent object is characteristic of narcissistic personalities, and is in sharp contrast to the transference involvements in other forms of character pathology where the transference may shift to reveal different, highly specific conflicts of varying psychosexual stages of development and with a highly differentiated awareness by the patient of the analyst as an independent object.... In [obsessive personalities], the exacerbation of or fixation at the infantile ego ideal is not accompanied by a primitive fusion of the self-concept with such an ego ideal, nor by a concomitant devaluation of object representations and external objects [Kernberg, 1970a, p. 64].

Furthermore, Kernberg states that the value system of the narcissistic patient is generally corruptible and contrasts with the rigid morality of the obsessive personality. Moreover, the obsessive individual feels strongly about social, political, and similar issues, and demonstrates an understanding of the emotional depths of other people while remaining "cold" himself. In contrast, the narcissistic patient shows superficial emotions of a quick and transient sort, but has a basic background of emotional blandness and indifference. It is typical for him to disparage the analytic process during his treatment, at the same time developing an intense transference. Transference resistances bring about paranoid developments. Such patients "learn" the method of analysis to defend themselves against their envy of the analyst. They see the analysis as a means of becoming "perfect," and, as Kernberg believes also, there can be dramatic improvement, a growing tolerance of depression and mourning being a good prognostic sign. I have already described George's depression and mourning as an indication of a crucial turning point of his analysis (see Chapter IX).

The course of Brown's analysis

I can provide only a bird's eye-view of Brown's analysis, and I shall not separate from his narcissistic transference the classical transference neurosis that at times covered it over. The picture was mixed most of the time, but it will be clear that the narcissistic transference

[279]

underlay all relatedness to objects until it was resolved. Compression of the four and a half years of psychoanalysis into this brief account may convey a false sense of rapid progress; in day-to-day involvement with this patient, however, many of the hours were filled with stubborn silence, monotonous devaluation of the other person, and his endless admiration of his own verbal productions. I did not interfere with the establishment of a narcissistic transference in accordance with both Kernberg's (1970a) and Kohut's (1971) technical points of view.

What follows is a clinical description of the actual analytical process rather than a formulation of manifestations from the theoretical point of view. The patient began with a rigid posture on the couch, giving forth endlessly, in a monotonous voice, accounts that seemed designed less as communication to me than as productions to elicit wonder. Within a few weeks he flew to his brother's resort, where he seduced a foreign woman who, like his analyst, spoke with an accent. During his hours he systematically itemized symptoms and events he thought an analyst should know, providing much "history" and many accounts of his phobia of high places. One aspect of this phobia was revealed in a childhood dream in which he had climbed a ladder to spy on his parents' second-story quarters above the floor where he lived with the other children and the servants. The customarily closed door to the second floor of the split-level house had become a symbol of the mysteries of adult life; in his dream, the ladder by means of which he tried to breach these mysteries was shaky, and he had to give up the attempt.

He insisted on keeping our relationship "formal"; he indirectly probed my "encouragement" and tried to make me helpless. He mocked free association, but said he hoped his psychoanalysis "would be a smashing success." He described an Oliphant cartoon with little figures marginal to the main picture, and said I resembled the marginal figures. The first year was full of complaints about his wife—how cold she was, how ungiving. In his narcissistic transference he saw me as an extension of himself; I was either a jewel in his crown or, at the other extreme, a sewer in which his resentments could be flushed away. The narcissistic core of his personality emerged: he was the earth's very center; his wishes were needs. He seldom mentioned his children unless one defeated him in competition. It was necessary for him not only to be Number One but the Only One.

Early in his analysis he reported what was probably a screen memory from the day his newborn brother was brought home. In it he was looking out of a garage on a gray day at a tree stump without branches. This represented his mother, whose upper parts—her breasts—were now cut off from him. He sensed that his turning inward toward his own resources had begun then; gray was the color of loneliness. He envied his brother then, and later envied me and my other patients. Most of his early memories involved sibling rivalry. Once he had let his brother's perambulator slip out of his hands into the path of a moving bus, and a tragedy had been narrowly averted. Although his family thought of this as accidental, the patient, with no felt remorse, knew he had attempted to free himself from his brother's competition for their mother's attention.

In spite of quick flare-ups of envy, he did not experience frustration for long; he became a push-button man, handling his frustration by summoning up a fantasy as though pushing a television control. He was in search of "an encouraging woman," later calling his ideal the "bountiful woman." The sight of a woman in an office or restaurant would set off elaborate daydreams, often daydreams in which he rescued the woman from rape.

He spent so much time daydreaming that his job was threatened during the first year of analysis. He daydreamed and masturbated at work and lying beside his wife at night, when he saw himself rejected unless she openly expressed admiration. He masturbated before getting up in the morning, and hung his soiled pajamas where his wife would find them. The genetic aspect of this behavior came from the revulsion with which his mother had dealt with his incontinence during an illness when he was four; it involved repetition compulsion and a need to test his wife's reaction. In the second year of analysis he came to my office soon after masturbating, with stained trousers, trying to repeat past events in our relationship. He was concerned about the control of elimination, and once locked himself with his child in the bathroom for two hours until the child eliminated.

In his transference neurosis his mother was symbolized by cold water, his father by a burning cigar. He had one of his infrequent anxiety attacks when he saw me smoking a cigar. The genetic aspect of this surfaced when it was revealed that once, during his childhood, when he had broken a family rule, his father had coaxed him to his side and pressed his burning cigar against the boy's hand. The possibility of felt anxiety in his transference neurosis led to recitation of his fantasies. He sometimes lay on the couch for hours without speaking, lost in fantasy; he reported having been in a state of bliss with a "bountiful woman" or in triumph over the oedipal father without the actual oedipal struggle. He was a magnificent bull in the ring where "bountiful women" pelted him with flowers, but where he did not face the matador. Faced with an oedipal situation, he had a feeling of self-castration; in the transference situation he escaped the oedipal struggle by a fantasy of having cancer, or by some other claim to special consideration.

In spite of analyzing the defenses against his oedipal fears and conflicts, he continued to disparage this insight and to treat me with indifference, demanding that his analysis bring him glory. In his second year his narcissistic core became more apparent; he fantasized an iron ball in which he lived and from which he reigned. It offered boundaries and an identity against the outside world, and accounted, as it hung high on shaky supports, for the pregenital aspect of his phobia of high places. He feared the collapse of his narcissistic world and betrayed his real lack of self-sufficiency and his lifelong need of others. The shaky support referred to his anxiety about knowing his oral needs and the eruption of devouring impulses.

At the end of the second year he reported a sleeping dream. Such reports were infrequent. In it he sat on a couch beside a man who represented his analyst; believing his companion to be female, he began to caress him, discovering with horror that he was caressing a man. Knowledge of his need of closeness to me was not only unacceptable but had homosexual implications. An interval followed in which he seemed to be in a typical transference neurosis and working on his homosexual fears and castration anxiety. Abruptly, he returned to his iron ball, and I learned more about his glorification of his lonely world, his self-admiration, his devaluation of me — whenever I was perceived as something other than an extension of himself, or something that failed to feed his narcissistic demands — and his envy of anything in the outside world that he considered good. He concentrated on protecting his narcissistic interests, going into a paranoid rage, for example, when his wife devoted herself to a visiting sister and failed to ask if there were something she could do for him. This sister belonged to him in his fantasies; when she married he briefly felt frustration, anger, and envy, and seduced the groom's sister on the wedding night in reprisal for losing "his woman." He felt no remorse for this behavior, believing that he had every right to meet his narcissistic needs.

During the latter part of the second year he was able to abort a daydream, hearing an inner voice object, "Here you go again! One more of your raped-girl fantasies!" I had once said this to him; his self-control here showed his internalization of me which was later lost by fragmentation, as indicated by his account of seeing the face of a newscaster fragmented in faulty television reception. And he did return to the daydream "on grounds of my curiosity" about its outcome.

During this time we were able to explore the meaning of his keeping others at arm's length, his fear of losing his omnipotence and of a breakthrough of his aggression, which he had not been permitted to tame in the sterile and controlled environment of his early childhood. The transference situation intensified and had a psychotic transference quality; at times he believed that I gave off heat that burned his head and arms. I *was* the "burning father." He managed to see, however, that he had kept the father stereotyped. His father had indeed been aloof, but before his marriage and his capitulation to the mother's "cold water," he had been "wild." The patient's desire to identify with his father as a youth was dangerous. If he became friendly and free he should have to admit weakness. He recalled with astonishment that once, while he was working as a lawyer in his father's office, he had seen his parent moved to tears over losing his brother. He speculated about his father's ability to express human emotion, and the anxiety that a man could entertain such warm sentiments initiated a regression into something like the Isakower phenomenon. Colored balloons seemed to fill his mouth as he lay on the couch. I felt that his mother's feeding had been not only nurturing but smothering. At times he panicked at oral expression; colors and shapes became "nebulous," and he became paranoid and afraid of being choked or smothered. I was a dark and shadowy character who recalled his childhood fear of shadows.

As the third year approached, he left analysis for a month, attending a professional meeting important to him because of the opportunity to study for the first time the "social aspects" of law, but also because it provided an escape from his intense oral-aggressive feeling. Just before the separation he came in preoccupied with the phrase, "too much of a good thing." He discussed the current drought, and fantasied being desiccated and in need of reviving water that I could provide. Analysis indicated the possibility that he had been abruptly weaned during his first year by a mother already embarked on a second pregnancy. He had never forgotten the "bountiful mother" who was "too much of a good thing." After a surfeit the *average* amount of oral supply constituted deprivation, and this explained his fear of drying up away from the mother-analyst. He agreed with this reconstruction, recalling aspects of his childhood relationship with his mother. Although she was cold, she had provided excellent food; dining was at the core of the family's interpersonal activity. The patient recognized a similar situation in his behavior toward his wife, who displeased him by her coldness but held him by her skill in providing good food. Behind his extolling of loneliness lay this intense relationship with the other for whom he could not acknowledge love-need because of his fear of rejection. He understood this before leaving for his month-long trip.

His relationships with others had considerably improved. His job had been in jeopardy a year earlier, but now he was promoted. Before analysis he had been without friends, but now he had many. His relations with his parents had improved, and he was a better father to his children; but basically he continued relating to me and to his wife from within the iron ball, boring me at times, and making any movement in the analytic working through in the transference seem hopelessly out of reach.

For a time after his return he seemed, on the surface, friendly to his wife and to me. He appeared to be examining his responsibility in keeping people at a distance, and his way of provoking rejection to prove that loneliness and fantasy offered superior safety, as when he approached his wife sexually at a time so inappropriate as to insure rejection. He was able to examine his vagina dentata fears and report primal scene memories. He had seen his father naked after intercourse, and he had concluded that the scars his father bore on his thighs and chest had been inflicted by his mother during the sex act. This shed light on his juvenile habit of tying a rope around his thighs and on his affairs with the judge's daughter, who, being extensively scarred, had externally represented the mutilated father and the castrated patient. He thus felt safe with her, although the relationship was also important to him as a means of gratifying his narcissism through the sense of superiority to her he felt because of her many social and physical disabilities. She had false teeth and thus could perform fellatio without biting. Once she had a malignant tumor which was removed, and she was a kleptomaniac. In comparison with her he himself was a superman.

Throughout these changes, however, the core narcissistic transference remained basically unaltered. He was afraid of my attack, and took refuge in his iron ball.

At the start of the fourth year of analysis I came to understand his specific fantasies and visual images as transitional objects. (I shall elaborate on this later.) As we worked through this interpretation he read an article about the teddy bear and the way in which some adults cling to such childhood treasures. When he retreated one day into a pet fantasy I said, "Now you have your teddy bear!" He reacted strongly, shouting, "I never had a teddy bear!" and went on to further insight about the smothering oral gratification followed by rejection in his early childhood, and his resort to archaic pathological narcissistic positions. He compared himself to a heroin addict and talked about his addiction to certain fantasies. Fantasies and other images slowly lost their magic. He became capable of remorse and sorrow and spoke of suicide. He could tell his wife that he loved her and play with their children. At the outset of his analysis he wore gray and light brown suits that reminded him of his "garage screen memory," and to interact with others he sat in his swimming trunks by the side of the pool waiting to be admired and adored. Now he wore colorful garments, became active in civic affairs, and supported liberal political movements. His professional reputation grew. He began to use me as a transitional object more than his own productions. He then came to see me as another human being and became curious about me personally. He said that although before analysis he had felt himself only a hanger-on in any crowd, he now felt included. Recalling Oliphant cartoons, he said, ". . . the little figures around the edge are important, even more than the main cartoon. I kept you outside the frame, but deep down I always related to you with intensity."

Termination phase

At the end of his fourth year of analysis, Mr. Brown started to talk about termination. Recalling his goal of having "a smashing psychoanalysis," he announced sadly that it had not made him a "perfect superman," but that he would be happy to be "perfectly average"—later dropping the "perfectly" from his specifications—and to rejoice in being a human being neither at the bottom of the heap nor at the top, seeing the joy and sadness of life. He added that he could now enjoy a game for the sake of companionship, whether or not he won. He became interested in repairing and decorating his house. I felt this activity symbolized his attempt at structural change within himself. He enjoyed doing this work with his wife, and referred with satisfaction to his having overcome his ladder phobia. He became preoccupied with putting a balcony in good order; this was interpreted to him as a wish to make his mother's breast good. After accepting this interpretation, he continued to enjoy the work, and I felt that he had attained sublimation. During this time he asked his mother about her feeding him at the breast; until then he had adhered to his belief that she had nursed him with breasts full of milk because of her diet of corn. He was, on one level, surprised to learn that she had attempted to nurse him over a period of a few weeks, but that she felt her milk was "bad" for him and transferred him to bottle feeding. On another level, neither the patient nor I was surprised. During regressive experiences such as the Isakower phenomenon, he had reported a visual impression of a skyline, and he understood that the "skyline" was made up of bottles standing side by side. He recalled a cartoon character who was able to smother people by placing his "water face" on them. It was necessary to re-examine our previous construction that he had been excessively and aggressively nursed.

By the beginning of the fifth year of his analysis the reporting of night dreams replaced the accounts of daydreams. They specifically referred to the recapitulation of his oedipal struggles. In one of them the undisguised father let him lose his way in an airport, but the undisguised analyst put him on the right path. Periodically he returned to his pet fantasies, but they had now lost their magic and no longer satisfied him. He asked about the pronunciation of my Turkish first name, saying that he would like to be on terms of first-name friendship with me after his analysis was terminated. He assimilated the events that predated his turning to psychiatric help and that had necessitated this step. He understood that his affair with the judge's daughter lacked substance and had almost psychotic qualities; he saw his lover as a "ghost" and the whole affair as "hazy." It was eerie how his narcissistic fantasies had materialized and blurred for him the boundaries between the real and the unreal. He could indeed have sex and other self-gratifications at will, just like the grandiose self of his fantasies.

At the completion of about four and a half years of analysis he reported a daydream quite different from his usual narcissistically oriented pet fantasies; this let both of us consider termination. His new daydream referred to Henry VIII, with whom he had been fascinated for some time, and whose biography he was reading. Seeing himself as omnipotent, divine, tyrannical, and the master of a collection of women, he openly associated himself with the King. In his fantasy, the patient was in England as a leader of a democratic colony newly formed under the aegis of a foreign power; it was designed to bring an easy-going democratic life style to England. He captured Henry and imprisoned him, gratifying himself with the awareness that he could kill Henry, but did not need to do so since the King was safely out of the way in prison.

He recalled how I had once referred to him as a tyrannical little king. He confided that whereas in the past he would have spent hours planning his future in every detail, and the outcome of his stories, he now felt satisfied that events in the colony would take their course. In the colony fantasy he was not internalizing me as an archaic aggressive image determined to fight against his grandiose self. The rest of the fantasy bore this out; in the book on Henry VIII a footnote referring to the Turks indicated their power at the time and described their onslaught at the gates of Vienna. In his fantasy it was not the aggressive Turks he turned to for help, but the benign foreign power. After making this report the patient spoke of having been surprised on the previous day by a strong awareness of his closeness to his wife.

Later, after reading the chapter on the death of Henry VIII, he provided further associations. Henry was a fat man "because he could eat whatever he wanted to,"

[291]

and thus he represented to the patient his infantile hungry self as well as the child-mother unit. The mother was perceived as having been as fat as Henry when she ate so much corn during and immediately after the time she was pregnant with the patient.

He began to perceive his penis, which in his narcissism he had seen as huge and existing for the purpose of screwing, as smaller and designed for loving. When he noticed one day that one side of his scrotal sac was smaller than the other, he had a fantasy that his testicles would atrophy. Consulting a physician, he learned that his testes were unequal in size. I suggested that he had noticed such common inequality even in dogs. It was his narcissistic investment that had made his scrotum unique — and glorified his "iron ball."

When he experienced rather intense sadness about our forthcoming separation, I told him I was now ready to discuss his wish to terminate and to help him set a termination date. He responded to this proposal with frantic activity and with a dream in which he stole money, stuffed it under his coat, and drove off "toward the sunset" on a bicycle. I interpreted his retentive defenses against separation.

That night in the bathroom at home he tore apart the toilet fixtures "by accident." He had a fantasy of being stuffed with fecal material and being anxious to leave a "big, beautiful piece" of it on my office couch as a gift that would so defile it that no other patient would ever use it and usurp his place. Thus he could keep me forever. He wanted to produce the perfect excrement, although he understood there was no such thing.

We discussed the possibility that if I established the termination date he might perceive me as rejecting him and want to retreat into his iron ball, whereas were I to wait for him to fix the date he might feel rejection in this response as well, since he might consider me indifferent to his struggles. It was finally in the course of discussing the concept of mutuality that we decided on a termination date.

During the last year of his analysis, Brown's interest in his son increased. The boy, seen by his mother as a fragile child, was having difficulty in individuation and was symptomatic at times. During the termination phase of his own analysis, Brown took the initiative in having a child psychiatrist see his son, although he had formerly been intimidated by his wife's expected "fury" at such a step. When psychiatric treatment for the child was begun at his insistence, however, he became delightedly aware, and very much surprised, that his wife's reaction was one of warm appreciation. He was able to report other instances of appropriately assertive behavior at work and in his daily life in general.

He had a fantasy a week before termination while driving in his car to attend an out-of-town business meeting. In the fantasy he had an automobile accident that damaged the left side of his face. He fantasied being taken to a hospital for facial repair; my office is in a hospital. One may connect the vulnerability of the left side of the face as one drives a car with its vulnerability in being the side revealed by a patient lying on the couch in my office.

His associations indicated that he was analyzing very

early pathogenic fantasies concerned with his struggle in psychic separation from his mother, reactivated by our approaching separation. The left side of his face was felt to rest on the mother's breast in the nursing situation. In recent months he had developed the habit of gently massaging the sides of his face while on the couch; now he could understand that he had been trying to put boundaries around his face. While talking about his fantasy he made an analogy, saying that his learning in analysis where the skin of his face ended was like a deaf man's trying to learn to speak by feeling his vocal chords. Again he recalled the cartoon character of Water Face, reviving the smothering aspect of early interaction with his mother.

He then discussed a film called "The Village of the Damned," which had made a strong impression on him. The strange children who appeared in this film possessed mysterious powers and were able to make others do their will simply by looking at them, but he thought they acted this way in self-defense. He thought that as an infant in his crib he might have felt in possession of such power, which he used because he felt that others might destroy him. In the past his intimate relationships had been blurred, but he had had no difficulty in separating himself from others in relationships that were not intimate. He recalled a previously repressed thought he had had during the affair with the judge's daughter, the thought of transforming her into an extension of his body. He felt now, however, that he could experience intimate skin contact with another without any doubt about the integrity of his own skin.

Termination was effected after five further sessions.

Brown's transitional fantasies

An examination of some of Brown's specific fantasies disclosed different levels of condensation and what I suggest was their underlying function as transitional objects. He seemed to be addicted to some of them, chosen from an endless store of possibilities; these he used over and over whenever he felt the need. There was some change in superficial content, but the basic themes remained unaltered. He named them, and sometimes instead of reporting them in the usual detail, he would simply say, "I had another of my so-and-so fantasies." Chief among their subjects were the bountiful woman, the raped girl, the magnificent bull, the greatest baseball player, and the iron ball. In the fantasy of the bountiful woman he would be adored by a woman who gratified him in every way on demand, supplying food, sex, etc. In the raped-girl fantasy he saved girls from rape and they became his slaves. As a magnificent bull he would be pelted with flowers by admiring women, but never face the matador. As the greatest baseball player he played magnificent ball, always alone in glorified isolation. The iron ball was itself his glorified Kingdom.

He based some of his real-life activity on them whenever possible, so that some of his behavior had dreamlike elements and lacked a reality base. His marriage had an appreciable element of the raped-girl fantasy, and he could experience it as being real and also unreal. His big love affair, so long glorified, also had a hazy quality. During the first year of analysis he spoke of it as the most

[295]

wonderful, ineffable love affair a man could experience, although it actually showed highly specific conflicts of varying psychosexual stages. For example, the mistress represented the mother and his sister, as well as his castrated father and himself. His castration fears were concealed by the scars on his lover's body, and his vagina dentata fears set aside because she was toothless.

The fantasies had like condensations of different levels of psychosexual implication. One aspect of the raped-girl fantasy concerned his presumption of his mother's rape by his father, based on his own birth nine months after their marriage; moreover, he had "raped" his wife before marrying her. In the fantasy of the magnificent bull he significantly refused to face the matador — the castrating father. His response to interpretations of this sort never led to anxiety that could be mobilized toward abandoning the fantasies. They were clearly narcissistic; a glorified self-image underlay them all. He was the magnificent savior of the raped girl who became his adoring slave, and something of the same sublime condensation carried over into the reality of his relationship with the judge's daughter.

Kernberg's (1970a) description of the fantasies of patients with narcissistic personality structure, with their fusion of the ideal self-image, ideal object image and self-image, and the elimination of dependence on external objects applies to this case. In his love affair, as well as in his fantasies of "bountiful women," it was hard to see where he ended and his lover began. They fused orally, as in kissing or fellatio, or merged through skin contact. Interpretation of these aspects, as well as the oedipal or other psychosexual aspects of his fantasies, did nothing to curtail their use, and I came to understand that they were illusions for the protection of his narcissism and omnipotence, and bridges between me and not-me. Kohut (1971) stressed that direct interpretation of the content of sexual fantasies of such cases, even retrospectively after the establishment of insight from nonsexual material, should be attempted cautiously and remain secondary to demonstration that the sexualization of defects and needs serves to discharge intense narcissistic tensions.

Brown abused his fantasies by excessive use, just as a child will abuse his transitional object. He would begin a "bountiful woman fantasy," finish it, start it again with a slight variation here and there in its unfolding, bring it to completion, and then repeat it with further variations — almost as though he felt the vicious zest of pulling and pinching a tangible object. Then he would cherish it for its comforting qualities when he went to bed.

The material for his fantasies came from what lay at hand. External stimuli, such as the sight of an interesting woman, altered by his inner preoccupations, fed his pet fantasies. Then he would be in the curious position of accepting or not accepting the external objects themselves. Use of the fantasies as though they were intangible representations of a transitional object protected him from the total fusion of self- and object images, from generalized psychotic manifestations, and from affects, especially those arising from gradual disillusionment. This activity recalls Fintzy's (1971) discussion of the covert transitional object of a borderline child (elaborated upon in Chapter VIII, see *Expansion of the concepts of transitional objects and phenomena*); although Fintzy speaks of inanimate objects rather than intangible transitional fantasies, his rationale is like mine. Following Modell's (1963) comment that the object relations of the borderline patient are arrested at the stage of the transitional object, he asks whether a fixation may not occasion a gradual lifelong transformation of transitional objects. He suggests that the covert existence of an unrecognized transitional object may magically undo the separation from the mother. "This instantaneous symbolic restitutive process permits [the patient] to traverse the road of daily living in comfort, for the wished-for, and perhaps sporadically experienced, Shangri-la of the first year has been reconstructed" (Fintzy, 1971, p. 111). When, during regression in Brown's analysis, the pet fantasies were reduced to "nebulous" thoughts or perceptual images, they were in a sense closer to the concept of transitional objects than when they were elaborate fantasies. Control by the use of transitional fantasies of that area in which inner and outer realities are separated but interrelated had to be worked through in analysis in order for my patient to be able to cross over to the progressive side by using his analyst as a transitional object. A less narcissistic object relationship then became possible.

In analysis my patient's understanding of his use of fantasies as transitional objects came slowly. When, at the end of the third year, he talked about me as though I were a slave subject to his wishes, I let him know— probably as a counter-response on my part—that ours was a two-way contract that could end if the joint work ceased to have meaning. This shocked him; the threat of separation increased his need of fantasies with which to conceal his separation anxiety. Not only were his fantasies abundant then, but he had a variety of visual images as well. For example, when I told him he was making a mockery of free association, instead of feeling anxiety he had a visual image about free association — a string of boxcars which, together, formed a train. Affect-laden ideas were transferred into visual imagery. When I was able to awaken his curiosity about this phenomenon, he explained that in these images as well as in his more elaborate fantasies he hypercathected all his perceptual senses, seeing, smelling, tasting, hearing, and touching what appeared in his fantasies. Each fantasy had for him, in accordance with Winnicott's description of the transitional object, "reality of its own."

I recognized that he was highly creative. At times I was fascinated by his beautiful analogies and the creative perceptual images that represented his feeling states, but I was sometimes bored by his repetitiousness and my awareness of the fact that he was caught up in his images. I reminded him of his recent frustration in the writing of a report highly important to his work. I encouraged him to think about putting creative energies to more adaptive and adult use, indicating that while his fantasies had no doubt had an adaptive value during his childhood in a sterile environment, in his adult life they were buffers against learning the nature of the realities of adulthood. Thus we began to interpret the use of fantasies as transitional objects. He asked for a guarantee that the surrender of his pet fantasies would make him a "perfect man" in real relationships. He felt that the experience of sadness and frustration in real life might take him back to his fantasies, but that the curiosity he felt about life undistorted by illusions would prevail.

Perhaps more important than his verbal acknowledgment of the fact that he had used fantasies as transitional objects was his working through his addiction to them; this occurred in the third year of analysis when, in transference, his use of me as a transitional object became obvious. I felt somewhat fused with him, just as he fused me with external objects. Later I separated myself from other objects for his benefit, as if I put a boundary around myself, as if I taught him that I was an individual in the external world, an object, and that if he could see me thus he could also see other things separately in the external world. He did not distinguish me from other psychiatrists he had known professionally or socially, but I insisted I was unique. He came to learn that I was not the foreign woman with whom he had slept at the start of the analysis and whom he thought of as his slave. During and after this phase he became involved in frustrating incidents, deliberately, I believe, to discover the nature of life.

Further commitment to reality was exercised in the analytic situation when on occasion I interpreted his frequently used phrases of "I guess" or "I think" as remnants of his noncommitment to the real world, his effort to keep his objects transitional. For example, when he said "I will have dinner with my wife at—I guess it's Holiday Lodge," knowing that he was well aware of the name of the restaurant, I interpreted his "I guess" as his effort to keep the dinner date with his wife both real and unreal. Further evidence that his specific fantasies were transitional fantasies lay in his discovery that he knew nothing of what started them to unroll at any given time, even after he learned to abort them once they had begun. Although he knew intellectually that his fantasies were his own creations, he felt no responsibility for them, and their apparently spontaneous appearance at times challenged his intellectual realization that he must have initiated them himself. It was only in the fifth year of analysis that he finally accepted responsibility for his fantasies. He then understood them as "pillows around me."

Whatever happened to Brown?

Three years have passed since Brown terminated his analysis with me. I have had no direct contact with him, so for all practical purposes I can say that I have no follow-up on him except for a few brief reports during the first year after termination from the child psychiatrist who was treating Brown's son. Brown and his wife had occasionally come to the psychiatrist's office for consultation. The psychiatrist found him appropriately concerned about his child's welfare, pleasant, and assertive. It was the psychiatrist's opinion that Brown's wife played an important role in the child's difficulty in individuating fully. She was described as being anxious to let the boy grow up, but at the same time "glued" to the child.

One year later at a social gathering I heard from someone who knew Brown that his good professional reputation had grown and that he was developing a prestigious career. My informant had gossip about Brown's having separated from his wife and awaiting a divorce. I did not participate in this "social" talk, nor did I mention that I "knew" Brown once upon a time.

CHAPTER XI

PRIMITIVE INTERNALIZED OBJECT RELATIONS AND NEUROSIS

We cannot speak of a pathology of internalized object relations in neurotics since arrival at the level of neurosis indicates the presence of an integrated self-concept as well as an integrated internalized representational object world. But, can we consider that a "strain" in the mending of primitive splitting, a "weakness" in the mended area, may be contributing to the perniciousness of a neurotic situation?

Primitive internalized object relations and transsexualism

Thus far we have considered how pregenital aspects of the treatment of schizophrenic, borderline, or narcissistic patients can be studied in new dimensions when a knowledge of the psychopathology of internalized object relations is applied to them. Manic-depressive psychosis was not investigated in this connection only because I have never analyzed a patient with this diagnosis.

In our continuing work with transsexuals (Volkan

and Bhatti, 1973; Volkan, 1974d, 1974e) we have found the application of the internalized object relation theory most illuminating. Our three years of work with these puzzling patients at the University of Virginia yielded evidence to support the view of Socarides that the transsexual's desire for sex change arises from the same factors as are present in the other perversions.

> The sexual pervert, including the transsexual, has been unable to pass successfully through the symbiotic and separation-individuation phases of early childhood and this creates the original anxiety from which sexual perversions arise. The source of the pervert's original anxiety emanates from this preoedipal period. Sexual perversion serves the repression of pivotal nuclear complex: the urge to regress to a pre-oedipal fixation in which there is a desire for and dread of merging with the mother in order to reinstate the primitive mother-child unity [Socarides, 1970, p. 347].

Our preliminary findings show that the male transsexual wants not only to be a woman, but to be an "all good" woman. The clinical picture of the transsexual, and observation of his behavior following surgery, shows that he is searching for a child-mother unity; I have found, however, that his goal is to be "all pure" and uncontaminated by aggression. Since he sees the penis as a tool of aggression, he demands its removal. To keep the unintegrated self-concept "pure" requires a continuous unconscious battle against its other half—the "bad" and aggressive component. Although this aggressive component can be removed by force, it never disappears altogether, but continues to threaten. Thus one sees within the feminine core of the male transsexual the defensive mechanism of primitive splitting of "all good" from "all bad" representations along affective lines. It is little wonder that after surgery has made the male transsexual into a "woman" his main symptom — preoccupation with the appearance of the genitalia — returns. Whereas before the surgery was performed the man was preoccupied with his penis, "she" is now preoccupied with the newly constructed vagina. It seems imperfect to "her" and "she" demands perfection. The search for perfection rather than the more immediate goal of physical change has been the defense against anxiety all along. Now "perfection" demands modification of the legs to a more feminine outline, reduction of the size of the masculine Adam's apple, etc.

It must be evident that I disagree with Stoller (1973) in his suggestion that "gender identity" (a set of convictions concerned with masculinity-femininity issues) is put at odds with the natural endowment in the male transsexual during the early mother-child relationship by some nonconflictual, nondynamic learning process like imprinting. The defensive organization of the female transsexual (Volkan, 1974) also shows a similarity to the defensive organization of patients with borderline personality organization.

Primitive internalized object relations and neurosis

The individual who has reached Stage IV in Kernberg's classification (1972a) is not psychotic or borderline. He is neurotic or "normal"; in either case we do not

[305]

speak of pathology of internalized object relations, but it may be well to consider that a "strain" in the mending primitive splitting, a "weakness" in the mended area, can be contributing to the perniciousness of the neurotic situation. The excessive preoccupation with the balancing of opposites displayed by the patient in the grip of an obsessive-compulsive neurosis is suggestive of this. Anna Freud (1966) does see in obsessional neurosis the possibility of early damage to the capacity for synthesis, and urges the analyst to pursue every mental disorder back to its earliest appearance in the life of the patient. She warns, however, that inasmuch as the first year of life is the focus of so much analytic interest, the anal phase may seem to many analysts an unduly late period for the *beginning* of the pathology of obsessive-compulsive neurosis. She cautions further that only those factors in the mother-child relationship that are truly *specific* for obsessional neurosis merit close attention in this connection. For example, if there is loss of a love object early in life, it is not the event as such that is significant for obsessional neurosis, but the child's belief that it occurred because of his having entertained a desire to be rid of the love object, and the guilt he feels on this account. Anna Freud suggests that only a few such specific factors contribute to the development of obsessional neurosis, among these being damage to the "synthetic function" and to the capacity for fusion of love and hate.

The obsessional neurotic has an integrated self-concept and an integrated internalized representational object world, but when, after considerable work, he deeply regresses in his analysis, aspects of conditions that pertain to pathological internalized object relations can be seen, especially unmended or poorly mended primitive splitting. I believe that the same observation can be made in other conditions as well. For example, the personalities involved in cases of hysterical multiple personality are kept apart by repression, and one may see behind them the remnants of primitive splitting or the fragmentation of different self- and object constellations.

One of my obsessional patients illustrated this. The initial development of transference in the obsessional analysand deals with the usual aspects of a transference neurosis, unlike that of the borderline individual. An escape from castration anxiety is accomplished by regression to the anal level, and this is dealt with only to disclose, after extensive work, an underlying layer in which primitive splitting plays a part. Alternating with or accompanying the transference neurosis there appears a split transference and evidences of reactivation of primitive internalized object relations. When, later, further regression comes about during analysis, the patient's fusion with the analyst (or his couch) becomes the dominant phenomenon, to be followed with (re-)integration of self-concept and object representations, whereupon the typical transference neurosis dominates once again. Its behavioral manifestations are generally confined to the analyst's office, although this is not the case with either the borderline or the schizophrenic patient.

The M-shaped scar

When he came into treatment, Hassan, a 28-year-old, 230-pound physical therapist, had taken the first steps to divorce his wife. There were no children. The wife, a social work trainee, appeared to have a narcissistic personality disorder. Hassan's father was an Arabian Catholic who had immigrated from Lebanon at 21 years of age, becoming in the course of time the owner of a farm and a country store in the new homeland. At the age of 45, he married Hassan's mother, who was 20 years his junior. She bore Hassan three years later, and another son 11 years after that. She was a converted Catholic of German-Dutch descent.

Hassan's presenting symptom was unhappiness at home. He felt obliged to submit to the often unreasonable demands of his wife. When she refused to have sexual relations, as she often did, he usually responded by working far into the night doing her housework—"just being nice to her, and unhappy." Other symptoms included the excessive use of intellectualization, reaction formation, isolation, premature ejaculation, intolerance of success, and difficulty in expressing emotions openly.

His parents had been occupied with their store during his childhood, leaving Hassan most of the time to the care of Colette, who was an unmarried mother of three children whom she left behind in order to continue in the patient's household, where she was a significant figure. Hassan did not give up the bottle until he was nearly five, but carried it about with him in behavior that reflected a deficiency in mothering provided him rather than any "generosity" on the part of those responsible for him. Even Colette's children referred to her as a whore. Hassan remembered her funeral, which took place when he was eight, without affect, although he had a strong visual memory of the event, even to the colors in the environment.

During Hassan's puberty his father returned to "the old country" for a year, and when he came back he accused his wife of being a whore. This accusation rekindled Hassan's oedipal difficulties. Since during his father's absence the boy occasionally shared his mother's bed, he was puzzled by his father's claim that she had been sleeping with other men. The threatened dissolution of his parents' marriage gave Hassan a brief fantasy of oedipal triumph, but his mother "betrayed" him by remaining and conceiving his brother. He then regressed in search of the oral mother, and became fat through overeating, thus identifying symbolically also with the pregnant mother. The father made excessive demands on his son, requiring that he do a man's work on the farm from dawn to dusk, and regularly beating him into submission. The boy had to swallow his outraged anger, which could be expressed only in disguised ways.

He was in his mid-teens when he suddenly realized, while hand-wrestling with his father, that he was the stronger of the two, and was frightened by this knowledge. The father sustained an injury while butchering, and was bedridden for a year as a result. Hassan seemed to need further repression of his aggression, and his moral masochism was crystallized as defense mechanisms of reaction formation, isolation, and hypertrophied intellectualization. He won a football scholarship because of his physique, and earned a college degree in physical therapy. He was injury-prone on the playing field, and had to have several operations. Before he graduated, he decided to be circumcised. Later, he married.

Hassan saw himself as hungry and hurt in his regressive fantasies, but also, paradoxically, as a powerful infant whose only goal was to be "filled up." He had a memory of exercising his power as an infant; at the age of four, still bottle-fed, he was taken to a movie theater, where he screamed during the show, "I want my God-damned bottle!", reportedly so convulsing the audience that a bottle had to be sent for.

The hypertrophy of anal-retentive aspects was most apparent. He perceived anal expulsion as not only dangerous to himself, but also to the environment. His superego had archaic features such as the fear of retaliation. One screen memory summarizes his problems as they initially unfolded in his analysis. He recalled being attacked by a fighting cock (the oedipal father and/or his penis) when he was three or four years old, and being left with a M-shaped scar (M = mutilated) on his face. He choked the cock to death (fear of his unneutralized aggression).

From transference neurosis to split transference, and back

The psychoanalyst who referred Hassan to me had told him I was Turkish. Placing stress on his father's origin, Hassan presented himself as an Arab during his first hour and indicated that in spite of the history of friction between Turks and Arabs he had always admired Turks. The tone of the transference neurosis that was to develop fully in analysis was thus set by his denial of aggressive feelings, his ready submission to authoritarian figures, and hidden rage.

At first he complained endlessly about his wife and his father's brutality. In the first months his silent rage was evidenced by his failure to pay his psychoanalytic bills on time. When this lapse was brought to his attention, he confided that he was using his analysis to separate from his wife and to facilitate his marriage to a girl who lived elsewhere, and who appeared in his fantasies as the ideal woman. Six months after he began analysis this girl married someone else. He exhibited affect at the news and wept briefly. He reported dreaming of the man who stole his girl. A preliminary attempt to relate this theme to the early experience of his father's returning from abroad and taking his mother away from him only increased his intellectualization. While he was unable to consider this material without intellectualization, he began to eat excessively, and referred to himself as fat, in a repetition of his pubertal history. His wife, who now became the oral mother, once more became his main preoccupation, and he felt himself to be the analyst's "slave" in an early mother transference. Toward the oedipal father analyst, on the other hand, he demonstrated an intolerance of success that was also reflected in his daily behavior. For example, when the instructor in an investment class he was taking began providing "hot tips" (= penis) for succeeding in the stock market, Hassan left the room, ostensibly because of coughing spells. He defended against castration anxiety by "losing" his penis—become so obese that his swollen body prevented a glimpse of it when he stood up. He complained, "I would do anything if I could see my penis." His obesity also confirmed his identification with a pregnant woman.

In this phase he displayed no angry affect in his hours and seldom allowed himself to feel rage, even outside analysis, since rage frightened him. He once reported an "outbreak" in which he almost had a fistfight with a man who took his parking space. He had been worsted in this encounter, for although he knew he was stronger than his antagonist he felt paralyzed in dealing with him.

Feeling crippled and mutilated, he likened his affliction to multiple sclerosis, of which disease he had an external representation in the person of one of his patients. In time it became clear that, while he submitted to his analyst, he nevertheless contrived to defeat him and invalidate his interpretations. When this was interpreted to him he poured out "bloody" stories. For example, his "vision" of "foamy red stuff" on the couch was associated with the blood of the animal his father had been slaughtering when he fell and sustained injury. During the fourteenth month of analysis, he showed an interest in "equal rights," and wanted to be the analyst/father's equal. This desire produced anxiety and once more he took refuge in a search for an "Earth Mother." His turning to mother at this point enabled the analyst and the patient to work together on the latter's classification of all women into "virgin-white" or "scarlet-red," and genetic aspects of having both the mother and Colette in childhood. Behind this classification we hit upon an unintegrated mother representation separated by primitive splitting into "all good" and "all bad." The reflection of this dominated the transference (split transference). Corresponding primitively split self-representations went into an interplay with the "all good" and "all bad" mother/Colette/analyst. He went back to a full-time transference neurosis, however, in that the analyst represented the ambivalently related father.

A year and a half after his analysis began Hassan prepared himself to separate from his sadomasochistic involvement with the wife whose behavior seemed to make the dissolution of his marriage necessary. After she spent a night with a black lover, she told her husband about her infidelity and they separated. Hassan became more passive during his analytic hours and began lying on the couch with his legs apart, trying to interest the analyst in coming after him. After this stage was worked through, however, Hassan was able to ride in the hospital elevator with a known homosexual without anxiety. He visited his wife and they had sexual relations for the first time in a year. He reported, "I took my manhood back from her." After this his efforts to separate in reality from his wife, and intrapsychically from his early mother, began in earnest. A second round of split transference came about with full force, and he experienced tension of (re-)integrating his mother/analyst representations and attempting intrapsychic separation from her.

The tension and anxiety produced were handled with even deeper regression. During his hours he began experiencing "presleep things," images of bright colors, a vision of a baby made up of a mouth and a hand. Sometimes he slept and snored during his hours. He wanted me to take away his "bad feelings" by "osmosis." I allowed his projections to continue long enough to be connected by means of interpretations with intrapsychic aspects. Hassan's reactivation of primitive internalized object relations was confined to his hours of therapy. His extremely regressed behavior on the couch did not prevent his re-establishing his separateness from me as the hour ended, or reintegrating his self-representation. In this he differed from borderline patients in analysis. As his analysis progressed, he returned once more to the manifestation of a typical transference neurosis.

Two years after entering analysis Hassan dreamed of being asked to play football and being told by the coach, "You can kick." After the game he was a hero for having kicked a field goal, but the actual struggle of the game was unseen, as if the dreamer wanted to escape the "working through" aspects of the oedipal struggle. The dream was interpreted as indicating his wish to reach oedipal triumph without a struggle with his father. A more direct involvement with the analyst (the oedipal father) then became evident. He talked about the story of a Turkish soldier and a "little Arab merchant"; the soldier was superficially superior, but the "little Arab" controlled the situation. During this process of working through Hassan exhibited more and more genuine friendliness toward his analyst and lost most of his fatness.

He found a new woman friend. His "fake" love for her slowly became a commitment. His relationship with his parents also changed, and they visited together successfully. Once Hassan allowed his father to hold his hand as he announced that he was an old man who should allow his son to become head of the family. Hassan then became harsh toward his younger brother, and his identification with the aggressor was interpreted to him. He could now regard his sibling rivalry and his rage against his "pregnant" mother. He began talking more openly about intimate sexual problems such as his premature ejaculation, which improved. He resigned a position that required him to swallow anger at a neurotic boss and suppress hurt pride. After much discussion with his analyst, he signed a contract for a better position elsewhere and transferred to another analyst in his new location.

Although Hassan did not come to termination of his analysis with me, I was able to see drastic changes in his general condition while he was my patient. At the time he left me for another analyst, I felt that his persistent attempt to sabotage the analytic process needed much work, as did his efforts to "silently" defeat the analyst/father, and his continuing inability to be open in his feelings. This account of his first two years in analysis does, however, demonstrate that pathological primitive internalized object relations may surface from time to time in the treatment of a neurotic patient. Although they appear only in periods of deep regression and are usually short-lived, they repay close attention in the treatment process. They do not characterize the entire course of the analysis, but, seen in context, they can provide insights that advance the patient's treatment significantly.

CHAPTER XII

CODA

The introduction to this book explains what it was designed to convey. Therefore I shall not attempt a summary of the whole volume, rather I shall comment on certain aspects of it.

This is predominantly a clinical book, a systematic study of the clinical correlates of the theory of internalized object relations. The theory describes the process whereby self- and object images are simultaneously formed from the multitudinous impressions of self and object made by interaction between the infant and his mother. In early awareness the infant perceives the objects that constitute his environment as either "all good" (gratifying) or "all bad" (frustrating); they are polarized, but, in the beginning, polarized images of objects are not differentiated from polarized images of the self. The ability to integrate opposite characteristics into the same representation of the self or object must await the unfolding of the capacity to differentiate self-images from internalized images of the object world, and to recognize that either constellation may contain "good" and "bad" possibilities within a unitary structure. Before the differentiated self-images and object images coalesce into more realistic representations, the mechanism of primitive splitting provides the unmoderated perception of any specific "other" — or of the self — as "all good" or, contrariwise, "all bad." Splitting that is "primitive" separates intrapsychic representations of self and object that are libidinally tinged from those that are tinged with aggression. Thus the separation occurs along affective lines.

Primitive splitting can be utilized as a defense before the ego achieves sufficient maturity to permit the use of repression in its place. Most of the patients described in this book — psychotics, patients with borderline or narcissistic personality organization — continued, into adult life, to use primitive splitting instead of repression as their primary active defense against anxiety. The psychotic patient not only cannot synthesize contradictory attributes of the self-image and of the object image, but he cannot always distinguish the self-image from the object image. Most of the time the person with borderline personality organization does not lack this ability to discriminate, although his psychic process is fixated at the early developmental stage of primitive splitting. The narcissistic personality, although organized at a somewhat higher level than the borderline personality, and possessed of a more cohesive (albeit pathological) self-concept, has similar difficulty in mending his representational split. His problem involves the failure to integrate his ego ideal and superego. Such failure betrays the underlying primitive splitting of "all good" and "all bad" self-object representational constellations.

Since it is usual to see in psychoanalysis and psychoanalytically oriented psychotherapy neurotic persons whose primary defense mechanism is repression, we may consider the patient's repressive forces as an essential issue with which to deal from the beginning of the treatment. Accordingly, we may have a tendency to apply to psychotic patients and to patients with borderline or narcissistic personality organization the same techniques we are accustomed to using with neurotics. I have tried to demonstrate in this book that success in treating the kinds of patients I describe in it depends on a focus, at the beginning of their treatment, on primitive splitting and its accompanying defenses, rather than on repression. This concept is a contribution from the theory of internalized object relations promulgated by those ego psychologists whose theoretical orientation I share.

I feel that the emphasis on primitive splitting, and the accomplishment of its mending as therapy progresses, require detailed clinical exposure in order to indicate how important the theory of internalized object relations is to clinical technique. I hope that the examples I provide here bear out my intent.

It is useful at the outset to demonstrate to the patient who uses primitive splitting how he is polarizing and separating segments of his experience, especially as they are reflected in interpersonal relations. But what helps these patients basically is full development of a transference that reflects their failure to synthesize representational self- and object constellations. The working

through of this failure by means of transference interpretations can then follow. The analyst or therapist
represents for the patient, through the split transference,
the patient's "all good" or "all bad" self- and/or object
constellations. The transference situation with the psychotic patient (psychotic transference) is considerably
more complicated since his self-images are not differentiated from his object images, and he merges with what
he externalizes onto the analyst.

In some of my clinical examples I have tried to show
the coalescence of differentiated and separated representations into integrated ones as the split transference is
worked through. This mending process may be accompanied by the eruption of emotion when "all bad" constellations approach "all good" ones. I recommend close
attention to primitive splitting throughout the treatment,
even later while dealing with manifestations of transference neurosis after primitive splitting has been overcome. These patients may briefly revert to this early
mode of operation in the termination phase.

I have gone at some length into the introjective-
projective relatedness that accompanies primitive splitting. Although the patient involves his split analyst or
therapist in his introjective-projective cycle, and thus
perpetuates this pathological relatedness, the therapist's
involvement in the cycle may cause the patient to assimilate the mended therapist's special functions into his own
characterological makeup. Such absorption grafts over
and alters the patient's psychic structure. I have suggested techniques to bring this about.

Patients who reactivate primitive internalized object

relations in transference as well as in their intimate interpersonal relations in daily living—that is, those who lack an integrated self-concept and an internalized representational object world—tend to use certain inanimate (nonhuman) objects or pet fantasies. This is their attempt to control the external object on which "all bad" self- and/or object images are externalized. I view these nonhuman objects or pet fantasies as reactivated transitional objects. The illusion of control over the transitional object reassures the patient that he has similar and absolute control over the external objects.

The theory of internalized object relations with which this volume deals has provided enormous help toward the understanding of important behavioral peculiarities of psychotics, patients with borderline personality organization, and the narcissistic personality organization. I have attempted to show not only ways in which this theory enriches our understanding of the therapeutic processes developed in such cases, but how it brings us face to face with new technical issues.

REFERENCES

Abraham, K. (1924), A short study of the development of the libido, viewed in the light of mental disorders. *Selected Papers on Psychoanalysis.* London: Hogarth Press, 1927, pp. 418-501.

Abse, D. W. (1955), Early phases of ego-structure adumbrated in the regressive ego states of schizophrenic psychosis, and elucidated in intensive psychotherapy. *Psychoanal. Rev.,* 42:228-238.

——— (1966), *Hysteria and Related Mental States.* Baltimore: Williams & Wilkins Co.

——— & Ewing, J. A. (1960), Some problems in psychotherapy with schizophrenic patients. *Amer. J. Psychother.,* 14:505-519.

Alexander, J. M. & Isaacs, K. S. (1964), The function of affect. *Brit. J. Med. Psychol.,* 37:231-237.

Archer, L. & Hosley, E. (1969), Educational program. In: *The Therapeutic Nursery School,* ed. R. A. Furman & A. Katan. New York: International Universities Press, pp. 21-63.

Arlow, J. A. (1963), Conflict, regression and symptom formation. *Internat. J. Psycho-Anal.,* 44:12-22.

Bak, R. C. (1953), Fetishism. *J. Amer. Psychoanal. Assn.,* 1:285-298.

——— (1971), Object-relationships in schizophrenia and perversion. *Internat. J. Psycho-Anal.,* 52:235-242.

Balint, M. (1955), Friendly expanses—horrid empty spaces. *Internat. J. Psycho-Anal.,* 36:225-241.

Berman, L. E. A. (1972), The role of amphetamine in a case of hysteria. *J. Amer. Psychoanal. Assn.,* 20:325-340.

Bettelheim, B. (1959), Joey: a mechanical boy. *Sci. Amer.,* 200:116-127.

——— (1967), *The Empty Fortress.* New York: Free Press.

Bibring, E. (1954), Psychoanalysis and the dynamic psychotherapies. *J. Amer. Psychoanal. Assn.,* 2:745-770.

Bibring, G. L.; Dwyer, T. F.; Huntington, D. S. & Valenstein, A. F. (1961), A study of the psychological processes in pregnancy and of the earliest mother-child relationship. *The Psychoanalytic Study of the Child,* 16:9-72. New York: International Universities Press.

Bowlby, J. (1969), *Attachment and Loss, Vol. 1, Attachment.* New York: Basic Books.

——— & Parkes, C. M. (1970), Separation and loss within the family. In: *The Child in His Family,* Vol. 1, ed. E. J. Anthony & C. Koupirnik. New York: Wiley Interscience, pp. 197-216.

Boyer, L. B. (1960), A hypothesis regarding the time of appearance of the dream screen. *Internat. J. Psycho-Anal.,* 41:114-122.

——— (1961), Provisional evaluation of psycho-analysis with few parameters employed in the treatment of schizophrenia. *Internat. J. Psycho-Anal.,* 42:389-403.

[323]

_____ (1967), Office treatment of schizophrenic patients: the use of psychoanalytic therapy with few parameters. In: *Psychoanalytic Treatment of Characterological and Schizophrenic Disorders*, ed. L. B. Boyer & P. L. Giovacchini. New York: Science House, pp. 143-188.

_____ (1971), Psychoanalytic technique in the treatment of certain characterological and schizophrenic disorders. *Internat. J. Psycho-Anal.*, 52:67-85.

Brierly, M. (1937), Affects in theory and practice. *Internat. J. Psycho-Anal.*, 18:256-268.

Burnham, D. L. (1969), Schizophrenia and object relations. In: *Schizophrenia and the Need-Fear Dilemma*, ed. D. L. Burnham, A. I. Gladstone & R. W. Gibson. New York: International Universities Press, pp. 15-41.

Bychowski, G. (1956), The release of internal images. *Internat. J. Psycho-Anal.*, 37:331-338.

Cameron, N. (1961), Introjection, reprojection, and hallucination in the interaction between schizophrenic patient and therapist. *Internat. J. Psycho-Anal.*, 42:86-96.

Darwin, C. (1872), *The Expression of the Emotions in Man and Animals*. London: John Murray.

De Saussure, J. (1971), Some complications in self-esteem regulation caused by using an archaic image of the self as an ideal. *Internat. J. Psycho-Anal.*, 52:87-97.

Eissler, K. R. (1954), Notes upon defects of ego structure in schizophrenia. *Internat. J. Psycho-Anal.*, 35:141-146.

Ekstein, R. (1966), *Children of Time and Space, of Action and Impulse*. New York: Appleton-Century-Crofts.

Engel, G. L. (1962), *Psychological Development in Health and Disease*. Philadelphia: W. B. Saunders.

Erhat, A. (1972), *Mitoloji Sözlügü*. Istanbul: Remzi Kitabevi.

Erikson, E. H. (1956), The problem of ego identity. *J. Amer. Psychoanal. Assn.*, 4:56-121.

Fairbairn, W. D. (1954), *An Object Relations Theory of Personality*. New York: Basic Books.

Fenichel, O. (1941), The ego and the affects. *Psychoanal. Rev.*, 28:47-60.

_____ (1945), *The Psychoanalytic Theory of Neurosis*. New York: Norton.

Ferenczi, S. (1909), Introjection and transference. In: *Sex in Psychoanalysis*. New York: Dover Publications, 1960, pp. 30-79.

_____ (1913), Stages in the development of the sense of reality. In: *Sex in Psychoanalysis*. New York: Dover Publications, 1960, pp. 181-203.

Fintzy, R. T. (1971), Vicissitudes of the transitional object in a borderline child. *Internat. J. Psycho-Anal.,* 52:107-114.

Fliess, R. (1953), On the spoken word in the dream. In: *The Revival of Interest in the Dream.* New York: International Universities Press, pp. 128-155.

Fox, H. M. (1957), Body image of a photographer. *J. Amer. Psychoanal. Assn.,* 5:93-107.

Freud, A. (1936), The ego and the mechanisms of defense. *The Writings of Anna Freud,* 2. New York: International Universities Press, 1966.

———— (1952), The role of bodily illness in the mental life of children. *The Writings of Anna Freud,* 4:260-279. New York: International Universities Press, 1968.

———— (1954), The widening scope of indications for psychoanalysis: Discussion. *The Writings of Anna Freud,* 4:356-376. New York: International Universities Press, 1968.

———— (1966), Obsessional neurosis: A summary of psychoanalytic views. *The Writings of Anna Freud,* 5:242-261. New York: International Universities Press, 1969.

Freud, S. (1887-1902), *The Origins of Psychoanalysis. Letters to Wilhelm Fliess, Drafts and Notes: 1887-1902,* ed. M. Bonaparte, A. Freud, & E. Kris. New York: Basic Books, 1954.

———— (1900), The interpretation of dreams. *Standard Edition,* 4 & 5. London: Hogarth Press, 1961.

———— (1905), Three essays on the theory of sexuality. *Standard Edition,* 7:130-243. London: Hogarth Press, 1961.

———— (1914), On narcissism. *Standard Edition,* 14:67-102. London: Hogarth Press, 1961.

———— (1917), Mourning and melancholia. *Standard Edition,* 14:237-258. London: Hogarth Press, 1961.

———— (1920), Beyond the pleasure principle. *Standard Edition,* 18:7-64. London: Hogarth Press, 1961.

———— (1923), The ego and the id. *Standard Edition,* 19:3-66. London: Hogarth Press, 1961.

———— (1925), A note upon the mystic writing pad. *Standard Edition,* 19:227-232. London: Hogarth Press, 1961.

———— (1926), Inhibitions, symptoms and anxiety. *Standard Edition,* 20:77-175. London: Hogarth Press, 1961.

———— (1927), Fetishism. *Standard Edition,* 21:149-157. London: Hogarth Press, 1961.

———— (1930), Civilization and its discontents. *Standard Edition,* 21:59-145. London: Hogarth Press, 1961.

_____ (1933), New introductory lectures on psychoanalysis. *Standard Edition,* 22:3-182. London: Hogarth Press, 1961.

_____ (1940), An outline of psychoanalysis. *Standard Edition,* 23:141-207. London: Hogarth Press, 1961.

Giovacchini, P. L. (1959), On gadgets. *Psychoanal. Quart.,* 28:330-341.

_____ (1967a), Psychoanalytic treatment of character disorders. In: *Psychoanalytic Treatment of Characterological and Schizophrenic Disorders,* ed. L. B. Boyer & P. L. Giovacchini. New York: Science House, pp. 208-234.

_____ (1967b), Frustration and externalization. *Psychoanal. Quart.,* 36:571-583.

_____ (1969), The influence of interpretation upon schizophrenic patients. *Internat. J. Psycho-Anal.,* 50:179-186.

_____ (1972a), The symbiotic phase. In: *Tactics and Techniques in Psychoanalytic Therapy,* ed. P. L. Giovacchini. New York: Science House, pp. 137-169.

_____ (1972b), Interpretation and definition of the analytic setting. In: *Tactics and Techniques in Psychoanalytic Therapy,* ed. P. L. Giovacchini. New York: Science House, pp. 291-304.

Glover, E. (1932), A psychoanalytic approach to the classification of mental disorders. *J. Men. Sci.,* 78:819-842.

_____ (1939), The psychoanalysis of affects. *Internat. J. Psycho-Anal.,* 20:299-307.

_____ (1950), *On the Early Development of Mind.* New York: International Universities Press, 1956.

_____ (1955), *Technique of Psychoanalysis.* New York: International Universities Press.

_____ (1966), Metapsychology or metaphysics: a psychoanalytic essay. *Psychoanal. Quart.,* 35:173-190.

Greenacre, P. (1952), Pregenital patterning. *Internat. J. Psycho-Anal.,* 33:410-415.

_____ (1953), Certain relationships between fetishism and the faulty development of the body image. In: *Emotional Growth,* 1:9-30. New York: International Universities Press, 1971.

_____ (1958), Early physical determinants in the development of the sense of identity. In: *Emotional Growth,* 1:113-127. New York: International Universities Press, 1971.

_____ (1969), The fetish and the transitional object. In: *Emotional Growth,* 1:315-334. New York: International Universities Press, 1971.

_____ (1970), The transitional object and the fetish: with special reference to the role of illusion. *Internat. J. Psycho-Anal.,* 51:447-456.

Greenson, R. R. (1954), The struggle against identification. *J. Amer. Psychoanal. Assn.,* 2:200-217.

_____ (1958), On screen defenses, screen hunger and screen identity. *J. Amer. Psychoanal. Assn.,* 4:242-262.

_____ (1969), The non-transference relationship in the psychoanalytic situation. *Internat. J. Psycho-Anal.,* 50:27-39.

Hamilton, J. W. (1974), Transitional fantasies and the creative process. *The Psychoanalytic Study of Society,* 6:53-70. New York: International Universities Press.

Hartmann, H. (1939), *Ego Psychology and the Problem of Adaptation.* New York: International Universities Press, 1958.

_____ (1950), Comments on the psychoanalytic theory of the ego. In: *Essays on Ego Psychology.* New York: International Universities Press, 1964, pp. 113-141.

_____, Kris, E. & Loewenstein, R. (1946), Comments on the formation of psychic structure. *The Psychoanalytic Study of the Child,* 2:11-38. New York: International Universities Press.

_____ & Loewenstein, R. (1962), Notes on the superego. *The Psychoanalytic Study of the Child,* 17:42-81. New York: International Universities Press.

Heiman, P. (1956), Dynamics of transference interpretations. *Internat. J. Psycho-Anal.,* 37:303-310.

Hendrick, I. (1951), Early development of the ego: identification in infancy. *Psychoanal. Quart.,* 20:44-61.

Heuscher, J. E. (1963), *A Psychiatric Study of Fairy Tales.* Springfield, Ill.: Charles C Thomas.

Isakower, O. (1938), A contribution to the pathopsychology of phenomena associated with falling asleep. *Internat. J. Psycho-Anal.,* 19:331-345.

Jacobson, E. (1953), Affects and psychic discharge processes. In: *Drives, Affects and Behavior,* ed. R. M. Loewenstein. New York: International Universities Press.

_____ (1964), *The Self and the Object World.* New York: International Universities Press.

_____ (1971), *Depression: Comparative Studies of Normal, Neurotic, and Psychotic Conditions.* New York: International Universities Press.

Jacobson, J. G. (1973), Reliving the past, perceptual experience and the reality-testing functions of the ego. *Internat. J. Psycho-Anal.,* 54:399-413.

Jessner, L. & Abse, D. W. (1960), Regressive forces in anorexia nervosa. *Brit. J. Med. Psychol.,* 33:301-312.

Jones, E. (1927), The early development of female sexuality. *Internat. J. Psycho-Anal.,* 8:459-472.

Katan, A. (1961), Some thoughts about the role of verbalization in early childhood. *The Psychoanalytic Study of the Child,* 16:184-188. New York: International Universities Press.

Kerényi, C. (1960), *The Gods of the Greeks.* New York: Grove Press.

Kernberg, O. F. (1966), Structural derivatives of object relationships. *Internat. J. Psycho-Anal.*, 47:236-253.

_____ (1967), Borderline personality organization. *J. Amer. Psychoanal. Assn.*, 15:641-685.

_____ (1970a), Factors in the psychoanalytic treatment of narcissistic personalities. *J. Amer. Psychoanal. Assn.*, 18:51-85.

_____ (1970b), A psychoanalytic classification of character pathology. *J. Amer. Psychoanal. Assn.*, 18:800-822.

_____ (1972a), Early ego integration and object relations. *Annals N.Y. Acad. Sci.*, 193:233-247.

_____ (1972b), Treatment of borderline patients. In: *Tactics and Techniques in Psychoanalytic Therapy*, ed. by P. L. Giovacchini. New York: Science House, pp. 254-290.

Klein, M. (1946), Notes on some schizoid mechanisms. *Internat. J. Psycho-Anal.*, 27:99-110.

Knight, R. (1940), Introjection, projection, and identification. *Psychoanal. Quart.*, 9:334-341.

Koff, R. H. (1961), A definition of identification. A review of the literature. *Internat. J. Psycho-Anal.*, 42:362-370.

Kohut, H. (1966), Forms and transformations of narcissism. *J. Amer. Psychoanal. Assn.*, 14:243-272.

_____ (1971), *The Analysis of the Self: A Systematic Approach to the Psychoanalytic Treatment of Narcissistic Personality Disorders.* New York: International Universities Press.

_____ (1973), Thoughts on narcissism and narcissistic rage. *The Psychoanalytic Study of the Child*, 27:360-400. New York: Quadrangle.

Kramer, P. (1955), On discovering one's identity. *The Psychoanalytic Study of the Child*, 10:47-74. New York: International Universities Press.

Lampl-de Groot, J. (1962), Ego ideal and superego. *The Psychoanalytic Study of the Child*, 17:94-106. New York: International Universities Press.

Lewin, B. D. (1946), Sleep, the mouth and the dream screen. *Psychoanal. Quart.*, 15:419-434.

_____ (1948), Inferences from the dream screen. *Internat. J. Psycho-Anal.*, 29:224-231.

_____ (1950), *The Psychoanalysis of Elation.* New York: Norton.

Lichtenberg, J. D. & Slap, J. W. (1973), Notes on the concept of splitting and the defense mechanism of the splitting of representations. *J. Amer. Psychoanal. Assn.*, 21:772-787.

Loewald, H. (1960), On the therapeutic action of psychoanalysis. *Internat. J. Psycho-Anal.*, 41:16-33.

REFERENCES

Mahler, M. S. (1963), Thoughts about development and individuation. *The Psychoanalytic Study of the Child,* 18:307-324. New York: International Universities Press.

_____ (1968), *On Human Symbiosis and the Vicissitudes of Individuation.* New York: International Universities Press.

_____ & Furer, M. (1963), Certain aspects of the separation-individuation phase. *Psychoanal. Quart.,* 32:1-14.

McDonald, M. (1970), Transitional tunes and musical development. *The Psychoanalytic Study of the Child,* 25:503-520. New York: International Universities Press.

McDougall, W. (1936), *An Outline of Psychology.* London: Methuen.

Meissner, W. W. (1970), Notes on identification. I, Origins in Freud. *Psychoanalytic Quart.,* 39:563-589.

_____ (1971a), Notes on identification. II, Classification of related concepts. *Psychoanal. Quart.,* 40:277-302.

_____ (1971b), Notes on identification. III, The concept of identification. *Psychoanal. Quart.,* 41:224-260.

Menninger, K. (1934), Polysurgery and polysurgical addiction. *Psychoanal. Quart.,* 3:173-199.

Meyer, B. C. & Weinroth, L. A. (1957), Observations on psychological aspects of anorexia nervosa. *Psychosom. Med.,* 19:389-398.

Miller, A. A., Pollock, G. W., Bernstein, H. E. & Robbins, F. P. (1968), An approach to the concept of identification. *Bull. Meninger Clin.,* 32:239-252.

Modell, A. H. (1963), Primitive object relationships and the predisposition to schizophrenia. *Internat. J. Psycho-Anal.,* 44:282-292.

_____ (1968), *Object Love and Reality: An Introduction to a Psychoanalytic Theory of Object Relations.* New York: International Universities Press.

_____ (1970), The transitional objects and the creative art. *Psychoanal. Quart.,* 39:240-250.

Moore, B. E. & Fine, B. D. (1968), *A Glossary of Psychoanalytic Terms and Concepts.* New York: American Psychoanalytic Association.

Murray, M. (1960), *The God of the Witches.* Garden City, N.Y.: Doubleday.

Niederland, W. G. (1956), Clinical observations on the "little man" phenomenon. *The Psychoanalytic Study of the Child,* 11:381-395. New York: International Universities Press.

_____ (1965), Narcissistic ego impairment in patients with early physical malformations. *The Psychoanalytic Study of the Child,* 20:518-534. New York: International Universities Press.

Novey, S. (1961), Further considerations of affect theory in psychoanalysis. *Internat. J. Psycho-Anal.,* 42:21-31.

Nunberg, H. (1955), *Principles of Psychoanalysis.* New York: International Universities Press.

Olinick, S. L. (1964), The negative therapeutic reaction. *Internat. J. Psycho-Anal.,* 45:540-548.

—— (1969), On empathy and regression in the service of the other. *Brit. J. Med. Psychol.,* 42:41-49.

——, Poland, W. S., Grigg, K. A. & Granatir, W. L. (1973), The psycho-analytic work ego: process and interpretation. *Internat. J. Psycho-Anal.,* 54:143-151.

Parkes, C. M. (1970), "Seeking" and "finding" a lost object: evidence from recent studies of the reaction to bereavement. *Soc. Sci. Med.,* 4:187-201.

Peto, A. (1968), On affect control. *Internat. J. Psycho-Anal.,* 49:471-473.

Pollock, G. H. (1961), Mourning and adaptation. *Internat. J. Psycho-Anal.,* 42:341-361.

Poznanski, E. O. (1972), The "replacement child": a saga of unresolved parental grief. *Behav. Pediat.,* 81:1190-1193.

Pulver, S. E. (1970), Narcissism, the term and the concept. *J. Amer. Psychoanal. Assn.,* 18:319-341.

Rangell, L. (1967), Psychoanalysis, affects and the "human core." *Psychoanal. Quart.,* 36:172-202.

Rapaport, D. (1942), *Emotions and Memory.* New York: International Universities Press, 1971.

—— (1953), On the psychoanalytic theory of affects. *Internat. J. Psycho-Anal.,* 34:177-198.

—— (1957), Cognitive structures. In: *The Collected Papers of David Rapaport,* ed. M. M. Gill. New York: Basic Books, 1967, pp. 631-664.

Reich, A. (1953), Narcissistic object choice in women. In: *Annie Reich: Psychoanalytic Contributions.* New York: International Universities Press, 1973, pp. 179-208.

Rosen, J. N. (1953), *Direct Analysis: Selected Papers.* New York: Grune & Stratton.

Rosenfeld, H. A. (1966), Discussion of paper by L. B. Boyer. *The Psychoanalytic Forum,* 1:351-353. New York: International Universities Press, 1972.

Rycroft, C. (1951), A contribution to the study of the dream screen. *Internat. J. Psycho-Anal.,* 32:178-185.

Sanford, B. (1966), A patient and her cats. *The Psychoanalytic Forum,* 1:170-176. New York: International Universities Press, 1972.

Schafer, R. (1968), *Aspects of Internalization.* New York: International Universities Press.

_____ (1973), Internalization: process or fantasy. *The Psychoanalytic Study of the Child*, 27:411-436. New York: Quadrangle.

Scheflen, A. E. (1961), Fostering introjection as a psychotherapeutic technique in schizophrenia. In: *Psychotherapy with Schizophrenics*, ed. J. G. Dawson, H. K. Stone & N. P. Dellis. Baton Rouge: Louisiana State University Press, pp. 79-106.

Searles, H. F. (1951), Data concerning certain manifestations of incorporation. *Psychiat.*, 14:397-413.

_____ (1960), *The Nonhuman Environment in Normal Development and in Schizophrenia*. New York: International Universities Press.

_____ (1962), The differentiation between concrete and metaphorical thinking in the recovering schizophrenic patient. *J. Amer. Psychoanal. Assn.*, 10:22-49.

_____ (1963), The place of neutral therapist-responses in psychotherapy with the schizophrenic patient. *Internat. J. Psycho-Anal.*, 44:42-56.

_____ (1965), Introduction. In: *Collected Papers on Schizophrenia and Related Subjects*. New York: International Universities Press, pp. 19-38.

Seigman, A. J. (1954), Emotionality—a hysterical character defense. *Psychoanal. Quart.*, 23:339-354.

Shengold, L. (1967), The effects of overstimulation—rat people. *Internat. J. Psycho-Anal.*, 48:403-415.

_____ (1971), More about rats and rat people. *Internat. J. Psycho-Anal.*, 52:277-288.

Smith, J. H. (1970), On the structural view of affect. *J. Amer. Psychoanal. Assn.*, 18:539-561.

Socarides, C. W. (1970), A psychoanalytic study of the desire for sexual transformation ("Transsexualism"): the plaster-of-paris man. *Internat. J. Psycho-Anal.*, 51:341-349.

_____ (1971), The desire to remain disappointed. *Brit. J. Med. Psychol.*, 44:35-44.

Speers, R. W. & Lansing, C. (1965), *Group Therapy in Childhood Psychosis*. Chapel Hill: University of North Carolina Press.

Sperling, M. (1963), Fetishism in children. *Psychoanal. Quart.*, 32:374-392.

Sperling, O. E. (1948), On the mechanisms of spacing and crowding emotions. *Internat. J. Psycho-Anal.*, 29:232-235.

Spitz, R. A. (1950), Anxiety in infancy: a study of its manifestations in the first year of life. *Internat. J. Psycho-Anal.*, 31:138-143.

_____ (1957), *No and Yes: On the Beginning of Human Communication*. New York: International Universities Press.

_____ (1965), *The First Year of Life*. New York: International Universities Press.

Stoller, R. J. (1973), The male transsexual as "experiment." *Internat. J. Psycho-Anal.*, 54:215-225.

Strachey, J. (1934), The nature of the therapeutic action of psychoanalysis. *Internat. J. Psycho-Anal.*, 15:127-159.

Suslick, A. (1963), Pathology of identity as related to the borderline ego. *Arch. Gen. Psychiat.*, 8:252-262.

Toplin, M. (1972), On the beginning of a cohesive self: an application of the concept of transmuting internalization to the study of the transitional object and separation anxiety. *The Psychoanalytic Study of the Child*, 26:316-353. New York: Quadrangle.

Valenstein, A. F. (1962), The psycho-analytic situation, affects, emotional reliving, and insight in the psycho-analytic process. *Internat. J. Psycho-Anal.*, 43:315-323.

Van der Heide, C. (1961), Blank silence and dream screen. *J. Amer. Psychoanal. Assn.*, 9:85-90.

Volkan, V. D. (1964), The observation and topographic study of the changing ego states of a schizophrenic patient. *Brit. J. Med. Psychol.*, 37:239-255.

_____ (1965), The observation of the "little man" phenomenon in a case of anorexia nervosa. *Brit. J. Med. Psychol.*, 38:299-311.

_____ (1968), The introjection of and identification with the therapist as an ego-building aspect in the treatment of schizophrenia. *Brit. J. Med. Psychol.*, 41:369-380.

_____ (1970), Typical findings in pathological grief. *Psychiat. Quart.*, 44:231-250.

_____ (1971), A study of a patient's re-grief work through dreams, psychological tests and psychoanalysis. *Psychiat. Quart.*, 45:255-273.

_____ (1972), The linking objects of pathological mourners. *Arch. Gen. Psychiat.*, 27:215-221.

_____ (1973), Transitional fantasies in the analysis of a narcissistic personality. *J. Amer. Psychoanal. Assn.*, 21:351-376.

_____ (1974a), Food, body shape and sexuality. In: *Marital and Sexual Counseling in Medical Practice*, ed. D. W. Abse, E. M. Nash, & L. M. R. Louden. New York: Harper & Row, pp. 412-421.

_____ (1974b), Death, divorce and the physician. In: *Marital and Sexual Counseling in Medical Practice*, ed. D. W. Abse, E. M. Nash, & L. M. R. Louden. New York: Harper & Row, pp. 446-462.

_____ (1974c), Cosmic laughter: a study of primitive splitting. In: *Tactics and Techniques of Psychoanalytic Psychotherapy*, 2, ed. P. L. Giovacchini, A. Flarsheim, & L. B. Boyer. New York: Jason Aronson, in press.

_____ (1974d), The transsexual issue. II, A cautionary psychiatric insight: a clinical report. In: *Marital and Sexual Counseling in Medical Practice*, ed. D. W. Abse, E. M. Nash, & L. M. R. Louden. New York: Harper & Row, pp. 393-404.

_____ (1974e), Psychological aspects of transsexualism and transsexual surgery. In: *Gynecologic Reconstructive Plastic Surgery,* ed. J. O. Stallings. New York: C. B. Mosby, in press.

_____ & Bhatti, T. J. (1973), Dreams of transsexuals awaiting surgery. *Compr. Psychiat.,* 14:269-279.

_____ Cilluffo, A. F. & Sarvay, T. L. (1974), "Re-grief" therapy and the function of the linking object as a key to stimulate emotionality. In: *Emotional Flooding,* ed. P. Olsen. New York: Behavioral Publications, in press.

_____ & Corney, R. T. (1968), Some considerations of satellite states and satellite dreams. *Brit. J. Med. Psychol.,* 41:283-290.

_____ & Kavanaugh, J. G. (1974), The cat people. In: *Transitional Objects,* ed. S. Grolnick & L. Barkin. New York: Jason Aronson, in press.

_____ & Lutrell, A. S. (1971), Aspects of the object relationships and developing skills of a "mechanical boy." *Brit. J. Med. Psychol.,* 44:101-116.

Waller, J. F., Kaufman, M. R. & Deutsch, F. (1940), Anorexia nervosa. *Psychosom. Med.,* 2:3-16.

Weigert, E. (1938), The cult and mythology of the magna mater from the standpoint of psychoanalysis. *Psychiat.,* 1:347-378.

_____ (1967), Narcissism: benign and malignant forms. In: *Crosscurrents in Psychiatry and Psychoanalysis,* ed. R. W. Gibson. Philadelphia: Lippincott, pp. 222-238.

Werner, H. (1948), *Comparative Psychology of Mental Development.* New York: International Universities Press.

Winnicott, D. W. (1953), Transitional objects and transitional phenomena. *Internat. J. Psycho-Anal.,* 34:89-97.

Wylie, H. W. (1973), Further considerations regarding treatment of narcissistic personalities by O. F. Kernberg. *Bull. Phila. Assn. Psychoanal.,* 23:333-337.

[333]

NAME INDEX

Abraham, K., 69
Abse, D. W., x, 5, 6, 7, 13, 18, 51, 113, 206
Adasal, R., ix
Alexander, J. M., 176
Archer, L., 198
Arlow, J. A., 184, 190

Bak, R. C., 39, 218
Balint, M., 35
Bergman, I., 237
Berman, L. E. A., 216, 224, 225
Bernstein, H. E., 64
Bettelheim, B., 220, 222
Bhatti, T. H., 304
Bibring, E., 169
Bibring, G. L., 171
Bowlby, J., xiv, 42, 71
Boyer, L. B., x, 89, 91, 95, 96, 108, 154
Brierly, M., 175
Burnham, D. L., 206, 207
Buxton, R., x
Bychowski, G., 32

Cameron, N., 80
Cillufo, A. F., 70, 223
Corney, R., 111, 116, 118
Cseh, W., xi

Darwin, C., 175
De Saussure, J., 243, 244
Deutsch, F., 18

Eissler, K., 176, 179
Ekstein, R., 220

Engel, G. L., 177
Erhat, A., 101
Erikson, E. H., xiv, 77, 78
Ewing, J. A., 118, 206

Fairbairn, W. D., xiv, 42
Fenichel, O., 61, 175, 177, 206, 207
Ferenczi, S., 22, 65
Fine, B. D., 35, 62
Fintzy, R. T., 208, 211, 212, 222, 223, 230, 297, 298
Fliess, R., 19, 129
Fox, H. M., 92
Freud, A., 17, 64, 81, 306
Freud, S.
  on affect as signal, 175, 176
  on character of ego, 31, 37
  on day residue, 148
  on development of perceptual functions, 61
  on ego ideal and superego, interchangeable use of, 251
  on ego psychology, 7
  on fetishism, 12, 217
  on identification, 64
  on infant's fantasy of controlling separation from mother, 66
  letter to Fliess on hysterical patient, 19, 64
  on mourning and melancholia, 65, 218
  on narcissism, 240
  on persistence of infantile omnipotence, 23
  on prehistoric ego structure, 10
  on protection by stimulus barrier, 60

[335]

SUBJECT INDEX

Abreaction
   defined, 169-170
   differentiated from emotional
      flooding, 191
   naming of constituent emotions
      in, 198
Affect
   perceived as control sphincter,
      loss of, 184, 191
   primal, 175, 177, 183
   "screen," 172
   strangulated, 169
   theory of, 175-176
Affectualization
   defined, 170-171
   similarities with intellectualiza-
      tion and acting out, 172
Aggression
   in borderline patients, 167
   cathecting self- and object im-
      ages, 38
   and constitutionally determined
      factors, 166
   and excessive frustration in in-
      fancy, 166
   in narcissistic patients, 267, 268,
      275
   neutralization of, 159, 160
   rhythmic discharge of, 182
   in transsexualism, 304
   see also Autoaggression
Ambivalence, ambivalent
   acceptance of, 167
   in grief, 72
   intolerance of, 57

mastery of in normal development, 167
relatedness, 269
Analyst
   an attitudinal model, 95
   introjected, 83, 84
   as "number one," 254
   "real" relationship with patient,
      81-83, 99
   see also Transference
Anorexia nervosa
   as acting out pregnancy wish, 18
   oral concept of sexuality in, 17
   see also Pregnancy
"Aphanisis," 184
Assassination and burial of President Kennedy, psychological effects of, 26, 27
Autoaggression, 174, 246

Bisexuality, 55, 102, 107, 149, 249,
   256
   symbolism of in fetish, 218, 228
Body defects and effects of early illness, 9, 11, 15, 16, 18, 103
Body image, 13
   an automobile, 113
   defective, re-enforced by mother,
      15, 17, 78
   illusion of defect in, leading to
      fetish, 211, 217

Childbirth, maternal injury in, 15,
   17, 32, 227, 261

taming by naming in, 198, 199, 229
Emotions, id and ego, 176
see also Affect
Enemas, 93
as maternal attack, 125

Fetish, 210, 216
combined with transitional object, 223-224
differentiated from linking object and transitional object, 217
"inner," 18
relation to loss, 218
representation of mother's illusory penis, 217
see also Childhood fetish

Head shaking
as first symbolic assertion, 151, 180
as identification with frustrator, 182
rooting reflex, 180
Hysteria, 171
multiple personality in, 56, 307
profusion of affect in, 172

Ideational flooding, 179
Identification(s)
as attempt to conserve libido, 66
with car, 113
with cat, 48, 231, 232
contribution of to superego and ego formation, 65
defined, 68
Freud's reference to orality in, 65
with machines, 220, 222
primary, 62
primitive, affective, 62
projective, 203, 249
with turtle, 205, 212-213

Incorporation, defined, 68, 69
"Instant mother," 210, 228
Internalization of object relations
in development of regulatory systems, 68
stages of, 41-42
types, defined, 68
Interpretations, 95-96, 168, 300, 320
"id," 97
"linking," 148
in transference with primitive splitting, 135, 173
Intimacy
blurred reality testing in, 274
difficulties in achieving, 39, 172, 226
fear of, 249
Introject
analytic, 81, 148, 149, 199, 270
defined, 70, 76
ferociousness disappearing, 130
as object representation, 76
release of, 182, 190
Introjection
"camera," 92, 146, 220
defined, 68
Isakower phenomenon, 153, 154, 211, 285, 290

Laughter
"cosmic," 149-153
as release of hostility, 152
Linking objects, 71-72, 75, 216
burden of anger in, 218
as defense against separation anxiety, 74
differentiated from fetishes and transitional objects, 73, 211
"living," 144
as token of triumph over death, 218